Zol Zayn Shulem
I: Zores

Zol Zayn Shulem I: Zores

(May there be Peace)

זאל זיין שלום

Loss, hatred, murder

Questions of identity from an autobiographical
perspective over more than three generations

———

Daniel Zylbersztajn-Lewandowski

© 2025 Daniel Zylbersztajn-Lewandowski

All rights reserved.

ISBN: 978-1-78324-378-5

Bibliographic information from the German National Library

The German National Library lists this publication in the German National Bibliography; detailed bibliographic data are available online at *http://dnb.d-nb.de*.

Automated analysis of this work, in particular to obtain information about patterns, trends, and correlations pursuant to Section 44b of the German Copyright Act (UrhG) ("Text and Data Mining"), is prohibited.

The Book

Zol Zayn Shulem – *May there be Peace* – is Daniel Zylbersztajn-Lewandowski's attempt to reconstruct and reflect upon the lives of his mother's and his father's families before and during the Holocaust, in Germany, Poland and the Netherlands. While the Munich-based side of his family survive the Third Reich by virtue of an earlier mixed marriage, the Jewish Berlin side and the Jewish branch in Poland are nearly all murdered, though some miraculously escape death. Zores (trouble), the first book of the series, documents in detail their individual lives and tragedies. Unlike many such histories which end at liberation in 1945, this book also examines the survivors' lives in Poland and Germany in the period immediately after the Holocaust. In the second book, Faroys (forward), the author looks back on his own life, lived in the constant shadow of the past as he grew up among Jewish survivors, mainly in post-war Germany but also in the Netherlands and Israel, and settled in Britain as an adult.

Daniel Zylbersztajn-Lewandowski

The German-Jewish, London-based author Daniel Zylbersztajn-Lewandowski has been the London correspondent of the German socio-critical left newspaper *taz*, one of Germany's main newspapers since 2012. He was born in 1969 in the Bavarian capital Munich, where he lived until he was 16. After completing secondary school in Israel, he moved to London in 1991 to study politics and history at SOAS. In 1995 he married his wife, who is a Sierra Leonean Kreo, a group of people who returned to West Africa following enslavement in the Americas through the trans-Atlantic-slave trade.

Contents

Foreword and Acknowledgements		ix
Chapter 1	The Cemetery	1
Chapter 2	The "Illiterates"	4
Chapter 3	The Lewandowskis	30
Chapter 4	No rent to *Saujuden*! Munich 1933	59
Chapter 5	Dachau	64
Chapter 6	1934-1935: Farewell to Munich	74
Chapter 7	Amsterdam 1935-1945	81
Chapter 8	Under Rommel's Command	96
Chapter 9	From Auschwitz-Birkenau to New York	103
Chapter 10	Escape to All Corners of the World	115
Chapter 11	"They Only Came to Murder"	122
Chapter 12	And the Heavens Did Not Open	144
Chapter 13	Treblinka	151
Chapter 14	Skarżysko-Kamienna	164
Chapter 15	The Cushion from Heaven	175

Chapter 16	I Still Looked Good	190
Chapter 17	The View from the Past	199
Chapter 18	Typhus	204
Chapter 19	Missing People, Questions and Answers	209
Chapter 20	Between Death and Happiness	214
Chapter 21	68516 – Buchenwald	218
Chapter 22	Hasag Camp Schlieben	227
Chapter 23	Hammer's Marmalade	237
Chapter 24	Death Train to Terezín	240
Chapter 25	The Emaciated Persons of Flößberg	246
Chapter 26	Train of the Dead and Half-Living	252
Chapter 27	Survival after Liberation	265
Chapter 28	My German Friends Grandfathers	276
Chapter 29	Judgements	278
Chapter 30	Amsterdam and Munich after the War	290
Chapter 31	The Lewandowskis in Munich	301
Chapter 32	Jewish Refugees in Munich	310
For a Leben, a Nayen		323
Literature, Sources and Archives		327
Descendants		353
Index		359

לְדוֹר וָדוֹר

Foreword and Acknowledgements[1]

"Nobody can force a goat to walk backwards."

Wolf Zylbersztajn, z "l

"Narrative is perhaps the most important form of symbolic memory. The person who remembers tries to place in chronological order what happened to him or her. Moreover, the narrative is a conscious and unconscious attempt at sharing and thus has an intersubjective aspect. The narrative reflects the state of the person, but the formation of the narrative helps to restore self-integrity. If an event, even a traumatic one, can be brought into a self-narrative and retold, then this is already an important part of the healing process."[1]

Tihamér Bakó & Katalin Zana in Transgenerational Trauma and Therapy (2020).[2]

What kind of goat is this, a goat that nobody can force to walk backwards. Is that an ordinary goat? Has anyone ever tried and succeeded to make a goat walk backwards? Perhaps it is a scapegoat that was sent to Azazel, and never returned? My father Wolf Zylbersztajn ben-Herszik-we-Szyfra

---

[1] The foreword in part I and II of the book series is the same
[2] Bakó & Zana (2020) p. 26, retranslated from German by author

z"l[3] was mostly thinking of the past whenever he quoted that old saying about that goat you could not force to walk backwards. It is said that the Messiah will one day reunite us living people with those who have gone before us. This may give hope to some, but my father, who lost his faith in a caring G-d during the Shoah, had none of it. Still, today he lies in eternal rest in the divinely blessed Jewish cemetery in Munich, awaiting the arrival of the Messiah, just like all those buried there. His soul possibly also hopes that "die Bayern" (the football team F.C. Bayern Munich) shall be blessed with another good season and that there may finally be peace between Israel and its neighbours.

My parents Wolf and Corrie gifted me the middle name Zwi, following my grandfather Herszl. Grandpa Herszl – I could never call him Grandpa affectionately – died during a typhus outbreak in the forced labour camp in Skarżysko-Kamienna, caused by the inhumane and unhygienic conditions to which "the clean Germans" subjected their enslaved Jewish labourers.[4] Zwi is the Hebrew term for a gazelle, i.e. in the broadest sense a deer or a goat (however, a goat itself is called an *ess* in Hebrew). Despite my name, I am neither able to undo the past nor am I able to reconstruct everything as history. *Zol Zayn Shulem* is only an attempted retrospective that won't be able to change anything about what was. Understanding and reflecting upon the past, however, strengthens our path into the future. It serves to pass it on to the next generation, in keeping with Jewish custom as we say:

Le dor va dor!
From generation to generation!

---

[3] It is not clear if his Hebrew name was ben Herszik, or ben-Zwi. The Munich Synagogue had the first version recorded, but often the Hebrew name was in Hebrew.

[4] I use both Herzl and Herszik to describe my grandfather. The two versions of the name thus refer to the same man.

Dedication

In honour and memory of my dear father Wolf z"l. and for my dear mum, Corrie Zylbersztajn. This book is dedicated to my daughter, her generation and all those who will follow her, and in blessed memory of all those who accompanied us, those who came before us, in particular those we were never able to meet.

In blessed memory of my aunt Roza Silberstein *z"l*, who barely survived Bergen-Belsen, and of Abraham Silberstein *z"l*, my uncle, survivor of Skarżysko-Kamienna, Buchenwald and of Terezín (Theresienstadt). In memory of my uncle Moshe Silberstein *z"l* and his wife Chaftje, *z"l*, my aunt, who both escaped the worst by fleeing early. In blessed memory of my murdered grandmother Szyfra, whom I would have liked to have seen and been able to hug, and in blessed memory of my uncle Fiszl, who was murdered as a young boy. In blessed memory of my uncle Dawid, who would experience the joy of liberation, but was unable to survive and live beyond that point and perished as a result of his starvation in Theresienstadt. In blessed honour of my grandfather Gerhard *z"l*: I am still fighting for your rights and against a world that all too easily chooses to forget what was done to you and so many others, and I would have liked to have met you and talked about your life. Through my research, I learnt that countless family members on my mother's side were murdered in Auschwitz and elsewhere. This book is also dedicated to their blessed memory, whose lives I only learnt about in fragments. May the memory of them all be a blessing.

In blessed memory of my aunt Gerda Cavallini *z"l*. Gerda always tried to answer my curious questions about her childhood and teenage years. She sadly passed away in the middle of the research for this book in August 2020.

In blessed memory of my dear cousin Hanni *z"l*, the daughter of my uncle Moisze and his wife Chaftjie, my aunt. Hanni succumbed to cancer on 1 Inyar 5781 (13 April 2021), one day after my father's Yahrzeit.[5] She tried to always share with me what she knew, even though that was little. Months before she left the world of the living, I was able to send her a Hebrew Google-translation of the then unedited preliminary chapters concerning our family in Szczekociny. Had she lived on, it was always my wish to share this book in its finished form with both Hanni and my aunt Gerda. Writing a book well and thoroughly takes a lot of time, hence I did not manage to finish before they left; however, the two of them are part of this book's *Ruach Ha Nefesh* (Hebrew for wind of the soul), as are all others that left the world of the living.

This book is also intended as a blessed memory to the many Shoah survivors who made the Bavarian capital of Munich their home, and where I grew up. The book is also written in gratitude to my wife, without whose support I would have struggled over many passages of my life and to the blessed memory of her family and ancestors who once passed through transatlantic slavery and, as soon as they were able, rebuilt their freedom in Freetown, West Africa, their Zion.

The deaths of our two families serve as a warning against overly blind arrogance, self-confidence and impetuous nationalism.

Yossi and Agnieszka (Aga Piskiewicz) Bornstein (Yossi is the son of a survivor from Szczekociny) have personally campaigned for many years for the remembrance of Szczekociny's Jewish family and history. It is thanks to Yossi's and Aga's initiative that I was able to travel to Szczekociny with my mother in 2011 and join all the other survivors and their descendants in the task of preserving the blessed memory and honour of the local Jewish kehilah (Hebrew community). Thanks also

---

[5] In the case of relatives, the Jewish year is often given after that of the current general calendar.

Foreword and Acknowledgements

to Yossi and Aga for allowing me to reproduce photos and quotes from the memoirs of Izyk Mendel Bornstein, their father and stepfather, and for providing me with the Polish translation of the book of remembrance "Pinkes Szczekociny" by the Jewish survivors of the Szczekciny community. I will always be honoured that you named your son Daniel.

Imran Manzoor became an indirect companion of this project, at least for the first part, because it was he who asked me years ago to talk to students in Swindon, England, about my family's experience of the Shoah. I first met Imran through my work for Oasis of Peace UK when I was their education officer. Later he accompanied me to the Jewish cemetery of Sosnowiec, where I recited a private Kaddish for my uncle. Thanks to the Sosnowiec Cultural Office for allowing me access to the cemetery. Thanks also to Imran's wife, Ewelina Chmielik, for her hospitality.

Thanks to the USC Shoah Foundation for interviewing my father and allowing me to use the material for this book and to Le Monde Diplomatique (Germany) for permission to reproduce the chapter "Ich werde Brite" (Becoming British) here, which was the inspired idea of Oliver Pohlisch, a colleague at *taz*.

I would also like to thank Stefan Walter and Wolfgang Heidrich of the "Flößberg gedenkt" (Flößberg Remembers) initiative for their information. Wolfgang walked me through dense bushes and forest to show me left-over traces of the Flößberg forced labour camp as well as its cemetery there, where those who lost their lives in the camp continue to be commemorated. Dr Jürgen Wolf guided me for several hours through the remains of Schlieben, passed on information and helping me with some improvements to the draft of this book without even being asked. Even before this book was published, he arranged for an appropriate memorial plaque to my father and his brothers in the memorial centre of KZ-Schlieben.

Thanks also to Krzysztof Gibaszewski, who not only tried to show me what's left of the Hasag factories in Skarżysko-Kamienna, but also took me to mass graves and execution places in the middle of the dense local forest. Unfortunately, his attempt to also show me the remains of Werk C was thwarted due to the war Russia had started against the Ukraine, but I must at least thank the Mesko company, which runs the current factory, for the short tour of their exhibition centre.

Pamela Castillo Feuchtmann was kind enough to take me on a tour of the Buchenwald Memorial Complex, where we also had a confrontation with a disrespectful family visiting the camp. Her commitment to education about what happened at Buchenwald is unparalleled. Thanks also to Šárka Neumanová from Památník Terezín, who authorised a tour of Terezín (Theresienstadt) for me.

I am grateful to Beata and Mirek Skrzypczyk for hosting me in their flat in Lelow, the village where my paternal grandmother lived, and showing me around Lelow and Szczekociny.

Thanks to my distant cousins Philipp Lewandowski, Steve Gundel and Frank Jones for their contributions to this book about their side of the Lewandowski family.

Angie Grützner helped with the deciphering of old official handwriting. Thanks also go to *Absolute Medien GmbH* for licences and rights. Many other archives and archivists in Munich, Amsterdam, Dachau and Berlin, as well as the German State Archives in Koblenz, helped to reconstruct parts of my family's history as best they could. Thanks to Thomas Pohl from the administration of the Jewish cemetery in Weißensee, Berlin, for information about those members of my family who are buried there.

Special thanks also go to Libor Schröpfer, who, as mayor of Holýšov, a small municipality in the Czech Republic between Domazlice and Pilzen, spent months trying personally to reconstruct my father's escape route from one of the German death transports by train to the Mauthausen extermination camp. It was important to Libor to honour the dead in this way, and I know that he did much more than was necessary.

Above all, Käthe Fleckenstein for the German edition, Susan Boobis and Kevin Avison for the English edition, but also Hannah Holtschneider and Eva Kollmar, deserve special praise for the final version of this book. They proofread the book page by page and scrutinised my lines and

Foreword and Acknowledgements

thoughts. They worked with love for the subject matter for days, weeks and even months.

I would like to thank once more my wife, my life companion of many years, and my daughter, for their patience, support and love. This book is also their book and would not have been finished without their help.

Without the very generous financial support of the following foundations, for the German edition, this book-series would not be in your hands. May it so honour the founders of the respective foundations.

Kurt and Hildegard Löwenstein/Losten Foundation
Irene Bollag-Herzheimer Foundation,
2mag AG, Kai Kress, Michael Fischer, Germany

The following amazing individuals supported "Zol Zayn Shulem" in its German crowdfunding drive: Eva Kollmar on behalf of Gregor Kollmar, Katy Elmaliah, Arie Meller, Jackie A. Boronow Danson, Alexander Diehl, Carlos Labraña, Silke Goldberg, Carl-Friedrich Laue, Victoria Hart, Catherine Brusky, Kirsten Wiseman, Gaby Coldewey, Bettina von Borries, Kim Segel, Guido Stefanec, Doo Ri Lichtenberger, Christiana Meredith, Erik Dege, Julia Orth, Kalmon Hener, Cornelia Topf, Josi Rosenfeld, Ina Lober, Rebekka Wedell, George Wilkes, Rena Beck, Margareta Burrell, Isabella Benson, Jan and Joost Gwinner, Michael Zur-Szpir, Tobias Müller, Hazel Seidel, Käthe Fleckenstein, Patricia De Souza, Paul Günczler, Friedrich-Wilhelm Höper, Lea Mühlstein, Joerg Nijmeijer, Marry Abberton, Rabbi Barbara Borts and seven people who wished to remain anonymous.

The following individuals supported the English edition crowd drive. Hazel Seidel, Doo Ri Lichtenberger, Roza Stegmann, Hilary Freeman, Ilana Treister, Steven Derby. Catherine Brusky, Ishmael Abberton, the Reay-Bartram Family, and a number of friends and supporters who chose to remain anonymous.

Thanks to my German publisher BOD.

Much of the music and songs mentioned in this series has been put together on Tidal and on Spotify under Playlist >>Zol Zayn Shulem<<

The future lies on the tracks of the past. It is forged in the fire and nothingness of absolute madness and beaten into a solid sword to fight for justice and humanity. And yet we pray for the time when we were promised by the prophet Isaiah that swords would be turned into ploughshares.

1

The Cemetery

פנקס שצ׳קוצ׳ין

שטשעקאטשינער יזכור בוך

(לעבן און אומקום פֿון א ייִדיש שטעטל)

העורך: ישראל שווייצר (בר-אברהם)

חברי המערכת:
מרדכי בן שלמה (גרייפֿנער)
חנוך בן פנחס (פֿרײמאן)
יצחק קופֿערברג

תל-אביב תש״ך — 1959
הוצאת ארגון יוצאי שצקוצין בישראל

Zol Zayn Shulem I: Zores

The following lines are taken line by line from the introduction of the Yizkor book concerning the Jewish community of the Polish town of Szczekociny. Yizkor books are special books written by survivors in memory of the community they lost and to or try to explain, what happened to them. It was important to me, to allow them to speak first, through their own words.

Our cemetery

Cease with all those questions already![6] *We don't know where our relatives and loved ones were buried and tragically killed by Nazi murderers. May God avenge their blood – do they even rest in a Jewish grave at all?*

Let the pages of this book, filled with memories, be their cemetery, the mazevot of these our brothers and sisters.[7]

Look – you who have survived these orphans and mourners, look and read those names with your own eyes and imagine that you are walking amongst their mazevot in their cemetery.

Here, on the pages of this book rest Your father, your mother, your sister, your brother, your grandfather, your grandmother, all your relatives.

shot – dishonoured – suffocated – burnt and buried alive!

Finally cease with all those questions! And let the ghosts of the images of these dark days appear in front of your eyes.

Allow your imagination to experience at least part of what these people had to experience, because your fate should have been the same as theirs.

Think that their eyes are looking at you from the lines you have written down. Their eyes remember and recall:

Original Polish is zatrzymaj się which means stop. Here freely translated by the author.

---

[6] Original Polish is *zatrzymaj się* which means stop. Here freely translated by the author.
[7] Mazevah, plural matzevot: Hebrew memorial stone, gravestone

The Cemetery

> *Mazevah, plural matzevot: Hebrew memorial stone, gravestone*
> *"Remember us – don't forget us!"*
>
> *And even if the Germans had succeeded in destroying our precious city, they only destroyed it physically – because the spirit of its Jewish inhabitants will always remain in our memories and in our hearts.*
>
> *Let the sacred memory of these people live in you forever and remain a sign for generations, so that your children and the children of your children will know that this book is a matzevah of almost 3000 Jewish souls who perished in a cruel way and to leave a testament for future generations:*
>
> *"Remember that! – Don't forget us!"*

From the introduction of the book *Pinkes Szczekocin* edited by Israel Szwajcers (2010). *Pinkes Szczekocin* is a book of memories written by the survivors of the town of Szczekociny after the Second World War to remember what happened to their community during the Shoah and to remember all that was destroyed.

With thanks to Yossi and Agnieszka Bornstein, in blessed memory of their father and stepfather.

2

The "Illiterates"

The "Illiterates"

My father Wolf Zylbersztajn's birth certificate. The first translation from Polish into English was by Agnieszka Bornstein (Piśkiewicz), rephrased by the author.

Szczekociny, 26 January 1919: 'The following took place in the municipality of Szczekociny (Poland) on the 26th day of January 1919 at five o'clock in the afternoon: Herszik Zylbersztajn, a leather worker, 28 years of age, who lives in Szczekocin, came here (to the registry), in the presence of the witnesses Mendel Lenczner, 58 years old, and Josek Mayer Szulmann, 56 years old, and he showed us a male child of whom he stated that it was born in Szczekociny on 16 January 1919 at eight o'clock in the evening by his wife Szyfra Rayzla, née (Landau), 32 years old.

According to the religious ritual, the baby was named Wolf. The certificate was read out in front of the witnesses and then signed by us. The father and the witnesses are illiterate.'

The registrar of the registry (of Szczekociny), Fabjanski.

Zol Zayn Shulem I: Zores

שצ'קוצ'יני

"We were a beautiful small town, a beautiful market, with beautiful houses – not small houses but two-storey houses!"

Wolf Zylbersztajn[8]

The birth certificate of my father Wolf was his official welcome from the Polish-Christian registration office of the town in which his parents lived.

Illiterates!? Were my grandfather and his acquaintances Mr Lenczner and Mr Szulman really illiterate? Most of the Jewish male residents of my father's town had studied Hebrew and Torah for some years in a *cheder* (religion school). They themselves spoke Polish as well as Yiddish. Leon Zelman (1928-2007), a compatriot of my father who grew up in Szczekociny and survived the Shoah, did not seem to think that there were many illiterate Jews in the town, as he wrote in his memoirs.[9]

You see, as a leather worker in this "shtetl" in Polish Upper Silesia, my grandfather was one of the town's relatively respected and important craftsmen. According to Zelman, he was neither a "*Schejner*" *(yid. lit. radiant ones),* one of the Orthodox Jewish scholars, nor a completely uneducated "Proste."[10] Could it be possible that subjective measure of antisemitism was shining through at the very beginning of my father's life? If so, this represented an early bad, omen.

The official birth of my father Wolf, the third son of my grandparents, had been officially registered ten days later and only after the

---

[8] Zylbersztajn, Wolf (2001), 3:17
[9] *Due to the high value placed on scholarship in the shtetl, illiteracy among Jews was practically non-existent. There were hardly any Jews who could not read, in contrast to the local peasant population."* Zelman (1995), S. 26
[10] *Schejner and Proste,* see Zelman (1995), p. 11

traditional "Bris" (Brit Milah)[11]. According to the Jewish calendar, the day of his birth, 16 January, was the day of the Tu Bishvat festival in 5679, a Jewish holiday dedicated to nature and trees.

Szczekociny, and likewise refered to as Szczekocin without the "y", is the name of this small Upper Silesian town in present-day Poland on the Pilica River, around 80 kilometres from Krakow. Leon Zelman wrote in his book, that on one side of the river there lived only Jews and on the other side a mixed Jewish and Christian population.

Szczekociny today, source (c) OpenStreetMap, Open Data Commons Open Database Licence (ODbL). CC BY-SA 2.0.

Jews and Christians lived side by side without bothering each other. The events of the year past quietly in this community. One year was like the other…

---

[11] Zelman (1995), p. 10

> *The Christians respected Shabbat, because that was when the Jewish shops were closed. The Jews respected Sunday.*[12]

The fact that there was a Jewish population in Szczekociny at all may have something to do with my ancestors. The Zylbersztajn and Schwrazbojm families are said to have settled there as the first Jewish people many centuries ago.

When I visited Szczekociny and neighbouring Leluw in 2022, I discovered small towns where everyone knew each other. People stopped in the streets to exchange the latest news and gossip.

Szczekociny was and is a town where time seemed to move more slowly, and the church bells can still be heard everywhere and at all times. In many ways it is a small and simple small town, and yet a universe for those who live there, a microcosm! Such places lack strategic and real economic significance in the wider schema of things. In its surroundings stand nothing but fields and forests beating to the everyday rhythm of rural life. Today, only the large lorries that are thundering through the streets remind of a world beyond the town's own limits. Back in the 1930s, even such lorries would have been a rarity. For Germans of the Third Reich, however, what existed here was enough to cause havoc to the town and its residents and to massacre huge numbers of the population.

How did it all once start for this town and its Jewish citizens? Mordchei ben-Szlomo Grajpner, a survivor of the Shoah and a native of Szczekoczyń who would later continue his life in Israel, had this today:

> *We lack real historical sources, as far as Jewish Szczekociny is concerned. It is speculated that Szczekociny was one of the first Polish Jewish communities. Older inhabitants of the town had said that the first to settle there were immigrants, actually refugees from Germany, and that most of these had come from the Szwarcbojm family), who had started dyeing workshops besides the river. The Zylbersztajn*

---

[12] Ibid. and p. 13

Family were also amongst these first settlers. Their trade was the making of glutinous glue out of leftover (animal) skins. Others who founded this Jewish community came here later.[13]

And before that? We can only speculate about the history of my ancestors before their arrival in Szczekociny. My personal DNA analysis may at least provide some clues. Whilst such analyses are based on calculations based on averages and cannot give total certainty, mine stated, that a partial Mizrahi ancestry was recognisable.[14] Mizrahi Jews in this context refer to Jewish populations that lived once roughly in the area between Baghdad and the Persian territories. Jewish people arrived there after the destruction of the First Temple of Jerusalem. The DNA analysis found living relatives of mine who were born in Aleppo, Syria and in Iraq, third to fifth cousins with whom I have common ancestors, no more than 300 or 400 years ago. Mizrahi migration to Europe is closely linked to Iraq, the Caucasus and trading centres such as that of biblical Babylon. Some Mizrahi Jews may have traded with the Iberian Peninsula during the Arab-Islamic rule that lasted between 711-1492 or even settled there. They were therefore probably also part of the Jews expelled during the Reconquista and the Spanish Inquisition of the 15th and 16th century. Some of these fled to the Ottoman Empire. In the 16th and 17th centuries, migration continued for some, for example via the Balkan regions, into various parts of Eastern Europe. Italian, Greek, Romani, Arab and Persian Jews were often forced to flee to Eastern Europe and were frequently regarded as *"Iberian Sephardim without distinction. Ashkenazi Jews, those Jewish people from Central Europe intermixed* with these groups for centuries."[15] One of the reasons behind the Jewish settlement was Casimir IV's invitation of Italian and Sephardic Jewish communities to

---

[13] Pinkes, p. 167 Translation by the author
[14] Mizrahi, hebr. Eastern
[15] Avraham (2010), own translation from English

Poland in 1475.[16] The role of the city of Krakow as a centre of Jewish learning since the 16th century may also be linked to further migration of Jewish people with a Mizrahi background. In addition, Upper Silesia and other neighbouring areas were connected to Italy and Sefad in the Galilee, another centre of Jewish religious scholarship during the Ottoman Empire.[17] In addition, the persecution of Jewish people by the Byzantine Empire drove Jews into Russian-Polish peripheral areas.[18]

I am unable to say if the Mizrahi link exists via my paternal grandfather (the Zylbersztajn family) or my grandmother (the Landau family) or both.

Five per cent of my DNA also point to Ashkenazi Jewish ancestors, and thus to the possible role of merchant Jews with connections to the Silk Road in the Middle Ages.[19]

However, centuries had passed between the actual settlement and my father's generation, and the memory of these migration routes had been forgotten. It is therefore no surprise that my father considered himself to be Ashkenazi when asked, but genetically, if my tests are to be trusted, the story is a different one. Without my DNA analysis, the Mizrahi ancestry would have remained completely concealed, its revelation is a gift of modern science to a forgetful humanity.

Other traces in my DNA point to ancestors in Asia Minor, Greece, Southern Europe and the Balkans, as well as traces of ancestors on the Arabian Peninsula and North Africa.

The German name Silberstein seems to have emerged later. It was put into Polish spelling as Zylbersztajn by most likely Polish bureaucrats. Silberstein is possibly a fantasy name adopted in the 18th century under Austrian rule, in which Jewish people could choose or buy their names.[20] Before that, Jewish surnames referred to their parents, usually their father

---

[16] Brook (2003), p. 8.
[17] Marks (2019)
[18] Brooks (2003)
[19] See e.g. Pullan-Sheffield (2016), Jiao-Yang et Al (2015)
[20] Gilad (2014)

The "Illiterates"

(such as Ben David or Ben Ascher), their tribal descent (such as Kohen or Levi) or their professions (Haddad, Schreiber, Hassan, Rabin).[21] In addition, as this book will demonstrate later, I am also strongly linked to Dutch people, via my maternal grandmother. And that is not all. One of my maternal great-grandmothers and one of my great-great-grandmothers were born as Christian Germans. In the end, however, ancestry refers to hair-splitting of different human migration routes within the last 2000–5000 years. Kevin Brooke (2003), who summarises the origins of the Eastern European Jewish populations in far more depth and better than I can do here, also concludes that there were multiple migration routes.[22] Ultimately, all people have the same ancestors before humans left the African continent 60,000-90,000 years ago.

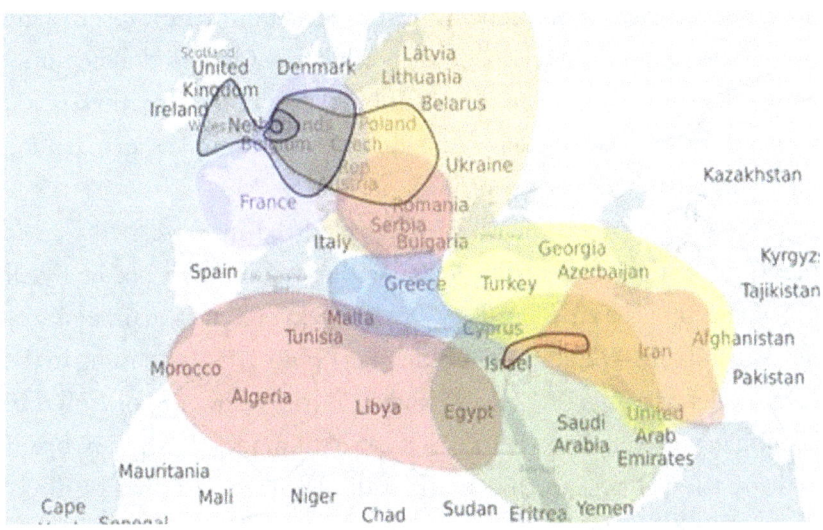

Spectrum of the closest verifiable human population groups I am descended from. The important thing is however that human history goes far beyond this analysis. In the end, all family trees from across the globe come together!

Source: My Heritage DNA analysis. Source (c) MyHeritage.com

---

[21] ibid.
[22] Booke (2003)

We often overemphasise the small external differences or migration routes created by geographical adaptation. Yuval Harari's book *Sapiens, A Brief History of Mankind*, may give those interested a deeper insight into the story of our common origins.[23] My point is, that the history of my family therefore neither begins in Munich, Poland or Babylon, nor with the Israelite tribes and Moses, but rather, as with all people, with the genesis of *Homo sapiens* on the African continent 300,000 years ago. In religious terms we are all but distant cousins too, created as humans in the image of G-d. It feels important to mention this. My intention is that this book should bring us closer together, rather than further divide us.

Concrete information concerning the history of my father's family can only be given from around the 20th century. At that time, around 5000 people lived in Szczekociny, just over half of them Jewish. Many of them were distantly related to each other according to the memorial chronicle *Pinkes Szczekocin* compiled by the survivors after the Shoah, which described the entire Jewish kehilah (community) as an extended family in the broadest sense of the word.

As already hinted, Jewish people have lived in Szczekociny since the 17th century, and it did not take long for them to become well known beyond the city's borders. One of them became a main figure of Hasidic Judaism – Rabbi Dovid Biderman (1746-1814, according to the Jewish calendar 5506-5574), also known as "the Lelower Rebbe." Rabbi Biderman was well renowned for his apparent modesty, as a clairvoyant and miracle worker. To this day, Hasidic Jews regard him as a direct descendant of the biblical King David.[24]

Biderman is said to have prophesied before none other than the French Emperor Napoleon that the later would not be victorious against the Russians. As a token of thanks for this prophecy, the Rebbe is said to have received the reward of a red cloak from Napoleon.

---

[23] Harari (2014)
[24] From Szwajcer, Isroel (Ben-Awrom) (2010) Pinkes Szczekoczyny, own translation.

The Jewish history of Szczekociny also includes an anecdote about a pious old Jewish man who is said to have once offered bread and water to the famous Polish leader General Tadeusz Kościuszko (1746-1817). In return, the old man supposedly was given a diamond-studded saddle cushion from the General, which according to legend was later transformed into a *parochet*, the prayer curtain of the synagogue in Szczekociny.[25] Shoah Survivors reported that the Polish State Museum had apparently shown an interest in the curtain in the 1930s.[26]

Another legend relating to the same General Kościuszko recites the story of a Jewish colonel by the name of Berek Joselewicz, who had fought alongside this general.[27] Much was also recorded about Rabbi Dov Bar Meisel (1798-1870, 5558-5630), who had participated in the November Uprising against Russia in 1831 and then again in the Polish January Uprising in 1863. In 1854, Bar Meisel had been invited to serve the Jewish community in Warsaw and two years later became chief rabbi of Poland. To the Jewish population such stories were important proof of their Polish loyalty.

How is one to imagine Szczekociny as it stood at the time of my father's birth? Firstly, around 1920 most of the houses would have still been wooden structures. Further, the town only saw the introduction of any electricity gradually, not all had electricity supply, and running tap water was completely unknown. Instead, water still had to be carried from wells. Horses transported people and most of the goods until well into the 1930s.

At number 20, right on the market square, known by everyone simply as "*rynek*," my grandfather Herszik owned a leather-shop, above which he and my grandmother Szyfra (née Landau) and their children lived. What my grandfather earned from his work as the town's leather worker (dad always referred to the profession as "leather cutter") sufficed for all essential necessities.

---

[25] from Szwajcer, Isroel (Ben-Awrom) (2010), own translation
[26] ibid
[27] Zelman (1995), p. 16

Leon Zelman recorded in his memoirs that "*the merchants and craftsmen led their lives as they seemed to have been marked out by God, in poverty and modesty. They did not serve scholarship; they spent their lives in the arduous pursuit of a meagre livelihood. Most of them were very poor.*"[28]

My father and his brothers and helped in the business and had learnt the family trade directly from their father, as it had been for generations. The hours of labour were long. Often it would be leather shoes and boots that he cut measured to specific sizes. Maybe he also prepared the leather for tefillin, the Jewish prayer straps, furniture upholstery, and perhaps was also involved in the making of saddles. As a child, I could often observe my father repairing shoes or re-covering chairs with leather, a skill that went all the way back to what my grandfather had taught him. My father kept small hammers, pliers and nails in a chest, where also a shoe-makers tripod was stored.

In his memoirs, Leon Zelman vividly recalled my grandfather, whom he referred to only as a cobbler, though my father would disagree to this label, in the following paragraph:

The cobbler's name was Silberstein, and I (also) enjoyed watching him, in particular, when I was given shoes that he had sewn by hand especially for me. He even had a small factory where the shoes were made by machine and a shop on the market square where he sold these. But Silberstein's hand-sewn shoes were something (particularly) special. Some craftsmen were philosophers, and even if they didn't want to change the world, they would talk for hours about the ways of life.[29]

Not only my grandfather Herszl (born 1890/5650), my grandmother Szyfra (born 1891/5651) and my father lived there, but also the rest of the family. Moisze (born 1909/5669) was the first son of my grandparents, Abraham was their second (born 1916/5781), my father

---

[28] Zelman (1995), p. 18 (translation by author)
[29] ibid

Wolf (born 1919/5679) was the third son, their fourth son was Dawid (probably born 1923/5689) and Fiszl (probably born 1930/5690) was their fifth, last and youngest son in the family.[30] My father's grandfather had also lived and died in the house at the end of his life, as my father recalled. Herszik's parents, my great-grandparents, were called Yaakov and Sarah and had another daughter, Orla Schwarzbojm.[31] The parents of my grandmother Szyfra, who had an older sister called Maria Laja (born 189/5659, married name Wajntrob), lived in the neighbouring village of Lelow. Their names were Josek Mendel Landau (born 27 September 1864/5624) and Sura Ryfka Landau (born Rzezak, 11 November 1862/5623), both hence my great-grandparents.[32]

Neither my father nor my uncles ever spoke about family members like my grandmother after the Shoah. They mentioned little about life before September 1939, when the German troops had marched into their town. Such memories about the good times of people who were all dead now, were too painful. This increases the value the memories

---

[30] Some dates of birth can only be assumed. Moisze, also known as Mosche. Moiszek and Mischa, was born on 3 May 1909 according to his Israeli death certificate. Abraham (also Abram) was born on 18 August 1916, according to his grandson Yaron Zylbersztajn. Wolf Zylbersztajn was born on 16.1.1919. Dawid's date of birth in the Buchenwald concentration camp records is 16 May 1925, but it is difficult to say whether this is the real date. Fiszl's date of birth is calculated according to the stories of his surviving brothers. My father had written 1930 for Fiszl in his entry at Yad Vashem, my uncle recorded instead 1925. It is clear that Fiszl was the youngest of the brothers. The description of my father that his youngest brother was still a boy in 1942 suggests 1930 as the more likely year of birth.

[31] According to a document from Abraham Silberstein (my uncle) on the death of his father, that he submitted to Yad Vashem. (Item 5676605). The Schwarbojm fled before the Germans arrived. I have no memory of my grandfather's sister, but I do remember her husband.

[32] Sura's parents were Perla (born Najberg 1821/5581)) and Abram (born 16.9.1824/5584) from Koniecpol, not far from Sczekociny. Their children were Sura, Cerka Ester, Dyna and Fajga. Abram's parents were the mohel Herszik Rzezak (c.a.1788-1857/5548-5617) and Matel Matla Rzezak née Nochemowicz, c.a. 1790-1881/5550-5621). Herslik's father was called Itzyk and was born c.a. 1770/5530. Herszik and Matel had eleven children. Icek, Masza, Esther, Maryna, Sura, Rayza, Dan, Dawid, Abram, Dwojra, Fajgla, Masza.

written down in "Pinkes Szczekocin" and those of Leon Zelman's memoir considerably.

Zelman, for example, wrote at length about the importance of Shabbat in Szczekociny:

> *Saturday was their big, beautiful day. On that day they treated themselves to their best of abilities, however little that may have been, none of them went without a feast, or without dressing up, and certainly not without the custom of inviting someone even more needy if they could somehow afford it.*[33]

Unlike larger towns, which tended to adapt to modern times, Szczekociny remained religiously more traditional. In fact, life in this small town only consisted of but three days, as Leon Zelman put it. The first of these days was Shabbat, the second was the Christian Sunday, during which Jewish youths, including Zelman himself, had the opportunity to indulge in exciting adventures into the neighbouring woodland, unlike on Shabbat, when that was not allowed. Thirdly, every Wednesday the town's market was held.[34]

Until 1939, there existed not only *stybl* – prayer rooms – and a synagogue in Szczekociny, but also two Jewish cemeteries. While many prayed faithfully every day, the faith of others slowly began to diminish. Zionist groups offered exciting authentically Jewish alternatives, whilst others may have flirted with a new surrogate Elohim (G-d) from neighbouring Russia – communism.

My father always emphasised that his family was not one of the particularly religious ones. Instead, he said, that he was a member of the Gordinia Movement, one of the many Zionist youth groups.[35]

---

[33] Zelman (1985), p. 13
[34] Zelman (1995) p. 10, p. 13, p. 31
[35] It was one of the many Zionist movements in the city, alongside Poale Zion and, Hitachdut, Ha-Noar ha-Zioni, Betar and Mizrachi. Gordinia's mission was above all to specialise in agriculture in order to have the necessary knowledge to cultivate the land when emigrating to beloved Yisroel.

His brothers, Abraham and Moisze, on the other hand, were attracted to the more conservative Zionist movement Cherut. Despite such interests, my father told me, that he attended synagogue alongside his father every week on Saturdays.[36]

Mordche ben Szlomo, a survivor of the Shoah, also recalled three groups within the Jewish population. The first, he said, was dedicated to Torah study. He described the second group as "farmers, who read the holy books" and the third as but "simple Jews", who were "craftsmen and merchants" who only prayed at the birth of their children and were active members of co-operatives rather than of religious services.[37] My father's family, I would guess, probably belonged to this third category, though my grandmother's grandfather Herszik Rzezak was still a mohel.[38]

Younger people were similarly divided into different groups. Children initially learnt free of any charges in the *cheder*. Between the ages of ten to twelve they began however to go their separate ways. The offspring of the more affluent families often studied at the *Melamed Dardacha* religious school. Others learnt the Gemara with older scholars, and some even sent their children to schools and later even universities abroad, to cities like Vienna or Paris.[39] Children from less well-off families or of non-religious backgrounds acquired the professions of their parents or those of others in the community instead.

Many of those who recorded their memories of the times before the Second World War in *Pinkes* also remembered the fun and the adventures of their younger years before the war. Isroel Gurtman in one who could not forget the beauty of the nearby lake and the forest "full of blackberries and raspberries," all in the immediate vicinity of the town. He described it as "a true paradise on earth."[40]

---

[36] Zylbersztajn, Wolf (2001), Cassette I, 4:40, Shul yid Synagogue
[37] Pinkes, p. 170.
[38] Mohel, person trained to perform trad, relig. Jewish brits (circumcisions).
[39] Zelman (1985), p. 17. The Gemara is the newer part of the Talmud, the collected work in which the writings of the Old Testament are interpreted and discussed.
[40] Isroel Gurtman (Kiriat Białystok) in Pinkes Szczekociny, p. 122

During the summer months, children would rush to the nearby lake to swim or to run around in the many meadows of the area.[41] Szczekociny's winters, on the other hand, were bitterly cold and harsh, "full of snow", as my father described it, often with the additional remark, "We still had real winters then." And it certainly had its attractions, such as ice skating on the Pilica River.[42]

At the rynek, that large, rectangular market square all the important shops were Jewish owned the survivors argued, and it included Leon Zelman's father's grocery shop. Rynek was the centre of the town. On market day all of the town's residents would meet there to shop and trade, and most likely gossip.[43] Tradespeople and farmers from the many neighbouring regions gathered here. Zelman labelled the place "an antipode of religious life and the centre of all important events and communication, which included a non-Jewish tavern."[44]

Zelman described the town's market day in vivid colours:

"Horse-drawn carts came from everywhere, farmers sold their goods, brought their animals (chickens, rabbits and goats), took home goods from the shtetl with the money they had earned and frequented the Jewish Inns. To us children, the key attraction on the square was Lentscher, the large café on placed on the corner of the market. It served the finest of cakes, and we used all of our last saved pennies to purchase a lolly or some chocolate on our way home from school."[45]

Those who left their memories of Szczekociny in *Pinskes* also mentioned distilleries, bakeries, tanneries, mills, sawmills and even a paper factory, whose owner was known to most people only by his nickname "Borech Papiernik".

---

[41] Ibid.
[42] Zelman (1995), p. 31
[43] Ibid.
[44] Ibid. p. 12
[45] ibid, p. 18f.

"Papiernik" once created the watermarks on Russian banknotes (the city was under the Russian Empire at the time) and became a legend because he apparently demanded the resignation of the then mayor, a man who was known to treat Jewish people very badly, as a token for his services.[46]

Other sources of pride for the community were the library, the cinema and the theatre with many theatre performances.[2]

The highlight of the town's weekly rhythm was the Shabbat. The Jewish Shoah survivor Icchok Kuperberg struggled to find the right words to describe Shabbat and Jewish holidays in Szczekociny:

You can't simply describe this joy, lack of worries, closeness and familiarity on the page of this book. Singing and dancing were everywhere. Everyone had the same feelings when somebody got married in the city. Without exception, they all felt the same joy, as if it had been their own hazene – wedding.[47]

Zelman called it all "a foretaste of the paradise on earth." Prior to Shabbat evening there women had to engage in many laborious tasks, including shopping and cleaning the house all washing and clothing the children under great pressure. The imminent arrival of Shabbat would be announced on Friday afternoons by the shamash who knocked on the windows of the Jewish inhabitants of the town.[48] Men and boys then hurried to the mikveh, the ritual bathhouse, and from there to the synagogue. From there they returned home for the Shabbat meal.[49] On Saturday mornings, after the call from the shamash, the whole family would make their way to the synagogue and then a sense of momentary peace remained for the rest of the day until the women celebrated the new onset of the week with the *Havdalah* Ceremony in the evening and everyone prayed for a good and blessed week.[50]

---

[46] ibid.
[47] Pinkes Szczekociny (Polish edition) p. 100, own translation, hazene, yid. wedding.
[48] Shamash – synagogue servant, *kehelah* – community, shul – synagogue.
[49] Zelman (1985) p. 10
[50] Ibid. p. 9 (freely translated by author) shul, yid. Synagogue. *Havdalah*: traditional

According to Zelman, everyone adhered to this Shabbat order.

No matter what social utopia one pursued or what social class one belonged to, Friday evening in the Shtetl had to be a wonderful evening, even if one lacked funds. It would be unthinkable without the sight of some chicken and fish. On Shabbat, people made time for each other and peace and quiet reigned. It was less the religion itself any longer, but this sense of peace that was still able to impose itself onto everyone in this shtetl, be they old or young, Rebbe or challutzim (Zionist youth), water carriers or socialist students, with a feeling of belonging together.[51]

Zelman also reported that the women of the Shtetl – he thought of women such as his own mother – were in his view, the real sources of its strength. He argued that they were stronger than the men because it was them who led the practical life. This was obvious to every child, he claimed.[52] His father, in contrast, was but a "distant figure" compared to her.[53]

Of course, it were also women who would bake the *challot* – the special Shabbat breads. These *challot* were prepared by them at home and then taken to be baked in bakehouses. According to my father, women often sold more bread to these bakehouses and not, as today, the other way round, when many Jewish people usually buy their *challot* from bakers.

Ben Pinchas, who also survived the Shoah, left the following memories concerning Shabbat in Szczekociny in Pinkes:

There is no one who would be able to describe in our (human) words the appearance of our city on the eve of Shabbat, its royalty and splendour – the Jewishness of the Queen of Shabbat. On Friday evenings, the face of our city was full of grace and at that time the entire essence of Judaism appeared in every part of the city,

---

prayer that marks the end of the Shabbat and the beginning of the new week.
[51] Zelman (1985), p. 22, loosely translated by author
[52] Ibid. p. 24
[53] Ibid. p. 25

fully immersed in Shabbat and taken over by it. And what light of Holiness of the Shechinah came over our city on the eve of Shabbat! The candles were inside in polished copper and silver and shone out of every house and window. And from the many streets and from inside the study houses, arose the evening melodies of "Lecho dodi likras kala, pnei Shabbat nekabala!" No pen can convey and describe the sensations that every single Jew felt in such moments of spiritual ecstasy, when everything brightened up with glory and Holiness. This was the wonderful synthesis of our city: sharp Talmudic wisdom – popular simplicity – and an abundance of popular humour.[54]

The synagogue of Szczekociny was located directly beside the market square and distanced only but 500 metres from the town's Christian baroque church. Izyk Mendel Bornstein remembered the shul as a living being:

It was one of the most beautiful synagogues in Poland, it was large for the (smaller) city (and community) that we were, and it was highly respected throughout the country. The Aron Hakodesh was fashioned with decorations and two cherubim and of golden trumpets. It was quite high to go up there, a few steps for sure, and there (inside) lay our sacred Toireh. The floor was made of marble, the curtain was light-coloured and velvety. The Ten Commandments were written out in gold lettering, and on the wall there was a picture of a large whale and a buffalo. For me as an eleven-year-old (boy), the pictures were so vivid that they came to life and made me afraid to be (t)here on my own. It was clear to me and to my friends that if the Messiah came, there would be enough whale meat for everyone (to eat). There was another drawing that represented the tree of Adam and Chava. The ceiling was like a celestial firmament with the colours and signs of the clouds, stars and the sun. It was such an extraordinary work of art, that I find it difficult to put in words. The

---

[54] Szwajcer (2010), p.192, own free translation. Shechinah – hebr. dwelling, Lecho dodi – trad. song sung after the lighting of the Shabbat candles.

entrance for women was twelve to fifteen metres high so that everyone could see and hear the chazans as they entered. Each woman had a stand for her prayer book. I remember as a child looking up (from below) to try to spot my mum there, but I never succeeded.[55]

The synagogue of Szczekociny the interior was destroyed by the Germans during their occupation. Photo from the archive of Yossi Bornstein.

---

[55] Bornstein (2009). Free translation by author. Aaron Kodesh – sacred prayer cabinet containing the Torah scrolls. Toire – yid Old Testament. Chazan – trad. Jewish Prayer singer, Chava – hebr. Eve

My own father was less enchanted by "the shul." He couldn't even tell me much about his bar mitzvah – nothing more than that people had thrown chocolate at him.[56] Perhaps the memories of Izyk Bornstein are of better help here, for example when he looked back at celebrations during the festival of Purim before the war. In *B-94, The Spirit of a Survivor* (2009), Bornstein reported on this "wonderfully funny festival" in the centre of the market square:

We would all wear different masks and costumes, it was sometimes hard to recognise each other. Some would walk on stilts three to four metres high, and there was usually a character dressed as a dancing bear who would dance around while people clapped their hands and laughed."[57]

Hanukkah, the winter Jewish festival of lights, was celebrated with dreidel games, latkes and ponshkes (pancakes and doughnuts), writes Bornstein. In his detailed descriptions he also recounts how two geese were slaughtered and prepared for the festival and how their left-over plucked feathers were saved for another festive purpose: goose feather filled pillows that could later become fitting wedding presents for a couple in the future.

Bornstein also left a mention about the non-kosher Brygalski Tavern of the town. He remembered that sometimes fights would erupt which were so intense that they required police intervention. Sweeter memories went back to the impressive bookshop of the Wojtasinksi-Family, Polish-Christian neighbours of the Bornsteins, with whom the family got on well. Bornstein confesses to having been a friend of their daughter Kazimiera.[58] Leon Zelman too mentioned non-Jewish friends in his memoirs.[59]

---

[56] Zylbersztajn, Wolf (2001), Cassette I, 6:00. The throwing of sweets in synagogue, after a first reading of a person is a Jewish custom.
[57] Bornstein (2009)
[58] Bornstein (2009)
[59] Zelman (1995)

My own father had only told me that "they (Jews and Christians) were all the same and all went to school together." The town library is said to have kept both Polish and Yiddish books and, as my father suggested, all the children of the town went to the same Polish primary school, regardless of their religion or ethnicity.

Bornstein also mentions other seemingly integral parts of Jewish life in Szczeociny. Just as in the story of Tevye, the milkman of the famous Yiddish author Sholem Aleichem, Szczekociny's Jewish community had "*shadchen*" – professional Jewish matchmakers. Whether my grandparents Szyfra and Herszl found each other through the efforts of such a matchmaker, I am unable to say.[60]

Foodwise, Bornstein recalled the delicacies of "Golden Joich" (chicken broth), lokshen, fried fish, roast beef, chocolate cake, cheesecake and apple pie. The latter delicacies were all favourites of my father and his brothers who survived the Shoah. They also loved pickles, sauerkraut, "gefilte fish", roast chicken and goose and various sausages and kreplach. Many also often served "fat carp from the ponds of Halperts (palace building) with butter or Lokshen to greasy 'Goldener Joich'".[61] Milk supposedly came directly from the cows (and not through merchants).[62]

More surprising, however, is Icchok Kuperberg's statement that Jews could also acquire unkosher forbidden meat in Szczekociny – he mentions explicitly ham – and even more surprising that this meat was scandalously sourced from some Jewish shops. Kuperberg names several people he knew, who sold these religiously unauthorised meats.[63]

One of the wealthiest residents of Szczekociuny was a man by the name of Jan Ciechanowski, Poland's ambassador to the United States in the 1920s and 1930s, who resided in the towns small castle, a bit like a large British stately home on the outskirts of Szczekociny. Bornstein

---

[60] Bornstein (2009)
[61] Memories of Isroel Gurtman, Szwajcer (2010), s. 124, own translation. Lokshen are egg based broad noodles, own translation
[62] ibid.
[63] Szwajcer (2010), own translation

remembered it well and marvelled over the fact that Ciechanowski, despite of his high status, openly greeted ordinary people like his father, which was quite unlike the behaviour of other persons of higher status.[64]

On Sundays, Jewish and Christian young people alike would stroll to the castle's gardens, where they could admire the welcome sight of all sorts of animals, from horses to peacocks. Looking back, Bornstein recalled also beautiful flowers and smells.[65]

The Jan Ciechanowski Castle in Szczekociny in 2022. Photo DZL.

A further insight into life within families in Szczekociny is provided by Itzyk Bornstein, describing the spot that remained reserved for his father at the dinner table and the fact that none of the children were allowed to approach their mother directly, but could only do so through their eldest sister.

We would never dare to approach our mother directly for anything. We would ask Sara (Bornstein's older sister) first, because we first needed her

---

[64] Bornstein (2009)
[65] ibid

agreement that we could disturb our mother. If she didn't agree, we were to accept that, even if we didn't like it. We also learnt to respect our siblings according to age.[66]

Pinkes Szczekocin brings the memory of other people back to life. One such family is that of the doctor Zelik Majzler, another, that of lawyer Chaim Simen Engländer or that of the town's philosopher Chaim Hersz Zwi Judkewicz. None of them survived the Shoah.[67]

Weddings were one of the highlights within the Jewish community of Szczekociny. It is almost hard to imagine now, but reportedly they could last for up to eight days. Almost the entire Jewish population took part in them. Another highlight was the street dances during the festival of *Simchat Torah*, as Itzak Kuperberg remembered:

> *The same joyful atmosphere as at weddings overwhelmed the town's Jews during Simchat Torah, the joyous festival concerning Torah. Everyone, without exception, danced in the streets and filled every corner with joy. All social distinctions between people vanished. Everyone became part of a dancing, celebratory crowd, and it seemed as if even the stones in the middle of the market were dancing along and enjoying the merriment of their Jews.*[68]

A personal memory my father and his brother Abraham retold, and which must have been an unforgettable night for family was an incident with a rat. My father's older Abraham, then just a young boy, was allegedly bitten by a rat on his most sensitive spot during his sleep. Whether true or not, people probably had to live with such rodents back then. According to their stories, my grandfather solved the transgression in an unconventional and spectacular yet unfortunate ending for the rat in question. He grabbed his shotgun

---

[66] Bornstein (2009)
[67] Szwajcer (2010)
[68] Szwajcer (2010), own translation

and one single shot did the job. It must have left a big impression on his young boys.[69]

The years of their childhood, the mid-1920s, were a time of great change for Szczekociny, especially concerning the cultural outlook of Jewish residents. Until that time, life had been dominated by religious community leaders. Awrum Szwarcbojm, my great-uncle (husband to my grandfather Herszik's sister), wrote about the first disputes between the uncompromising and traditional Orthodox community and the emerging Zionist movements.[70] By 1924 the town had two community representatives, one from each camp. This was seen as a victory by the progressives.

> *This victory encouraged new demands on a constant level. Their aim was to put Jewish urban life on the tracks of progress and culture and, above all, to contribute to the realisation of the Zionist ideals.*[71]

These developments were later reflected electorally. In 1929, the nationalists, as Szwarcbojm described the non-orthodox Jewish members of Szczekociny's Jewish council, held a majority of six of the nine seats in the community for the first time. In 1934, Szwarcbojm himself was elected to the council of the Kahal. It may have continued, but 1934 was going to be the last test, as subsequent elections were not held due to the German invasion of 1939.

Szwarcbojm reported that the Jewish council of Szczekociny was one of the first of any Polish town to support boycotts of German goods in solidarity with Germany's Jewish population. How unfortunate that only a few years later they themselves became victims of Nazi Germany.

---

[69] orally told stories of my father and his brother
[70] Also spelled within this book as Schwarzboim and Shwarzboim, depending on the source quoted.
[71] Awrum Szwarcbojm in Szwajcer (2010), p. 89,

The market square in Szczekociny, where all the shops were once Jewish, in August 2022. One of the houses in the background was my grandfather's. Photo DZL.

My father told me next to nothing about such things. A possible explanation for his silence was suggested by Itzyk Bornstein, when he wrote the following:

> *These wonderful memories are also immensely painful for me. They made me deeply sad because of everything that came so suddenly. What was a peaceful existence was, in the most brutal way, destroyed with death. Every time I look back, I long for those who were murdered and were lost forever. I can only imagine what happened to all my schoolmates and teachers after the Nazis set up a ghetto in Szczekocin and imprisoned the Jews of my town before they deported them to Treblinka.*[72]

Still, before 1939, if one is to believe Bornstein, there were traces of antisemitism in Szczekociny. From the stories he and others left us, Jewish and Christian residents of the town had certainly worked closely side by side. And yet, he said this: "*Sometimes they would call us 'Moshek'. That was a bit insulting, but nobody got upset about it. We needed them,*

---

[72] Bornstein (2009) retranslated by author

they needed us," he continued.[73] In fact, Jewish religious households, required non-Jews to perform certain tasks for them during Shabbat, but non-Jews also served as maids and in other posts. Bornstein remembered non-Jewish Poles who spoke Yiddish, and that his mother was baking Easter bread for her Christian neighbours.[74]

When I asked my father about antisemitism before 1939, he was dismissive:

"We got on well with the Poles, we didn't have any problems. I also had Polish acquaintances. We (Jews) attended the (regular) Polish middle school. We absolutely had no trouble with anyone!" [75]

Leon Zelman too confirmed this. He wrote:

"We young Jews didn't feel like we lived in a ghetto in (this) shtetl. No differences existed between Jews and Christians. At worst, when a farmer felt cheated by a Jew on market day, it was because his (the Jewish person) superior education was always suspect (to them, the farmers). We didn't feel discriminated! To the contrary, some even looked with pity upon the Christians who didn't honour the Sabbath and therefore didn't know about its blessing." [76]

The only thing that once came up, as far as he remembered, were debates amongst the elders of the town, following the death of the political leader Marshal Pilsudki in 1935, and a law that aimed to prohibit kosher meat in Parliament.[77]

---

[73] Moshek – pol. Moses
[74] ibid.
[75] Zylbersztajn, Wolf (2001)
[76] Zelman (1995), S. 29
[77] Ibid. p. 14-15

3

The Lewandowskis

Jacob Lewandowski (1832-1885), picture supposedly painted
by Lovis Corinth (1858-1925).

Source Lewandowski (1981)

My great-great grandfather Jakob Lewandowski, recorded as Lewandowsky with a "y", was born on 27 February 1832 (5583) in the small town of Schöneck near Dresden, today renamed as Skarszewy, due to the once German area becoming part of Poland after 1945.[78] The town prided itself of both a Catholic and Protestant parish church, as well as a synagogue. Jacob's Jewish parents were Blume (née Zamory) and Markus Lewandowsky (both born 1799) and came from the same area. Whilst nothing is currently known about those two, it was their sons Jakob's professional specialisation in women's underwear, bodices and corsets, that would soon determine the direction of the family for four generations.

When Jacob was born in 1832, legal and political equality reforms that would have an immense impact on the freedom of Jewish people were under way. Up until the 19th century, restrictions and discrimination of Jewish people existed in many places. One of the first to institutionalise equality was an invader, Napoleon. Due to him, changes were introduced in Prussia in 1812, whilst many other German-speaking states remained unchanged. Not only that, in 1819 the "Hep-Hep Riots" flamed up, after the Bavarian Parliament debated the possibility of the emancipation of Jews. It led to members of many guilds and students marching through cities such as Würzburg, Frankfurt am Main and even Hamburg protesting against equality for Jews. They carried out countless attacks and acts of intimidation. Following the Prussian and British victory over Napoleon, Jewish residents of Bremen and Lübeck felt compelled to leave their cities.[79] Not even those in Germany who

---

[78] My great-uncle Alfred however believed that the family came from Kladau (Klodowa) near Dresden (in Lewandowski, 1981). In fact, both places, Kladau and Schöneck, appear in various family documents, it may be that the family lived in Kladau. Schöneck can be found on Jacob Lewandowsky's death certificate and is also the birthplace of his later wife Minna. A Lewandowski family from Posen, who also had a son by the name of Jacob, born in 1838, does not seem to be related, as that Jacob Lewandowski became a pasty maker and remained in Poznan all his life, see https://www.genealogieonline.nl/shirekchamove-tree/I03549.php (retrieved July 2020).

[79] Klärsn (2010): 1815-1833: Emanzipation und Akkulturation.

favoured equal rights for Jews wished to fully accept Jews as equals. What they principally desired was that Jews should sever their links to their religion and traditions in return for equal treatment. In other words, Jews had the right to become German equals through the process of shedding off their Jewishness.[80]

Berlin address book entry 1886.

By 1848 and 1849, when political and legal emancipation was finally said to be the intention of a total of 26 German states, only five small German states actually implemented the later. Of these, none had a sizeable Jewish population.[81] It took further debates and efforts on the equality issue until finally emancipation took hold under Bismarck.[82]

Meanwhile, lectures on the apparent differences of human races and on eugenics emerged and spread almost in parallel to the liberalisation.

For my great-great-grandfather, emancipation probably meant that he was able to marry a non-Jewish woman. Jakob Lewandowski's wife was Minna Sielmann, born as a Catholic in Schöneck in 1825 without great obstacles.[83] As far as is known, the couple not only stayed together for the rest of their lives but had seven children. These were

---

[80] ibid,
[81] Brenner et al. (1986), p. 298
[82] ibid
[83] Born on 28 May 1825.

probably Malwine 1852-1878, Max/Marcus (1852-1912), Adolph (1853-1902), Herrmann (1853-1904), Ernestine (later Wolf, 1855-1940) and Hans-Ludwig (born c.a. 1855-?), and my great-grand father David (1857-1929).[84]

Unfortunately, not much can be said about the life of Minna or Jacob only that, according to the family saga, Jacob opened a small textile shop in Kladau in 1856.[85]

Due to the legal changes that gifted Jewish people their status as equals, Jews were able to work their way up without the previous restrictions. Jacob Lewandowski seems to have been one of the beneficiaries, possibly bringing with it the end of insecurity and poverty for him and his family, though through hard work. This followed general trends. Poverty among Prussian Jews fell generally by 40-50 per cent (amongst all Jews) in the first half of the 19th century, settling at just 2.5 per cent in the year by 1858 (Prussia).[86] It was around this time of growing security, that my great-grandfather David was born in Kladau on the 20 February 1857 (5617), with his father's business having just opened the year before.

---

[84] Hebrew years: Malwine (5642- 5673), Max/Marcus (5612-5672), Adolph (5612 -5672), Herrmann (5613-5664), Ernestine (later Wolf, 5615-5700) and Hans-Ludwig (born c.a. 5615-? And David (5617-5689). A few dates about some individuals. Adolph Lewandowski was married to Michalina Amalie (born 1859) Ephraim. They had two children: Eugen Lewandowski (Dr jur.,1882-1923) and Walter Lewandowski. Hermann Lewandowski was married to Emma Sachs. His name appears in a newspaper advert at the time of his engagement as Herrmann, as well as in telephone directory entries and on his death as Hermann with an "r." Their daughter **Frieda (born 20 October 1900) was murdered in Auschwitz in 1943.** A document from the Third Reich lists her as a shorthand typist. See https://collections.arolsen-archives.org/en/document/128450671 (retrieved 7.2.2022) of Ernestine Lewandowski, there is a newspaper advertisement that she married Louis Wolff on 01.02.1886. She later married Louis and would have two children with him, Georg Wolff (1894-1942) and Helene Neumann (née Wolff, later wife of Albert Neumann).

[85] Lewandowski (1981)

[86] Klären (2010): 1815-1833: Emanzipation und Akkulturation.

Obituary of Minna Lewandowski who died on 19 April 1900 in Berlin. Image from My Heritage.

By 1871, the year emancipation was legally settled, the family appears to have moved to Berlin. Again, this move was similar other people of Jewish faith. In fact, between the years of 1852 and 1871, Berlin's Jewish population increased from under 10,000 people to 36,000.[1] Here in the capital of the new German Empire Jacob Lewandowski would lay the foundation stone of one of Germany's most successful corset businesses.

Ad. by Gebr. Lewandowski in "Berliner Tageblatt" 25.4.1908.

Eight years later, the Lewandowskis appeared for the first time in the Berlin address book with an entry for Köpenickerstraße 112, where they were listed as "Corset Manufacturers Gebrüder Lewandowski Hermann and Max."[87] In addition, there was an address book entry stating Blumenstraße 13 in Berlin-Spandau as the company's address.[88] Ernestine, the only sister of the "Lewandowski Brothers" is also listed in the address book. Remarkably, it says there, that she is the actual owner of a corset shop in Central Berlin's Rosenthalerstraße 21. That is quite an achievement for a woman in her own name at the end of the 19th century, with equality only just emerging. The rights to engage in politics and to vote would only follow decades later. But Ernestine may actually have held a key position in the family venture of the "brothers." In fact, it is almost inconceivable that a manufacturer of ladies' corsets could have been successfully established without the participation of women. Jacob Lewandowski was probably an excellent tailor and businessman, just like his sons, but without daughter Ernestine, indeed without Jacob's wife Minna, it seems implausible that this corsets manufacturer could ever have gone far. After all, it was all about female bodies, and they had to be accurately measured in an age that at least officially demanded respect and decency. Jacob's wife Minna and his daughter Ernestine, and possibly also, many years after them, my great-grandmother Luise (the wife David Lewandowski, see later) may have played a decisive role in this. Even my grandfather Gerhard married a seamstress almost 50 years later – my Dutch grandmother Maria – who, like the others, was also involved in the business and manufacturing side of things.

That said, from a contemporary perspective, the corset was certainly still a garment that was forced onto female bodies by harsh convention. Whatever we may think of it today, the ideal of beauty for a woman

---

[87] Gebrüder, German for Brothers. There is a huge housing estate there today in its place. The Lewandowskis were not the only company on this site. See https://www.xn--kpenicker-strasse-zzb.de/Koepenicker112.html (accessed 12/10/2022)

[88] Nothing remains of that building either, and visitors will discover only a modern school building on the site (Wilhelm Leuschner Secondary School).

in the 19th century was a waist of merely 40 cm. As a result, women had themselves laced and pressed into these corsets, almost as a form of voluntary torture.

Bruno Lewandowski's company, mentioned in a jubilee prospectus (Lewandowski, 1981).

The corset of the 19th century, which my great-grandfather and his sons specialised in, was therefore both fashion for "moral decency", and part of the erotic idealisation according to the fashion of the time.[89] Towards 1900, the shape of this elaborate garment changed into the so-called bodice-holder, which increased the emphasis of the bust and shifted the abdomen slightly backwards.

The Lewandowskis provided whatever the latest trend demanded, and soon became so popular that the new Lewandowski shop at Berlin's Blumenstraße 13 was too small. Eventually there would be 56 shops across German speaking countries carrying the Lewandowski name.

Berliner Gebr. Lewandowski shop, fitting the corset. Still from the advertising film, the corset fitting, by Julius Pinschwer, 1910, edited by absolut Medien in Julius Pinschwer, classic of the advertising film.

The shop at Leipzigerstraße 113 in Berlin was probably one of the main show rooms with its huge window display. Its shopfront can still

---

[89] Barbier & Boucher (2005) p. 164

be admired today, though the last time I visited, it served as furniture shop (if it is not the same shop it is very similar to the one displayed in film material). The main Berlin branch is said to have been however located at Alte Jacob Straße 20-22. Today that building no longer exists.

It may have been expansion plans that made my great-grandfather David Lewandowski move to Bavaria after opening a branch in 1885 on the other side of Germany, in Danzig, today Gdansk.[90] In the same year he established the southern German headquarters of the family business in his own name in the Bavarian capital of Munich. Not long after that, he opened branches in the most prestigious Munich shopping streets, such as at Theatinerstrasse 49, 1911 (with an extensive show-window and an in-house orthopaedic and repair workshop), Rosental 2, Neuhauserstrasse 13, Augustenstrasse 13 and, naturally for Munich, even by today's standards, at the city's heart, Marienplatz (number 18). In addition to conventional undergarments and corsets, they supplied medical-orthopaedic articles such as hernia bands and other medical support underwear.[91] A promotional leaflet from the 1960s describes the early days in these words:

> *The opening of the retail shop with customised and hygienic workshops in Munich's Rosenstrasse in 1889 was a sensation for Munich at the time with its perfectly shaped corsets and pretty decorations, especially the new spiral corsets. The company soon built up a good reputation thanks to its personalised and professional service. The titles of royal merchants to the court of Queen Maria Theresa of Bavaria, Princess Ludwig Ferdinand and Princess Adalbert of Bavaria and Infanta Eulalia of Spain and their frequent personal purchases from the company, as well as the diploma of honour from the 1924 Amsterdam Exhibition, are proof of the high reputation of this Munich company.*[92]

---

[90] According to a promotional leaflet c.a. 1960, privately owned by Philipp Lewandowski
[91] Ibid. p. 10
[92] Advertising leaflet c.a. 1960, privately owned by Philipp Lewandowski

Whilst the business grew, racism and hatred against Jews also continued to spread in parallel. Munich's first modern antisemitic association (the Deutsch Sozialer Verein) was founded in 1891. Four years later, in 1895 an audience of some 5,000 people came to listened to an antisemitic lecture by Hermann Ahwardt.[93] I currently have no knowledge of how the Munich-based Lewandowski family perceived these developments. Given the rapid growth of the company, they may have focussed more on business things, but at the same time, I am sure it was noticed.

David Lewandowski at the height of his success.

Jacob Lewandowsky passed away rather early in his life in 1885 (5645). Minna, his wife, followed him only three years later. But the fortunes of

---

[93] Brenner (2019), p. 34

this German-Jewish family business that he had set up perhaps, as suggested earlier, with the women in the family also involved, were already recognisable.[94] Jacob's sons, in particular my great-grandfather David and his brothers Max, Adolph and Herrmann, now managed branches of their father's business throughout the German Reich, with all items initially manufactured in their own factory.[95] Photos from this period depict a huge Berlin-based textile factory with large industrial buildings typical of the time, in which there were large weaving and sewing machines.

The size of the factory not only meant that Jacob, Minna and their children had been successful, but also suggests that they had probably expanded the family business with the help of a loan and which they used to their advantage. The achievements of Jacob Lewandowski(y), even with only the few fragmentary details that are so far known, allude to an ambitious, most probably non-stop working business man, who himself had grown up in modest circumstances.

And yet, apart from telephone book entries and surviving adverts and a few photos, not much more could be found about the family when writing this book series. Was this due to the destruction and looting during the later Third Reich? If there is more, maybe we shall discover it in the future.

Other Jewish families achieved equal fame through emancipation and hard work. At the time, 70 per cent of all German-speaking Jews resided in Berlin. They included prominent figures such as the department store owner Georg Wertheimer, the AEG founder Emil Rathenau, the banking house Carl Fürstenberg, the publisher Samuel Fischer and authors Kurt Tucholsky, and Max Liebermann and Lotte Cohn, to name but a few.

In the Bavarian capital of Munich, Jewish people also succeeded in breaking through prior glass ceilings despite a smaller Jewish population of only 11,000 people. Famous names included not only the Feuchtwanger family, but also the Cohen family and their chain of shops "A.B.Cohen"

---

[94] Death certificate recorded on 25 February 1885.
[95] I couldn't find out what the son Hans-Ludwig did.

that specialised in silk fabrics and furniture and who became royal Bavarian suppliers. Other notable success stories of Jewish business people were the Uhlfelder Department store and the textile merchant N. Stark, located at "Stachus 5" and the royal furniture manufacturer Ballin.[96]

It was trade that seemed to provide opportunities for Jewish people testing the freedoms of equality. A stunning total of 66 percent of Bavaria's Jewish people earned their living with trade, a further 19 percent in industry and crafts; the Lewandowskis seemingly combined the two.[97]

David Lewandowski's business card mentioning some of the royal clients. (Photo Lewandowski 1981).

It was not until the early 1920s that this opportune time for Jewish people withered due to the spread anti-Jewish sentiments, leading one Thomas Mann to describe Munich as becoming a city of stupidity."

---

[96] See Robert Brunner: Münchner Geschäfte, in Baumann (1995), pp. 109-127 and Heide Grunewald: Max Uhlfelder 1884-1958 in Baumann (1995) pp. 128-148 and Marguerette Strasser: N. Stark, also in Baumann (1995), pp. 134-146. On Ballin, see Tobias Mahl: „Die „Arisierung" der Hofmöbelfabrik Ballin in München. In Baumann and Heusel (2004), pp. 54-69

[97] Franziska Schott: The elimination of Jews from Munich's economic life in Baumann (1985), p. 149

David and Luise Lewandowski. From Lewandowski (1981).

Not unlike his father Jakob, David Lewandowski did not seem to be discouraged by supposed religious boundaries in marrying Luise Bertha Lenz (1866-1933), a German Christian.[98] Whilst his own mother Minna, born a Catholic, seems to have converted to Judaism, Luise remained a Christian.[99] In general, mixed-marriages, such as between Jews and Christians were no longer unusual at the turn of the century.[100]

The years around the turn of the century in this family, as for many others, seem to have been a time of religious intermixing and part of the *Haskalah* (Jewish enlightenment), and of greater opportunities and more equality. Jewish people in Germany finally had the same opportunities as

---

[98] Luise was born on 22 January 1866 in Rastenburg and died on 30 June 1933.
[99] She was buried in 1900 on the Jewish Weißensee Cemetery in Berlin.
[100] Even the much-quoted Jewish philosopher Martin Buber married Catholic woman who, like Minna Lewandowski, later converted to the Jewish faith.

everyone else, and in some families that meant that different members of the same family could belong to different religious affiliations.

Luise's and David's children were baptised. The decision to baptise children was, however, not always a choice of faith. Heinrich Heine and Walter Rathenau were not the only ones to be baptised in order to overcome social barriers.

But the wed-locked Lewandowski couple was still separated in death, with my great-grandmother Luise having been buried in Munich's Christian Nordfriedhof cemetery, and my great-grandfather David one kilometre further in Munich's New Jewish Cemetery.

Main shop at Theatinerstraße 49, Munich. My great-grandfather David Lewandowski seated, fourth from the left. My great-grandmother Luise on the right, my grandfather Gerhard Lewandowski, sixth from the left, Lewndowski (1981). It is possible that the photo was taken at the opening in 1911. Photo Lewandowski (1981).

Friedrich Wilhelm Lentz (1823-1881), the father of Luise and therefore also my great-great-grandfather, came from the German town of Königsberg, where he worked as a gunsmith. His wife, and Luise's mother, was Wilhelmine Lentz, née Koesling (1824-1899) and hence my great-great-grandmother.[101] She came from the town of Bantenberg, which lies at the border of what is now the Czech Republic and Poland.

David and Luise had four sons, Gerhard (1891-1956), Bruno (1895-1953), Alfred (1908-1983) and Willi (Wilhelm, 1904-1966).

Striatum of Prince Regent Ludwig Ferdinand of Bavaria.

---

[101] According to information on My Heritage, the parents of Wilhelmine Elisabeth (Wolf) Koesling and Johann(es) Koesling were master coopers. Johannes Koesling's father was Christoph Koesling, born c.a. 1765

Gerhard Lewandowski first from the left during the First World War. Own photo.

An insight into the life of the family in the years 1915 and 1916 can be found in the diary of my grandfather Gerhard Lewandowski. Supposedly he wrote many diaries, but so far only one has been recovered thanks to my late aunt Gerda. In it, he reports the lifestyle of a young member of the Bavarian well to do society. I found traces of splendour and extravagance through his visits of the finest Munich restaurants and hotels, as though this was normal. He also describes frequent visits to the theatre and the "English Gardens" of Munich, one of the big city parks.

The other side of the family in Berlin also did well at the turn of the century. One of the first ever advertising films in Germany was made in the year 1910 about Lewandowski Corsets. It was shot by Julius Pinschewer, a Jewish-German film pioneer, who later was forced to flee to Switzerland after 1933. The significance of the brand "Lewandowski Brothers" becomes clear through the names of the other companies that had such pioneering and exclusive advertising films prepared for them. They included the seasoning brand Maggi and the sparkling wine brand Kupferberg, both known to this day. The Lewandowski advertising film shows one of the Berlin shops – possibly the shop in Leipziger Straße in Berlin – with two customers in corsets. The sales assistant professionally laces up one of the corsets and then adopts a respectful distance from the distinguished lady customer in the frame, who is examining her fine underwear in the mirror with satisfaction. Her undergarment is decorated with elaborated ruffles. As mentioned earlier, it is women who take centre stage for the Lewandowski brand, no man can be seen here, except for some individuals rushing past in front of the shop.

David Lewandowski's shop in Theatinerstraße, 1912.

There is more, that indicates the grandeur. On June 5th, 1914, the Lewandowski Brothers had a brochure with their latest collection enclosed inside the Berlin newspaper *"Berliner Tagesblatt."* It read:

"Only through its enormous turnover can the corset house Lewandowski Brothers achieve (this) outstanding performance, both in terms of the quality of the material and in terms of the fit and the (seasonal) flavour of the corsets. The corset brochure enclosed (for you) today is so rich in illustrations, specialities included, that (it) certainly (can be described as) a firm favourite. We hope it will be an enjoyable read for all readers."[102]

Munich Phone Directory 1918.

The extended Lewandowski family in Berlin experienced other successes. Eugen Lewandowski (1882-1923, 5642-5683), the son of Adolph

---

[102] Berliner Tageblatt and Handelszeitung, Friday 5 June 1914, p. 15

Lewandowski, not only became the first member of the Lewandowski family to earn a university degree, but also entered a profession previously denied to Jews. The entry of an "Inaugural Dissertation" in 1909 was most probably his doctoral thesis.[103] Its title suggests discussions and issues of property law.[1] Tragically, Dr Eugen Lewandowski's success was however short-lived; in 1923, only 41 years old, he suddenly died. "A life full of work, a life full of love", was the inscription his family had put on his gravestone.

The interior of the Werk Building in Berlin. Photo from Lewandowski (1981).

As an advertising leaflet from the 1960s proudly remembers, in Munich, David Lewandowski's company succeeded in receiving the status of royal merchant.[104] Advertisement and a business card of the time stated this with pride.[105]

---

[103] Is the contract of sale in respect of a property subject to the formal requirement of § 313 B. G. B.? Ein Beitrag zur Lehre vom obligatorischen und dinglichen Vorkaufsrechte", Schöneberg-Berlin, Buchdruckerei von Gebhardt, Jahn und Landt, 1909.

[104] It is reported that they were royal purveyors to the court of Marie Therese of Austria-Este, the wife of Prince Ludwig III of Bavaria (1845-1921), Princess Adalbert of Bavaria, the mother of Prince Ludwig Ferdinand, Princess Amalie, the Infanta of Spain (1834-1905), Princess Maria de la Paz, the Infanta of Spain (1862-1946), and her younger sister Eulalia, also Infanta of Spain.(1864-1958).

[105] Lewandowski (1981)

Lewandowski Werk Building in Berlin.

In addition, the David Lewandowski company was listed in Munich's telephone directory in 1913 and 1914.[106] Her Majesty Maria Therese is said to have personally attended the opening of the shop in Munich's Theatinerstrasse. A handwritten note from Prince Ludwig Ferdinand of Bavaria to David Lewandowski also dates from this time.[107]

While my great-grandfather David was a migrant from the German-speaking East, such honours from the Bavarian Royal Family must have meant a lot to his four sons, who were all born in Munich. They were now fully and completely part of the upper echelons of the Munich establishment.

As the son of a well-to-do family, my grandfather Gerhard, being the eldest son, also socialised in artistic and intellectual circles, which, according to his daughters, included meeting people such as Thomas Mann, Jakob Wassermann and others. That was not unusual, as this

---

[106] According to Duke Franz's office and the secret state archives of Bavaria, documents relating to the purveyors to the Royal Bavarian court were destroyed in a fire. Duke Franz's office advised me to look at the entries in the Munich telephone directory. The company is listed there as a purveyor to the court of Her Majesty the Queen.

[107] Lewandowski (1981)

generation of well to do Jewish citizens of Munich tended to be rather liberal. Not the least because they were excluded from right-wing nationalist parties and associations but because they were increasingly described as supposedly un-German and foreign nationals, for no other reason but their religion. But we may put that point to the side for now, as my grandfather did not, due to his Baptism, understand himself to be Jewish and according to his diary, most of his friends and colleagues were also non-Jewish Germans.

Bruno Lewandowski as a non-commissioned officer in the telephone section (later the communications unit of the German military) Photo from Lewandowski (1981).

At the outbreak of the First World War, the Lewandowski company now owned two factories in Berlin and 64 shops with over 4000 workers.[108] The employees were said to receive social welfare services even before comparable initiatives were introduced by the state, at least

---

[108] Lewandowski (1981)

that is what is described by my great-uncle Alfred Lewandowski in his anniversary publication in 1981.[109]

My grandfather appeared to have had a good time during his initial military service. Before and after duty, he spent time in some of the finest and most expensive restaurants and theatres. It is fair to say that both Bruno and Gerhard Lewandowski served under the conviction that they were as German as anyone else. This is evident from entries in which my grandfather wrote about "our heroes and the enemy." He himself was a member of the Bavarian Red Cross medical service on the Ukrainian Eastern Front and in Alsace. The pleasurable excursions were soon replaced with the sombre reality of war.

Gerhard Lewandowski, 1918, own photo.

---

[109] Ibid. p. p.1

My grandfather wrote the following from Polish Wlodowa on 1st September 1915:

The hero's cemetery lies quietly – only the trees move in the wind, a picture of great suffering. Just now I look (up) from the door and see again the Russians throwing a corpse naked and dirty into the grave, there in the sack (lies) a man who died of cholera – quickly a small cross (is erected) over it –) that (man) was a hero – lying so abandoned in foreign soil.

What is man?
What is this war for?
That's how it is here in the field hospital behind the front line.

Just having started serving, my grandfather fell seriously ill and was ordered to spend six months in the Bavarian Alpine town of Garmisch-Partenkirchen for treatment, where he lodged in a private hotel next to the military field hospital at his own expense instead of staying in military accommodation. From there he wrote about several visits by his mother and his later first wife Anny. Once healthy again, he was sent to serve in Kolmar in Alsace alongside the French border.

From there he wrote about how he transported seriously injured soldiers from the frontlines between France and Germany in his military ambulance van. He speaks of his constant fear of French air raids. After the war, he would receive a Cross of Merit for these years of service. I can remember seeing this award as a child in my grandmother's house.

My grandfather Gerhard was thus one of many Germans on the German frontlines. His father David is listed on his and each of his brothers' birth certificates as a father of "Mosaic faith." How did this man, my great-grandfather, live out his Jewishness? Did he ever attend the "*Hauptsynagoge*" (main synagogue) in Munich, opened in 1887, in Herzog-Max Straße, near "Stachus" and which not only espoused the new equal rights given to Jews, but also the integration of the Jewish liberal Reform community into non-Jewish society? This liberal reform movement, which originated in the Jewish community of the German town Kassel in 1810, had spread rapidly throughout Germany at the beginning of the 19th century, encouraged by the winds of emancipation. In Munich, such developments of reformed faith and assimilation to the wider non-Jewish society were also recognisable, not the least through the organ that was placed inside the synagogue and the synagogue's mixed-gender choir.

Orthodox Judaism became the tradition of the minority of Jewish citizens in Munich, although the later immigration of Jewish people from Eastern Europe made sure it remained sizeable. Their place of worship in Munich was a different synagogue, the Ohel Jacob Synagogue.[110] Yet questions remain; how exactly David practised his Jewish faith, did the family keep Shabbat on Friday evening, did my great-grandfather not work on Saturday, observe Passover and did he attend synagogue on Yom Kippur? All of this cannot be determined until further evidence emerges.

The birth certificate of one of his sons, Bruno, tells us that the boy was baptised in St Luke's Church in Munich. My grandfather's diary reports numerous visits to churches. And instead of Passover, my grandfather Gerhard revealed degrees of excitement about Easter and Good Friday in his diary, at least during the First World War.

Prior to Munich becoming the nest of German fascism, it would first come under the spell of socialist ideals under the so called "*Räterepublik.*"

As purveyors to the royals of Bavaria, the Lewandowskis must have been, royalists, out of self-interest or conviction. Nevertheless, there could have been a divide within the family between a more liberal and a more national identity. In a later note after the Second World War, my grandfather stated that between 1918 and 1919 he was a consultant and head of the Bavarian Red Cross under Albert Roßhaupter. Roßhaupter was briefly Minister of State for Military Affairs during the Kurt Eisner government of the *Räterepublik.*[111]

---

[110] Munich's contemporary main synagogue, which opened in 2005, bears the same name.
[111] Note that is part of his court representations in the early 1950s

Michael Brenner, a historian who specialises on Munich's Jewish community during the interwar years, investigated the position Munich's Jewish residents found themselves in as antisemitism steadily grew after World War I. For him, the conservative merchant and former representative of the Orthodox Jewish Munich community Siegmund Frenkel (1860-1925), and the anarchist and anti-militarist Erich Mühsam (1878-1934) personified two distinct and polar currents within Munich's Jewish society. In an exchange of letters, the two argued about who was more representative as a Jew. However large the divide may have been between the two, ultimately, they were both treated abominably by the German National Socialists and without any distinction. Maybe this could hint also to a kind of political and spiritual separation among the Munich Lewandowski brothers Gerhard, Bruno, Alfred and Willi, although I already have put into question, whether the family at this time should be viewed at all as a Jewish family. Among the brothers, my grandfather Gerhard must have been one of those who were extremely critical of Nazism. It was he who would eventually be targeted by the ever more visible Nazis, as evidenced by the attacks on synagogues, graffitied walls and shops and other disturbing events prior to their rise to power in 1933.

The "*Thulegesellschaft*," the pamphlet "*Münchner Beobachter*" (later the "*Völkischscher Beobachter*"), the NSDAP, even the later Prime Minister Gustav von Kahr (and the police chief Ernst Pöhner, alongside Adolf Hitler) regarded Kurt Eisner (the son of a Jewish royal merchant in Berlin) and others as Jews who were "in their nature" collectively anti-German and anti-Bavarian. It did not matter how little or how much Eisner and others identified with Judaism, and how many others involved in the movement of the Räterepublik were not Jewish at all.[112] Michael Brenner wrote that Eisner owned a suitcase full of inflammatory antisemitic post addressed to him. Some of the letters vilified him as the "King of the Jews" and a "Galician Jew from the East" who should leave Germany for Palestine.[113]

---

[112] see Brenner (2019)
[113] Ibid. p. 10-132

The assassination of Kurt Eisner by Count Anton von Arco, who tried to push aside his own Jewish family origins and who wanted to make an impression upon the Nazis through his murderous crime, was but a beginning. There was more to come. Gustav Landauer and Eugen Levine followed him, and there were the attacks on Magnus Hirschfeld and, in 1922, on Walter Rathenau. In 1921 swastikas were smeared onto Munich's synagogues during Passover. Increasingly, posters of nationalist Germans, or Nazis, there may have been little distinction, appeared all over the Bavarian capital.

After the 6th of April 1924, following Hitler's attempted coup, the nationalist "Völkische Block" gained 35 percent of the votes of the Munich electorate. During that time, a sizeable group of the later Third Reich leaders found themselves in Munich, later labelled the "*Haupstadt der Bewegung*" [capital of the (Nazi) movement]. In all, 132 of Adolf Hitler's 188 speeches up until 1923 were held in the Bavarian capital.[114] Furthermore, on 17th October 1923, Gustav von Kahr ordered the expulsion of 1,500 so-called, "Galicians" or Eastern European, Jews. It followed his call three years earlier for the expulsion of "undesirable foreigners."[115]

So much for the emerging dark political clouds. As for the Lewandowskis, that was only part of their trouble. They struggled with changing fashion trends after the First World War. The constricting corsets that the Lewandowskis had specialised in for decades suddenly became unpopular. Part of the fashion change were "waist girdles" which facilitated the ever growing participation of women in sporting activities and their deployment in "men's professions" during the First World War.[116] In spite of that, the Lewandowskis appeared to be able to maintain their position as a trusted fashion brand. It was not until several

---

[114] Brenner (2019), p.194
[115] Ibid. p. 265 Kahr's attempt to get closer to the National Germans at the expense of Jewish people did not help him. In 1943, as he had not stood by Hitler in 1923, he suffered the same fate as Röhm, and was murdered by those he sought to impress.
[116] On this see Bauer (2014)

years later that at least the Bavarian Lewandowski company began to suffer more heavily during the great global economic crisis.

Besides its financial impact, the economic depression of the 1920s was doubly serious for the Lewandowskis, because it brought about the short-lived trend of the *garçonnes*, a fashion, which emphasised women's masculinity, with shorter skirts and, above all, no corsets[117].

The Lewandowski company in northern Germany was now also fragmented and divided into six smaller companies.[118] David Lewandowski in Bavaria tried his best to adapt the company, despite the loss of its important status as exclusive merchant to the royal Bavarian court following the republican revolution and the aforementioned fashion changes. His sons Gerhard, Bruno, Alfred and Wilhelm were heavily involved in the endevour. They even set up a new business "die Bayerische Korsetts-Industrie GmbH." Postcards sent by Bruno Lewandowski during these years reveal that he travelled extensively. He wrote his fiancée several cards, reporting from trade fairs and exhibitions in Milan, Lucerne and Venice. Philipp Lewandowski, the grandson of Alfred Lewandowski, told me that he keeps a box full of such postcards, and thinks he recognises Marrakesh on one of them – perhaps more holiday than business.

Based on these cards, Phillipp assumed that the brothers must have been relatively well off until the stock market crash in 1929. Wilhelm, for example, continued to run the family business in the "*Pschorrbau*" in Munich's Neuhauserstraße 19 after his father's retirement. Nevertheless, numerous Lewandowski outlets were forced to close between 1926 and 1933, a process that was not least also linked to the death of David Lewandowski himself on 28th August 1929 (5689).

He was however still to witness my grandfather's marriage to his long-time friend and later fiancée "Anny" Anna Amalie Walburga, née Eichenseher (1891-1939) in 1926. Neither my grandfather nor any of the other sons of David Lewandowski married Jewish partners, in stark

---

[117] Bauer (2014) p. 6
[118] Lewandowski (1981), p. 2

contrast to their Berlin relatives, such as the children of David's own brother Max.

The depression ultimately led to the closure of the company's shop in the eminent Residenzstrasse 11 in Munich. Elsewhere, Lewandowski shops remained open, not just in Munich. I found three branches in Amsterdam for 1925, but they were no longer tied together as one company and had little if anything to do with the Munich businesses.

Telephone directory entry in Amsterdam 1925.

Eventually around 1926, demand for corsets had virtually disappeared. The Bavarian Lewandowski Brothers sold brassières instead. The once natural fibres gave way to nylon (from Dupont), although there was a brief reprieve for the old corset tradition and the "hourglass style" between 1926 and 1939.[119]

How many shops Gerhard, Bruno, Wilhelm and Alfred held when Hitler rose to power is not completely clear. What is certain, however, is that Bruno Lewandowski was able to run a shop throughout the Hitler years. It can also be assumed that Gerhard owned at least one business in Augustenstrasse 83. Soon after 1933 he was forced to give that up, however.[120] Alfred Lewandowski mentioned that he had acquired a bandage factory (H. K. Schmidt & Co) at that time.[121]

---

[119] Bauer (2014), p. 6-7
[120] Testimony of Otto Meyer. September 1951, see chapter four. "No rent to "Saujuden"!
[121] Lewandowski (1981)

This was not just the time for major political changes, but also a period when the lives of the Munich Lewandowski brothers began to take different directions. The reason behind it was in part most certainly their public position towards the Nazis. My grandfather in particular allegedly made no secret of what he thought about the new rulers. This openness would soon come at a considerable cost to him personally. In contrast, his youngest brother Alfred enlisted 1939 as a German Wehrmacht soldier in the Afrika Korps at the relative late age of 31 (see later).[122] Bruno and Willi appear to have lived in Munich throughout, for Bruno and his family with terrible consequences.

---

[122] Lewandowski (1981), p. 3

4

No rent to *Saujuden*! Munich 1933

My grandfather on the list of admissions to KL Dachau by the
Political Police (later Gestapo). Archive documents.

When the Nazis rose to power in 1933, my grandfather Gerhard Lewandowski was probably rather cynical about it. For months, indeed long before 1933, he had certainly been able to observe how shopkeepers in Munich had been harassed for no other reason than being Jewish. In Munich such behaviour was already reported to occur during the 1920s. After the Machtergreifung in 1933 things worsened at a fast pace. Initially Jewish civil servants were removed from their positions because of their religious affiliation. Then, on 9th and 10th March 1933, paramilitary units of the NSDAP, SA and SS threatened businesses they classified as "Jewish." A total of 280 Jewish persons were forced into so-called "protective" custody. Many of these were just ordinary businesspeople.[123]

My grandfather Gerhard was also arrested in 1933 and, as if he were a serious criminal, and was later forced to spend a whole six months in captivity.[124] His crime? Alleged jokes about Ernst Röhm, the head of the SA (see later for a twist in the story). His Jewish ancestry through his father and grandfather certainly also became an issue.

My mother and my aunt Gerda told me time and time again that their "dad wasn't the type that would just shut up." It can be assumed that as a veteran of the First World War, he had an aversion to the self-declared apparent "true" defenders of Germany, but also as a person who came from a well-respected Munich family.

However, it was one of his tenants in his Munich apartment at Beichstraße 9 (located in Schwabing, parallel to one of Munich boulevard, Leopoldstraße), who was responsible for the start of my grandfather's early persecution. My grandfather had a five-roomed apartment. Part of the apartment was sublet to a Herr Braml, as the man was referred to in the legal documents after the war. Braml no longer wanted to pay rent to "*Saujuden*" (Jewish Swines) after the *Machtergreifung*. He promised my

---

[123] Franziska Schott: The elimination of Jews from Munich's economic life, in Baumann (1995), p. 150 and p. 152.

[124] According to the file of the proceedings of the Supreme Restitution Court File B 215/1824 S. 3, Koblenz State Archives

grandfather's brother-in-law that he would make sure via the "Political Police" that his landlord, "this *Saujude*" ended up where he supposedly belonged.[125] Where *did* he belong, you may ask?

Soon after the Nazis got into power, Heinrich Himmler ordered the opening of the first concentration camp in a former industrial area of the small town of Dachau near Munich. The Jewish community of Munich soon found out what the purpose of the Konzentrationslager (KL) was, when dead bodies of Jewish persons were sent to them in sealed lead coffins with strict instructions not to open them. However, so that they could pay their last respects, members of the Jewish burial society did not follow these instructions. They removed the bodies from the coffins, and the marks on the bodies left them in no doubt that what they found were signs of torture.[126]

This was only the beginning of severe actions against Jewish people. On the 23rd of March 1933, "Jewish" department stores received the attention of a mob in uniform, presumably motivated by the election results. "April Boycott Actions" followed the very next month. This time, Jewish doctors, lawyers and businesspeople became the target.[127]

Max Uhlfelder, the owner of one of Munich's most famous department stores at the time, was one of those they sought out. His department store was located in Munich's Rosental district, today the home of Munich's City Museum and in 1928 spread out over 7,000 square metres of retail space with a total of 550 employees. Uhlfelder was arrested on 9th March 1933, accused of having allegedly made a "denunciation." He was then locked in a cell for three days. Barely two

---

[125] Affidavit, Max Stöckl, 15 June 1953 in the files of Gerhard Lewandowski, Munich State Archives. My grandfather's tenants are also mentioned in Otto Meyer's letter on case 9789 Court of Restitution, 16 November 1950, Gerhard Lewandowski file, Federal Archives, Koblenz. Political Police: these were the predecessors of the Gestapo, in some documents they are listed as the latter).

[126] Doris Seidel in Bauman & Heusler (2004), p. 34 after Peter Hanke (1967): The Stories of the Jews in Munich between 1933-1945, p. 79.

[127] Ibid.

weeks later, a Nazi militia marched to the store and put up posters in his store and on advertising pillars in its vicinity. On these, the Nazis' unmistakable message to "Reich-citizens" and to Jews could be read: "Don't buy from Jews!" And "Jews out!" A mass rally against an alleged "Jewish Campaign of Lies" was also announced.[128]

On the 1st of April 1933, a man in SA uniform appeared in front of another shop with Jewish owners, the Starks Department Store situated at Munich's Stachus, a prominent location in the city centre. The SA man barred entry to customers and left a "Don't buy from Jews" poster in the shop window. In the same month, so-called "*Verpflichtungsscheine* (liability-notes)" were also handed out, with which supposedly "Jewish" businesses had to certify that their company was "purely German." or in other words, not owned by Jewish people.[129] Then, in August 1933, Jews were banned from swimming in Munich's public baths.

My grandfather's business was also targeted by the "brown clan." His former lawyer Dr Otto Meyer wrote in a testimony on 14 September 1951, that my grandfather was forced to give up his shop in the Augusten Staße 83 as early as 1933, for "*rassenpolitischen Gründen* (racial-political reasons)," in other words, his Jewish father made him the target of Nazi persecution. The letter also reveals that he appeared to have made a living as an insurance man for Rheinland AG. An insurance man? The National Socialists must have ended my grandfather's career as a representative of the proud Lewandowski business. It was a significant loss for Munich, because as the oldest of the sons of David Lewandowski, he most likely had an established name and regular customers, some of whom probably went back years, to times his father was still alive.[130]

---

[128] Heide Grundewald: Max Uhlfelder 1884-1958 in Baumann (1995), p. 129.
[129] Schott in Baumann (195) p. 150
[130] Entschädigungsakte Gerhard Lewandowski, Bayerisches Staatsarchiv

Eidesstattliche Versicherung

Als ehemaliger anwaltschaftlicher Vertreter des Herrn Jethu Lewandowski in der Angelegenheit betreffend die Räumung seines früheren Anwesens Haus Nr. 9 an der Reichstr. in München weiss ich, dass Herr Gerhard Lewandowski in dies Hause vor seiner Emigrierung nach Holland eine Pension führ und daraus ein nachhaltiges Einkommen von 200 - 250 Mark pr Monat erzielte.

Ausserdem bezog er als Versicherungs-Inspektor bei der Rhei land A.G., Direktion München, ein Gehalt von monatlich rund 250,- Mark (einschliesslich Provision). Alles in allem hatt er so ein gesichertes Auskommen.

Ich weiss auch, dass Herr Gerhard Lewandowski ein Ladenges an der Augustenstrasse 63 in München aus rassenpolitischen Gründen schon 1933 aufgeben musste.

Die Richtigkeit vorstehender Angaben versichere ich an Eides statt.

München, den 16. September 1951

(Dr. Otto Meyer)
Rechtsanwalt

5

Dachau

After my grandfather had been arrested by the Political Police (predecessor of GESTAPO), he was deported to the newly created Dachau Concentration Camp on 29 November 1933. There he would have to remain as a prisoner for over six months.

As already mentioned, KL Dachau was already partly a camp in which prisoners were tortured and murdered. This is confirmed by numerous sources, although most of the prisoners at this time still survived their incarceration. Prisoners, both men and women, were nevertheless forced to carry out extremely hard labour there.

In the beginning, prisoners were ordered to create the camp out of the remains of a dilapidated World War I ammunition factory. Five watchtowers were erected from which snipers could keep an eye on prisoners. The entire camp was surrounded with electric barbed-wire in addition to the building of a separation wall. During their unpaid forced labour, prisoners were often brutally beaten, usually by groups of guards. There are accounts of victims fainting or even dying due to the severe injuries they sustained. Some prisoners were also "encouraged" to commit suicide; others were executed by being shot.[131]

---

[131] Richardi (1983)

What may have happened to my grandfather inside Dachau ought not to be trivialised or pushed aside as less significant than the serious crimes committed against my father and his family (see later). I do not have details but the testimonies of others leave little to the imagination. Inside the "medieval barbaric penal institution", as the Munich decorative painter and communist Martin Grünwiedel described Dachau after his own months of interment there, also still in 1933, the deprivation of freedom, the daily threats, beatings, humiliations and intimidations, were all intended to break people who, for whatever reason, did not support the Nazi state or were seen as a threat to it. In the words of the Dachau camp commander at the time:

"We don't know sentimentality. Those amongst our comrades who can't see blood don't fit in with us! The more of these bastards we shoot down, the fewer we have to feed."[132]

This was the advice given by SS-Brigadeführer Freiherr von Maisen-Ponikau (SS Brigadier-Leader) to his men during an assembly in Dachau, right after he had taken over the command of the camp, replacing the allegedly still relatively benign supervision by the Bavarian state police.[133]

Those who failed to welcome the rise of Adolf Hitler and of the SS and SA, or who were perceived as political opponents (such as communists and socialists, but also simply Jewish people) were to be "re-educated." In reality, this meant nothing else but intimidation, or sometimes murder.[134] By the end of December 1933 the death toll of people who had died in the preceding months counted at least 22.[135]

Some of these murders were so heinous and so degrading that at the beginning of the Nazi era, the Bavarian state prosecution service

---

[132] Richardi (1983), p. 54 (translated by author)
[133] Ibid. p. 54
[134] ibid.
[135] Shortly before the liberation in 1945, there would be around one hundred deaths per day in Dachau

investigated some of these. At that time, they still doubted the excuses and apologies they had received by the SS. It was not until the Nazi leadership had Munich's senior public prosecutor, Carl Wintersberger, a man who courageously fought against the injustices, removed from his post in August 1934, that the investigations by the Bavarian public prosecutor's office ended.[136]

Politicians from the KPD, Germany's communist party and the SPD, the German social democratic party, and especially people with a Jewish family background, were recipients of extra harsh treatments. They would be harassed on a daily basis and, according to eyewitness reports, some were so badly maltreated that their death soon followed suit, often as a direct result of targeted and brutal merciless beatings. Examples were the cold-blooded murders of Wilhelm Franz and Dr Delvin Katz, in which the camp leadership feigned self-defence and suicide. Carl Wintersberger, who was still in office at the time, did not believe the Nazis excuses for their deaths.[137]

Other prisoners, such as Dr Erich Braun, a Jewish doctor and social democrat from Coburg, survived the atrocities and were able to escape KL Dachau, which later enabled them to describe the conditions they had experienced there. To start with, "prisoners" were often beaten upon their arrival. During the arrival roll call, prisoners were then given disciplinary and punishment orders. The concentration camp leaders deprived the prisoners of all rights and informed them of what was now punishable by immediate death. These rules had been introduced by Theodor Eicke, who had taken control of the camp after the sadistic SS-duo Anton Hoffmann and Hans Steinbrenner had been dismissed. Eicke turned out to be no more humane than his predecessor.

While Steinbrenner and Hoffmann were known to be impulsive and that they would sporadically become violent and never gave a thought if a measure they took, was in effect committing murder, Eicke would

---

[136] Richardi (1983), p.218
[137] Ibid. p. 210

introduce a system that was not just intended to discipline the inmates. Its other purpose was to teach SS personnel that those under their control were people for whom they had to feel no mercy. They were not to receive even a glimpse of humanness.[138]

One of the strangest camp rituals liable to severe punishment was bed-making. Beds were instructed to be made totally crease-free each and every morning. Where a bed had not been "properly made" according to the opinion of the supervising SS camp guards, it served as a pretext for a punishment order. However, this policy triggered a high level of solidarity among the inmates to help each other with the task. In general, the often shared socialist or communist background of many prisoners ensured that in 1933, the first year of the running of the camp, the inmates constantly looked out for each other. People who were beaten for example, were immediately tended to by fellow inmates, Kapo (internal camp police run by inmates) supervision posts were given to trustworthy, well-known comrades, and paramedics and doctors tried their very best despite a lack of resources – perhaps my grandfather too, as he was an expert in first aid, thanks to his experience in the services of the German Red Cross during the First World War.[139]

It was only after the arrival of convicted criminals – as opposed to those who were accused of having "hostile" political views – that solidarity-based support became a more complicated affair. The SS soon capitalised on the differences between the political and the ideological prisoners and others, by making prisoners with criminal backgrounds informers and kapos.

All those who survived their initiation beatings at arrival were given "camp clothes" and utensils. These were "a white drill suit", a pair of boots, a shirt, a pair of pants, socks and eating utensils, a glass for drinking, a toothbrush, and a bar of soap. Compared to camp conditions in

---

[138] Ibid. p. 121 Kapos were lower "policing" posts, usually people that were inmates themselves, that carried out orders
[139] Ibid. p. 73

later years, such spare provisions were "luxury." As a matter of procedure, to in part dehumanize them, prisoners' hair was shorn weekly. Those whom the SS particularly despised had to endure hair clippers with blunt blades and were handed old, tattered clothes to further humiliate them.[140]

The beds and clothing provided for the inmates, were meagre, yet they were at least something. Nevertheless, many froze at the onset of the first winter of 1933 because stoves were only available from mid-December of that year. But even that came with its own challenges, for once they were provided, their stuffy, sooty smoke choked the air in the living quarters. Notably however, there was one luxury, if you can call it that. Unlike many other camps later, there was also a fresh water supply, even hot water (the later however, was sometimes misused as a form of torture by guards), and there were usable, functioning toilets.

Although in each room a total of 54 people were accommodated, everyone still had a little space they could call their own in the simple three-storey wooden beds, which were fitted with straw sacks. They also had a pillow and a thin woollen blanket to cover themselves. It was also possible to wash your own clothes. But that being said, Dachau meant that the foundations for the later mass murder in concentration camps had been laid. As is well known, Dachau became the model for many later Nazi camps.

Like everyone else, my grandfather Gerhard must have been forced to work. This work, accounts tell us, consisted mainly of construction or road work, or digging jobs at a nearby gravel pit. On their way to their workplaces forced labourers, who were always guarded by SS men, were ordered to sing cheerful German folk songs as loudly as they could, to give the locals the impression that everything they saw and witnessed was of no great concern and quite in order. One of the "jolly" musical favourites was the song "*Schwarzbraun ist die Haselnuss* (black-brown is the hazelnut)," an ironic and sinister take on the uniform colours of the National Socialists.[141]

---

[140] Richardi (1983), p. 72f.
[141] Ibid, p. 82

It was not the only form of sarcastic humiliation. The inmates were served their meals in a dining hall that had caricatures of people the Nazis disliked drawn onto its walls. Reportedly these included an antisemitic drawing of the publisher Georg Bernhard, depicting him with Jewish religious side locks and a kippah, and SPD leader Philipp Schneidermann, shown with a needle through his forehead. Another wall depicted an SA man with a swastika flag emblazoned with the Hitler slogan "Über Gräber, forwärts!" (over graves, forwards).[142]

In spite of everything, living conditions, which for most of the inmates were traumatising and among the worst they must have ever experienced in their lives at this time (with exception of those who were veterans of the First World War, perhaps) in 1933 and 1934 at least the Dachau concentration camp was not yet comparable with the later death camps and murder factories. However, during the "Night of the Long Knives" in 1934, the concentration camp would be transformed into an execution yard. Prisoners, perhaps including my grandfather, were able to observe how newly arrived people were executed on the spot. As is known today, the camp's leader Eicke had become a close confidant of Hitler's leadership circle a few weeks before that . This explains why the camp had become the chosen location for preparatory exercises by the SS for its strike on the rival SA. It would be Eicke himself who, together with the leader of the Dachau guards, Michael Lippert, shot Röhm on direct orders of the Führer, after Röhm had been deported to the Stadelheim Prison near Munich.

The same development may have caused the release of my grandfather from Dachau on 1st May 1934, given that the reason he was being held in Dachau was in particular the alleged citation of insulting jokes concerning Röhm. However, the allegation about those jokes was not quite what granted my grandfather the stay in Dachau: In August 2023, I came across a typed statement by my grandfather amongst my mother's documents, in which he details the circumstances of his arrest and incarceration:

---

[142] Memoirs of Wenzel Rubner, in Richardi (1983), p. 76f.

Zol Zayn Shulem I: Zores

Gerhard Lewandowski
Munich, Grillparzerstr. 51
Munich 28 October 1953

Report on my persecution by National Socialism.

I was a member of a regulars' table society that met at Café Grünwald (in Munich). Sometimes we had to go to Café Plendl in Rosenstrasse for security reasons because we couldn't speak entirely freely in Café Grünwald as sometimes there were informers there. I was also a member of the board of the medical table of the German War Association, which had its premises in the Mathäser Bräu (a beer cellar in Munich). I spoke there as part of our weekly meetings and also took a stand against National Socialism before and after the rise to power. Our chairman Klob, who later became a well-known National Socialist, warned me even before the rise to power not to be so outspoken, but to exercise restraint. I resigned after the rise to power, because I didn't want to and couldn't continue to work under such circumstances, nor did I want to be cut off from speaking freely. When Kolb heard that I had been sent to Dachau, he said, I was told, that a guy like that ought to be there. I was imprisoned several times in June, July and August 1933. I was arrested again in November 1933. When I was interrogated at the police station I was told, "You tell mean jokes, for example: "A German woman doesn't smoke", a joke about Röhm. My accuser, the (my) lodger Braml, had confirmed this (to them). I told the police that I hadn't told that joke, but rather, that Braml himself, who had been sitting at my dining table in my flat, recited this joke. I then had answered to Braml in the strongest possible terms (with words) against immoral national socialism and said, yes, you see, that's how the new rulers are, they offend religion and race as well as humanity and can therefore never have lasting success. Braml then went on to say that our empire would last 1000 years.

Of course, I didn't mention this self-accusing fact during the Gestapo interrogation. Braml also repeated all my anti-state statements to the police. I was interrogated again the following day by the Gestapo in Ettstrasse (a Munich police station until this today) and was questioned about my personal details. After a few days, I found myself in Dachau. That was at the end of November 1933. The Gestapo had also imposed a mail embargo on my incoming and outgoing mail, apparently to control my correspondence because of my political views. The Gestapo also often stopped at my house at Beichstraße 9 to find out why I wasn't showing the (swastika) flag (outside the building).

On 1 May 1934, I was released from Dachau and had to report to the police all the time as a person hostile to the state. In the summer of 1934, I was arrested again for making anti-state statements and suspected of racial defilement and indecent relations with young girls. I was taken from my furnished room in Utzschneiderstrasse; three Gestapo men behaved in a very mean way towards me, slapped me in the face, dragged me into their car and said, "We'll soon have you finished off. But they turned back at Forstenriederpark after I had informed them that I had turned to the Reichsstadthalter Epp (lit. Empire's City Holder) for protection a few days earlier. I also wanted to get married at the time, but this marriage was prohibited on orders of the NSDAP. When I told the Gestapo that I had approached Epp concerning my marriage, they turned (the car) round and took me to Ëttstraße. There I was literally thrown down the stairs into the cellar, had a sack pulled over my head and was beaten with sticks and bull whips until I collapsed (and fell) into unconsciousness. When I woke up in the cell the next morning, I was lying on the floor covered in blood. A whole group of SS men, at least ten of them, had taken part in the abuse.

After 14 days I was provisionally released thanks to the intervention of the lawyers Lermann and Meyer. I was given a letter by the Gestapo, which explained that I was never to be seen again

> and (that) could say (to others as a reason regarding the injuries sustained) I had fallen down the stairs). I immediately made plans to flee to Holland. I went to see lawyer Lermann, who also confirmed my intention, saying that there was a high risk that I would be arrested again ... I therefore had to abandon everything, my house, my apartment, my business and my job, and lost my entire livelihood as a result.
>
> *Gerhard Lewandowski*

Dachau had many personal consequences for my grandfather. It was not just the imprisonment; it also seemingly had an impact on his marriage. Here it is worth noting that on 28 December 1933, one month after his incarceration in Dachau, the registry office of Munich received an application for divorce on behalf of Anny, his first wife. The divorce was recorded later on 24 May 1934. Of course, there could have been any number of reasons for this divorce. But maybe it was also an attempt to protect Anny. Or was she afraid, or was it a lack of capital to support herself, or maybe something else entirely?

When my grandfather fled to the Netherlands, Anny didn't join him but remained in Germany. My grandfather allegedly wanted to remarry after the divorce, but the NSDAP, as he wrote, had forbidden him to do so. One thing is certain, it must have been a desperately complicated time, in which the order of the world my grandfather knew fell apart.

Dachau

Eidesstattliche Versicherung.

Ich unterfertigter Max S t ö c k l, Kaufmann in München, Glockenbach 7/3 links versichere Nachstehendes an Eidesstatt mit dem Auftrage diese Versicherung an Eidesstatt dem zuständigen Gerichte zum Zwecke der Glaubhaftmachung zu überreichen. Ich weiss, dass eine falsche Versicherung an Eidesstatt mit Gefängnis bestraft wird.

Ich habe für Herrn Lewandowski die Verwaltung des Hauses Reichstrasse 9 übernommen, weil Herr Lewandowski als Eigentümer diese Verwaltung nicht mehr zu führen wagte, nachdem ein Mieter namens Braml ganz besonders aufsässig gegen Herrn Lewandowski war und von ihm nur per Saujuden sprach. Dieser Mieter Braml hat offenbar auch die anderen Mieter gegen Herrn Lewandowski verhetzt. Herr Lewandowski hatte durch die Verfolgungen im dritten Reich sehr zu leiden, obwohl er Halbjude war. Offenbar wurde er für einen Volljuden gehalten, jedenfalls wurde er so behandelt.

Als ich nun einmal zu dem Mieter Braml kam, um die Miete zu kassieren, erklärte mir dieser ohne weiteres, für diesen Saujuden zahle ich keine Miete mehr und als ich dagegen protestierte, sagte er, ich werde Sorge tragen, dass dieser Saujud dahin kommt, wohin er gehört, Sie scheinen ein Judengünstling zu sein, dann bringe ich Sie auch nach Dachau. Ich erklärte ihm, ich nehme pflichtgemäss als Schwager diese Verwaltungsgeschäfte wahr, ich bin kein Judengünstling. Trotz dieser Auseinandersetzung wollte er keine Miete. Und als ich einmal wieder zu ihm kam, verweigerte er mit den gleichen Worten, er zahle dem Saujuden keine Miete, wiederum die Miete. Unmittelbar darauf kam mein Schwager, Herr Gerhard Lewandowski, nach Dachau. Ich hatte damals die Überzeugung, dass dies auf Veranlassung des Braml geschah, wie mir auch mein Schwager selbst erklärte, man habe es ihm auf der Polizei gesagt, dass sich Braml gegen Herrn Lewandowski eingesetzt hat. Auf Grund dieser Erfahrung habe ich dann weiter gegen Braml nichts mehr unternommen, weil ich fürchtete, ich käme dabei selbst unter die Räder. Diese Vorgänge spielten sich im Jahre 1933 nach der Machtergreifung ab. Herr Lewandowski weilte dann etwa bis im Mai 1934 im KZ. Nach seiner Entlassung setzte sofort wieder das Treiben gegen Herrn Lewandowski ein, er wurde neuerdings als Jude und wegen staatsfeindlicher Betätigung verhaftet. Ich kann die einzelnen Verhaftungen zeitlich nicht so auseinanderhalten, ich weiss aber, dass Herr Lewandowski mindestens 3 bis 4 mal verhaftet worden

- 2 -

war und dass er bei seiner letzten Verhaftung auf der Polizei fürchterlich misshandelt wurde, er war grün und blau geschlagen. Hierauf ist Herr Lewandowski sofort nach Holland geflüchtet.

München, den 15. Juni 1953

Another testimony, concerning my grandfather Gerhard Lewandowski, from his former brother-in-law Max Stöckl in 1953, confirming the arrests and incarcerations and the flight of grandfather. Own archive.

6

1934-1935: Farewell to Munich

My grandfather's release from Dachau in 1934, after some six months of forced imprisonment, was clearly not the end of his ordeal. Even though the Munich National Socialists were no longer able to arrest him for making comments about Röhm, my grandfather's tenant Braml continued insulting him as a "pig Jew" right in his home and refused to pay his rent. Instead, this man with the Bavarian surname ensured that my grandfather continued to be arrested. Brutal beatings and house searches were the consequences thereof.[143]

The Nuremberg race laws now classified my grandfather as a "Second Degree Mixed Person" and that made things only more difficult, even though such persons were allowed to marry German non-Jewish spouses.

According to the written testimony of his once brother-in-law, Max Stöckl, the Political Police had beaten my grandfather "black and blue" after further arrests (at least three to four times). This was nothing but grievous bodily harm against a defenceless person, carried out in the name of the German state.[144]

---

[143] Testimony of Max Stöckl in my grandfather's later lawsuit for restitution of his property.
[144] Ibid.

1934-1935: Farewell to Munich

After the last arrest, my grandfather was held and "treated" in a local "Gestapo prison" for another two months. Paul Lermann, his lawyer, who saw my grandfather shortly before his escape to the Netherlands, described my grandfather's body as being covered in "blue and green marks," and added that these were caused through the beatings by the Politische Polizei, the Political Police."[145]

> Verfolgung eingesetzt hatte.
> Kurz vor seiner Emigration nach Holland, man darf wohl sagen Flucht, kam Herr Lewandowski noch zu mir, nachdem ihn die Gestapo vernommen hatte. Herr Lewandowski zeigte mir da seinen Körper, war entsetzt über diese Behandlung eines Menschen. Blau und grün geschlagen, verschwollen und mit Striemen bedeckt war Herr Lewandowski, was nur eine Folge zahlreicher und grausamster Schläge sein konnte. Herr Lewandowski ersuchte mich seine Sachen zu regeln, er gehe weg, was ich nur zu sehr verstehen konnte. Für mich war es aber nach näherer Überlegung eine nicht zumutbare und unmögliche Aufgabe in diese Verhältnisse einzugreifen zu können, wenn ich mich nicht selbst der Gefahr aussetzen wollte, dafür politisch verantwortlich ... ich ... selbst Parteigenosse

> Passierte es mir doch kurz vorher auf der politischen Polizei, dass man mir dort sehr deutlich sagte, als ich für einen Polen vorsprach, was ich für ein Interesse hätte als deutscher Anwalt für einen Polen einzutreten. So kam es zur Versteigerung. Meine Überzeugung nach hätte Herr Lewandowski, wenn diese politische Verfolgung nicht hereingespielt hätte und wenn er überhaupt nicht Halbjude gewesen wäre, ohne weiteres seine Verhältnisse so ordnen können, dass überhaupt ein Versteigerungsverfahren nicht eingeleitet worden wäre. Schwierigkeiten sind eben dadurch entstanden, dass Herr Lewandowski als politisch Verfolgter aus seiner normalen Geschäftstätigkeit verdrängt wurde. Leider besitze ich keine Akten mehr, aber ich glaube mich bestimmt zu erinnern, dass das Haus auf dem Notariat Hieber um 24 000.- RM versteigert wurde ...

Part of the testimony of the lawyer Paul Lermann, Adalbert Str 25 Munich, on 20 September 1951. own archive.

One inmate of Dachau was Hans Beimler. He had ended up in the concentration camp a few months before my grandfather, and having survived, he left a detailed testimony of what was to be understood

---

[145] Letter from Paul Lermann, inventory of my mother, 20 September 1951

under "treatment" of the Third Reich Political Police in 1933. He wrote that he had been beaten with rubber truncheons by several people at the Munich police headquarters. This happened while he was forced to stretch across a table. Beimler counted a total of 60 to 70 blows before he passed out.[146] According to other accounts, victims often had a woollen blanket tied around their heads "so that screams of pain could be muffled and therefore not heard by others."[147] This correlates with my grandfather's testimony.

My late aunt Gerda was once told by acquaintances that my grandfather had only just survived the beatings, as she confided to me.

M grandfather Gerhard Lewandowski, an opponent of the National Socialists, was eventually told that he "better not get caught again. Should there be a next time, he wouldn't be allowed to leave Dachau!" There can hardly be any doubt about what such a promise meant, then or now.

After the war, various court documents confirmed that my grandfather had been detained in a Munich police station between 20 November 1933 and 29 November 1933 and had then been sent to Dachau as an "enemy of the state" only to be released on 1 May 1934. However, they also confirm that four months later, on 13 September 1934, he was arrested for alleged "racial defilement" and held in the police prison for a total of 17 days, until 30 September 1934. Several house searches are also mentioned.[148]

At some point during this time, the rest of the former Lewandowski Brothers' businesses, in particular the Berlin branches, were "aryanized" and confiscated, alongside the "Arnold Obersky Mieder-und-Korsetts-Warenfirma (Corset and Corsetry Company)," whose owners were also Jewish. They were now declared possession of by the National Socialist state and henceforth operated under the "aryan" new name "*Wegens*".[149]

---

[146] Meiler (2019), Beginning of torture p. 31-45

[147] For example, in the case of Josef Zäuner in Hornung Walter (1936): Dachau eine Chronik, quoted here by Richardi (1983), p. 160

[148] Federal Archives file on Decision 246, Case 484 of the United States Court, Gerhard Lewandowski, v. Bayerische Vereinsbank and Katherina Glasbrenner, 9 July 1952.

[149] s. 216 in n Berliner Konfektion und Mode: die Zerstörung einer Tradition,

It can be assumed that any business that my grandfather still ran or owned in early 1933 (we have learnt about a shop in Munich's Augusten Straße which he was soon forced to give up) attracted the attention of the National Socialists, which must have had a further impact on his financial situation. The historian Andreas Heusler summarises such affairs in one sentence: "Most Jewish businessmen suffered from a considerable drop in sales after the NSDAP rose to power and were increasingly forced to fight for their economic survival."[150] Even though my grandfather did not consider himself Jewish at this time, this may only have been true of him personally, as the Nazi state reportedly perceived him in relation to his Jewish father and by virtue of the pseudo-scientific racial order an enemy of the state.

With the explicit help and support of numerous German friends and acquaintances, my grandfather speedily left his home in Munich after his last traumatic arrest, and fled to the Netherlands. He was registered in Amsterdam for the first time in 1935. In 1933, following the ascendancy of Hitler, some 700 Jews left Munich. The Nuremberg Race Laws of 15 September 1933 triggered further emigration waves. Between 1st of March 1933 and 16th of May 1938 some 3,500 Jewish people out of the previous population of 11,000 had left the Bavarian capital.[151] Whether this data would include my grandfather, who thought of himself as a Christian, albeit with a Jewish father, I cannot say, but there were certainly also many people who had to flee for political reasons. However, my grandfather's chosen destination of the Netherlands was rather an exception, though not unheard of. Most people with a Jewish background travelled or intended to travel to the United States, Palestine, Switzerland or even South America, some headed for France. Socialists and Communists would choose Spain, to join the fight against fascism from there. However, there existed another "escape route." Doris Seidel reported that especially for 50- to 80-year-olds, the "escape route" could also sometimes be called suicide.[152]

1836-1939, by Uwe Westphal, Edition Hentrich (1992)
[150] Baumann and Heusler (2004), p. 204
[151] Seidel in Baumann & Heusler (2004), p. 49
[152] Ibid. p. 50

The historian Franziska Schott stated that the sum of reprisals (boycotts and harassment) had a truly recognisable impact from the mid-1935. By this time, bankruptcies and closures of Jewish owned businesses, and probably also of all those who were considered opponents of the Nazi regime, became a frequent occurrence. The harassment and destruction of Jewish businesspeople and professionals robbed them of their ability to make a living. It created a situation where savings and property had to be given up in order to survive.

When talking about the consequences of National Socialism upon Jewish individuals, it is often the dispossessions on the basis of racial laws that are discussed, but not what was lost through the constant encroachments on their ability to make a living or simply to live at all.

As an example of such harassment, one can look at the misfortunes of the Jewish couple Emil and Lina Katz. The couple had owned a clothing shop in Munich's Giesing District and protested in front of a mob against a smear written on their shop's windows. It read: "Juden Raus!" -*Jews, get lost!* Emil Katz, to his credit, courageously hung up a "counter-poster" on which he proudly referenced his military service on the German frontlines during the First World War. When the police were eventually called, Emil Katz pointed furthermore to his war medal, an Iron Cross. But his resistance was in vain. Two years later, the entire Katz family was forced to emigrate from Germany to the United States.[153]

From January 1938 onwards, all trade and business licence extensions to Jews were rejected as "politically unreliable." There were also new labels indicating the "quality" of goods: They read "*Goods from Aryan hands*" and "*pure Aryan product.*"[154]

After *Kristallnacht*, Hermann Göring imposed a "cleaning fee" of one billion Reichsmark on all Jewish businesspeople whose shops had been smashed during the Antisemitic riots for the "service" of (destroying and) clearing up after the pogroms. This step was intended to liquidate

---

[153] Schott in Baumann & Heusler (2004)
[154] Schott in Baumann & Heusler (2004p. 153

Jewish property under the pretence of supposed legal measures. It also blamed the victims of the night of ferocious violence for the destruction it had caused.

On 10 November 1938, 169 Munich businesses belonging to Jewish owners closed, many more following in the wake of forced closures. Of the 600 businesses still owned by Jewish Munich residents at the end of 1938, only 27 remained by the end of 1939.

Among the businesses affected were the Volkskunsthaus Wallach and Kunsthaus Bernheimer (art shops) and the Aufhäuser Bank. Their owners were deported to Dachau in 1938, five years after my grandfather had been there.[155]

After my grandfather fled to the Netherlands, his apartment – estimated to be worth some 50,000 Reichsmarks in 1935 – was forcibly auctioned off at the Hieber notary's office in Munich for just 24,000 Reichsmarks.[156] His furniture, paintings and other possessions were also confiscated if not outright stolen. And yet, my grandfather's early flight to Amsterdam can still be described as a lucky escape. In 1935, the year he fled Munich, many others still strongly believed that things would get better again; but especially after 1938 things only got worse.

In his own family my grandfather was the exception with all the troubles he had to endure. Bruno, my grandfather's brother, on the other hand, is said to have continued his business during the war. I will come back to the story of Bruno and the other Lewandowskis later.

I would like to pause for a second and ask what could have been going on in the mind of a person who was treated like my grandfather in the very city in which he was born and raised? Here was a man who had been repeatedly beaten up as an alleged enemy, who saw himself as a German of Christian faith and as a Munich resident, and who had served his country during the First World War. This model German citizen was then forced to run away from his hometown and birthplace.

---

[155] Ibid. pp. 153-15
[156] Witness statement, P. Lermann, in court file of Gerhard Lewandowski

My grandfather's later return, more than a decade later, may indicate that he never accepted how others saw him then, but continued to see himself as part and parcel of Munich – as a native.

I don't think he ever accepted, or was able to accept, that National Socialism had risen and had been upheld by the active or silent approval of many Germans. Many people who were treated like my grandfather turned their backs on Germany during and after the war, never to be seen again. In my view, my grandfather's post-war attempt to regain his possessions and rebuild a life in Germany would later become just as tragic a detail of his life as the terrible things he had to endure between 1933 and 1935 and as will be reported in the next chapter, between 1940 and 1945.

7

Amsterdam 1935-1945

Foto fünfter September 1943

Ihr Lächeln ist Trauer.

Ihr Leben ist Tod.
Die Sonne scheint,
mitten im Krieg
Das Rad sich dreht,
wie Wasser, wie Leben

Die Schritte sind eilig.

Bombenalarm
Das Leben ist heilig,
der Krieg auch.

Bist Du nicht ich?

Ich sehe mich
in Deinem Gesicht.
Was ist denn geschehen?

Zol Zayn Shulem I: Zores

Mein Kind ich kenne Dich nicht.
Meine Zukunft,
die weiß ich nicht.
Die linke Straße von gestern
ist eine Einbahnstraße.
Wenn die Zeiten sich ändern,
dann kauf ich Dir dies,
dann kauf ich Dir das,
für den Wechsel Deiner Heimat.

Gabriele, meine Hand,
die Dich hält,
ist bald nimmer mehr.
Dann geh ich allein und denke an mich,
wenn Du Rosen stellst auf's Grab.

Ich will Dir zeigen diese Welt,
selbst wenn es uns verboten.
Der Stern auf Deinem Kleid
soll uns die Lust am Tag nicht nehmen.
Die Sonne, der Wind beiben immer unser.
Das erkennt sogar des Wolfes Welp'
(ist Jude ist Mensch)

Komm, soll sie sich drehn'
Die seltsame Welt!
Wir leben heute für immer!

Photo, fifth September 1943[157]

Her smile is sorrow
Her life is death
The sun is shining.
In the midst of war
The wheel turns
Like water, like life

The steps are hurried.
Bomb alert
Life is sacred.
The war is sacred too.

Aren't you me?
I can see myself,
inside your face
What has happened?

My child, I don't know you.
I don't know what my future holds.
The left those roads of yesterday.
It's a one-way street.
When times change,
I'll buy you this,
then I'll buy you that,
for the change of your home.

Gabriele, my hand that holds you,
is soon no more
Then I'll go alone and think of myself.
When you put roses on the grave.

---

[157] Poem, Daniel Zylbersztajn-Lewandowski, December 1991

I want to show you this world,

even if it is forbidden to us.
The star on your dress
should not take away our enjoyment of the day.
The sun and the wind will always be ours.
Even the wolf's puppy recognises that
(it is a Jew, is a man)

Come, let it turn, the strange world.

We live forever today!

My mother Corrie on her fifth birthday in Amsterdam, in the middle of the war and the occupation, with her father Gerhard Lewandowski. Own photo.

I have a few acquaintances who speak of the Netherlands with high praise. They claim that people are more tolerant there, and many talk about beautiful Amsterdam with its neighbourhoods, coffee houses and teashops. For my grandfather the town would soon change to become a very dangerous place.

Gele (Gerhard Lewandowski), the shopfront of my grandfather's business under the family home at Haarlemerstraat 29 in Amsterdam in the 1940s. Own photo.

My grandfather travelled a lot; he and his brothers had, I assume, been to Holland and even London before, perhaps on road trips in expensive cars in the years following the First World War.[158]

Because the Dutch maintained political neutrality during the First World War, my grandfather's idea to flee to the Netherlands was not as strange as it seems. Other refugees chose the Netherlands also, including

---

[158] Statement by Philipp Lewandowski, who has postcards of the family from those years. iehe

the family of Rudi Oppenheimer (1931-2019), whom I was able to interview shortly before his death in London, or the family of Edith and Otto Frank, and thus Margot and Anne Frank.[159]

It was only after the Anschluss of Austria three years later in March 1938, and the consequent German invasion of Poland in 1939, that the Netherlands seemed to be as safe as other places one could try to escape to, such as Great Britain, the United States, Palestine, Shanghai or South America. For my grandfather, the Netherlands appear to have been more than a temporary place though, as he attempted to re-establish a business there and allowed himself to fall in love with a local Dutch woman of Christian-Lutheran background. In 1938 they were expecting their first child – my mother!

My grandfather had already known my grandmother Maria in January 1938 or December 1937, possibly even earlier. It is documented that my grandfather first settled at Haarlemerstraat 54 in Amsterdam in the second half of 1935 and officially registered there. Haarlemerstraat was already one of the many narrow and particularly busy shopping streets in the heart of Amsterdam at that time. Almost every one of the small three-storey houses, made of red brick had a shop with a large window display. The area seemed to suit him, because after a few years in Amsterdam, he moved just a few doors up. Documents state that on the 12th of July 1939 he lived in Haarlemer Straat 29, the house where my mother would grow up. Her parents. my grandmother and grandfather ran a corset shop on the ground floor. The living quarters were on the upper floors. To my immense frustration, given everything else that has been destroyed in my family's history, this house no longer exists in its original form. In its place is a newer house, possibly built sometime after the end of the Second World War.

---

[159] Zylbersztajn-Lewandowski (2018.11)

Amsterdam 1935-1945

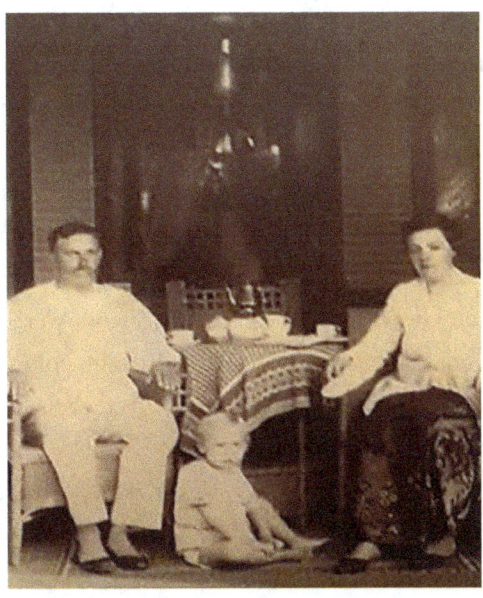

Arie and Cor Schutt, picture most probably taken in Indonesia around 1915. The child in front is my great-uncle Reyer. Own photo.

My grandmother was born on 31 August 1916 in Vlaardingen, an old town close to the Dutch port city of Rotterdam. She was the second child of Arie Valk, who came from the village of Ridderkerk, and of "Cor", short for Cornelia Petronella Valk, née van't Woudt, who was also from Vlaardingen. Both Arie and "Cor" were born in 1886. Records of the van't Wout family can be traced in Dutch registry offices dating as far back as the 17th century.[160]

---

[160] Arie, born 10 November 1886, Martha born 21 August 1886, Cornelia was the child of Reijer van t' Woudt (1848- 1910) and Margje Cornelia Aletta van t' Woudt (née Vlaming) (1851-1921) both from Vlaardingen (The Vlaming family can even be traced back to the 16th century, where a Willem den Dubbelden was mentioned as a precious metal worker. He lived in Wassenaar – 34 kilometres from Vlaardingen). Most of his ancestors seem to have been craftsmen, one worked in shipbuilding and another as a painter. Reijer was a decorative painter. He himself was the child of the basket maker Wilem (1817-1895) and the seamstress Jacoa (1815-1869) van't Woudt (née Liscet) and also came from Vlaardingen. Her father was Jacob Adrianusz Liscet baptised in 1788 in Vlaardingen and her mother Cornelia Pieters (née van den

What can be said about the ancestors on both sides is that the van't Woudts were mostly simple craftsmen. Ancestors, who can be traced back to the 18th century were basket makers, decorative painters or seamstresses and had lived in Vlaardingen for several generations. I could not discover any direct connection to the Dutch trade in enslaved African people, even though they lived near one of the most important trading harbours.[161] Because the families often had many children, it cannot be ruled out entirely, however. My Dutch ancestors were neither Dutch nobility or aristocracy that enriched itself through colonial trade. As far as I can tell, they were born relatively poor, lived their lives as such, and died in no better position.[162]

My grandmother's older brother, Reyer, was born four years before her in in the year 1912 and her younger sister "Martha", Margje Cornelia Aletta, nine years after her.[163]

My great-grandfather Arie Valk, was, according to one source, the leader of a crew of sailors on Dutch transport ships that travelled to colonial Indonesia. So here is, in the end, a minor colonial link. When his years of service in this position came to an end, Arie seems to have worked in numerous other professions, for example, there are registry

---

Berg, baptised in 1788 in Vlaardingen). Wilem (II) (we call him II here) was the son of the father of Wilem (I) (1784-1863) and Hendrina (1788-1859, née Hofman) van't Woudt (both from Vlaardingen). The couple had six children: Wilem (II), Adriana, Huibertje Mojet, Arij, Hendrina and Jannetje. Hendrina's father Adrianus was also a basket maker (1735-1805), his wife Huibertje Mojet (died 1824) worked as a seamstress, basket maker and 'shop elder', which probably meant that she ran the business. They both lived in Vlaardingen. Her father was Jan Johannes Mojet (baptised 1710 in Gorinchem – 50 km from Vlaardingen) and her mother Metje van der Garde (baptised 1708). Source: Dutch archives via MyHeritage.

[161] In total, Dutch trading ships are said to have forcibly enslaved at least 600,000 African people.

[162] Enthoven (2016) and Zeeuwsarchief: The Voyage – History. This was important for me to check. The Dutch West India Company (Geoctrooieerde westindische Compagnie,1621-1792) was one of the main drivers of the global transatlantic trade in enslaved people at the time, with 383 ship transports.

[163] Reyer was born on 19 May 1912, and sister Martha on 4 September 1925.

entries in which he is listed as a chicken farmer and others as a construction worker.

Remarkably, I came across also a photo of Arie's parents. Arie Valk (1856-1928) and Maria Strefland (1853-1927) which shows my two great-great-grandparents seemingly in their Sunday best, Maria with the Bible in her hand.

Arie appears to be out of focus in the picture, which makes him appear absent-minded.

Arie Valk (1856-1928) and Maria Strefland (1853-1927). Photo: via My Heritage.

The couple's clothing suggests the family's self-portrayal as a married couple of Protestant Dutch decency and members of the petty bourgeoisie. Perhaps the picture suggests a couple that tried to make the best of a life within their limited sphere with a degree of established recognition from within a small community. Maria smiles contently in this and another photo, and unlike her husband who looks straight into the camera. This photo opportunity may have been a special occasion to her, and she probably was pleased to have it taken. She seems, if I do not read too much into it, to grasp that the picture will capture her and Arie like a painting that will serve as a memory in the future. If so, she was right.

What am I to think of the two of them looking at us from this photo of the past, long after their lives have ended, without having much other information about them? My guess is that they were people who wanted to act properly and responsibly. Maria's holding of the Bible could suggest just that. Years later, one of their sons, who will also be called Arie, would make the right decision alongside his wife Cor and grant their young daughter Maria permission to marry my grandfather.

The parents of my grandmother, Arie and Cor, must have known what was going on in Germany and what had happened to the suitor of their daughter in Munich.

My mother, left, 1942. Own photo.

Maria and Arie, died in Schiedam, near Rotterdam, but lived for a long time in the neighbouring town of Ridderkerk. That is all I know of their lives, besides the details of Arie's work on the ship and his later jobs. My grandmother, named Maria after her grandmother, became pregnant when she was 21. She and my grandfather, by then then 44-year-old, married on 22 June 1938 in Amsterdam. My mother was born three months later on 5 September 1938 (5698). Gerhard and Maria gave their little girl three names: Corrie after her maternal grandmother, Luise after her paternal grandmother and Wilhelmina after the Dutch Queen.

Expelled from Munich, with a young family, my grandfather had made a new life for himself in Amsterdam as well as possible. But dark clouds were already gathering on the horizon. The invasion of Poland in 1939 and the start of the war were not the only obvious signs of this. On 12 September 1939, my grandfather's former partner and first wife Anny passed away at the age of just 47 years in Munich. The reasons given on her death certificate are "cardiac insufficiency and shrunken kidney." I understand the two conditions to affect each other and amongst the probable causes are heigh weight, smoking, infections and inherited conditions.[164]

In Amsterdam the real tragedy was to take place on 10th of May 1940, not just for my grandfather but for 25,000 Jewish refugees from Germany. On that day Germany occupied the Netherlands. Seventy percent of the Dutch Jewish population which still counted 140,000 people in the year 1940, would no longer be alive after 1945. Given that information, I was quite surprised to be able to find my grandfather's name, occupation and address in the 1942 edition of the Amsterdam telephone directory.

---

[164] See Kidney research UK: Cardiovascular and Kidney Diseases. *https://www.kidneyresearchuk.org/conditions-symptoms/cardiovascular-disease-and-kidney-disease/* accessed 17.02.2025

Amsterdam telephone directory 1942, 49361 Lewandowski, G. Corsetten, Haarlemerst. 29 My grandfather is registered here despite the German occupation. Amsterdam.

In spite of the occupation, my grandfather continued to be listed there as *49361 Lewandowski G., Corsetten, Haarlemerstraat 29*, in between Levy, Löwenstein and Lewin, family names that are clearly Jewish.

The occupation of the Netherlands had severe consequences for my grandfather. He would now have to retreat occasionally to his parents-in-law in Schalterdalweg 59 and 61, Beekbergen, not far from the City of Apeldoorn. The houses were deep inside a large, forested area, quite a contrast to densely populated Amsterdam. Perhaps it was hoped to be a place where eager Germans and National Socialist Dutch agents would not be on the hunt for Jewish people. In the large house where my grandmother's parents Cor and Arie lived, there was not only space under the roof, but there was also, I was told, a barn that had been converted into living quarters. Nevertheless, my grandfather and his family still travelled to Amsterdam often so that "dad (could) try to earn some money", my mother told me. What she knows is from the perspective of the young girl she was then. Not only was her father often not there. Her mother is said not to have had much patience for motherly tasks, and as soon as my mother was no longer breastfed, her attention went elsewhere. It was my mother's grandmother Cor and her father who gave her the necessary affection. A photo from 1943 (see beginning of chapter), in the middle of the war, shows my grandfather holding my mother's hand on her fifth birthday on Sunday the 5th of September. My mother has a small present in her hand; it looks like a pinwheel. My grandfather appears to be wearing his best suit, in honour of his daughter and the happy occasion. If you look closely, you can spot X-shaped army barriers in the back lined up against a house.

Things were not always that happy. The following story, told to me by my mother, may indicate how difficult this time must have been for my grandfather. She said, that sometime after 1940, my grandfather is said to have thrown himself into one of the many canals out of desperation in an apparent attempt to take his own life. It is hard to say how much of this she herself witnessed as a child and what she may only have learned later. However, according to what my mother knew, bystanders jumped into the water to save my grandfather. Such extreme degree of desperation can certainly not be understood without the prior experiences and traumatisation in Munich and in Dachau and before that, perhaps during the First World War. My grandfather must have feared the worst.

As already mentioned, my mother was frequently in Beekbergen with her Oma and Opa. She told me that there were a few children from the neighbourhood with whom she had contact, but not many. One of my mother's early memories is how she used to watch her grandfather grow roots from cut branches to plant new trees, or how he made compost in the woods. Flowers and gardening remained my mum's hobbies, even after all that was left for her to tend in later life was but a balcony and houseplants.

All this was amid the Second World War.

From left to right, my grandmother Maria, my mother Corrie, my great-aunt Martha (Margje) Valk, and my aunt Gerda, c.a. summer 1944 in the background my grandfather's shop, with a large sewing machine appearing through the window. Own photo.

My mother remembers that she was always warned during the war years -, that she should not go near any Germans. I don't know whether she understood at the time that her father had also been a German citizen. She told me that back then her father only spoke Dutch to her.

It was not the only complication for the family. Through a document from the Amsterdam city archives, I learnt that Reyer, my grandmother's brother, was on a job placement as a carpenter in the German city of Kassel, 400 kilometres away. He held a permit given to him via the German-Dutch Labour Office. He was therefore employed deeply in

Hitler's Germany as a hired foreign labourer. On the other hand, perhaps it provided for some cover.

Apart from these spare memories my mother never said much about those childhood years, only remembering warplanes flying over the forest and Canadian soldiers. But those two memories she mentioned frequently.

From 1943 onwards at least my mother's loneliness finally came to an end when her sister Gerda was born, with whom she would remain in close contact for most of her life except for the last few decades. However, at first she may probably have felt even more left out, as the attention of the grownups must surely have shifted towards her more needy baby sister.

8

Under Rommel's Command

The story of my family is not just about concentration and extermination camps, expropriations, occupations, flights, escapes, murders and other fates. The life of one man in the family seems to contradict everything you read so far. To my mother, who many years later "re"-converted to Orthodox Judaism, it was an uncomfortable fact. She always much preferred to speak of her paternal grandfather, a man whose Jewishness was undoubted and who was put to rest in the New Jewish cemetery in Munich. Or she would mention her distant cousin Max, from the Berlin side of the family, who had fled to Chile and had remained Jewish.

Allow me to introduce you to Alfred, my grandfather Gerhard's biological brother. He not only managed to not attract any attention on himself by the authorities of Third Reich Germany, it seems that he didn't even have to work hard to hide his partly Jewish family background, although according to the so-called racist Blutschutzgesetz (Blood Protection Act), he was to be considered a "half-blood" or "Quarter Jew." Whilst his biological brother Gerhard (my grandfather) had to flee to Amsterdam to save his life, he, Alfred, was drafted into the German Wehrmacht (or he may have joined as a volunteer) and served, it seems, with some considerable pride in the Afrika Korps under the command of Germany's so-called "Desert Fox," General Erwin Rommel.¹⁶⁵

Alfred Lewandowski in North Africa, picture
Lewandowski anniversary catalogue (1981).

A letter from his brother Bruno, dated 16 May 1943, reports that he, Alfred, had just been given the task of an interpreter due to a wound he had sustained, but that he normally had the task of a military driver.¹⁶⁶

The jubilee booklet celebrating the Lewandowskis' 150th year as an established company, published by Alfred in 1981, makes no secret if his Wehrmacht service. He even made sure to include a picture of himself showing him sitting topless and with a pith helmet on his head atop the

---

¹⁶⁵ Lewandowski (1981), p. 3
¹⁶⁶ Letter in the possession of Philipp Lewandowski

front of a Wehrmacht Army Vehicle, presumably somewhere in North Africa. He had no qualms about adding this photo as proof of his service. The fact that his father, grandfather and grandmother were Jews, or that his brother had been beaten to near death and was incarcerated in Dachau, he had conveniently overlooked, nor did he give any indication or information concerning the grim consequences the Third Reich had for the Berlin side of the entire Lewandowski family there, who were after all, Alfred's uncles, aunts and cousins, nor that the Berlin Lewandowski chain had been aryanized (more on all of that later). Anyone reading this celebratory anniversary publication had to assume that what was being presented here was the story of a "good German family and its business history" who had done their "duty" in both world wars. Not a hint of a Jewish background, whatsoever. It is impossible that he was not aware concerning his brother's life or that he did not know about the fate of his cousins, great-aunts and uncles from Berlin (see later). He had left these details out by nothing but deliberate choice.

Moreover, his years under Rommel did not need to be mentioned in this family anniversary publication. What did all of that have to do with the history of one of Germany's largest and proud corset manufacturers? I needed to have a closer look at the man under whom Alfred served.

During the first decades of the post-war period, Rommel was recognised as the figure of the "decent", heroic soldier. Propaganda material from Nazi newsreels emphasised Rommel's supposed "heroic" image. Rommel was ordered by Hitler to hold out in El Alamein in Egypt following his defeat to the British military. Contrary to the orders he had received from Berlin, Rommel withdrew his troops. The Allies also drove the development of something of a "Rommel myth", reported as a respected force against which the British struggled, but ultimately won.

Another myth concerning Rommel is his alleged involvement in the Staufenberg plot, which is considered less probable today than it had been in the past. Clearly, this alleged involvement in the plot served the Nazi-leadership as a reason for his forced suicide. But this does not mean that questions about Rommel can be left to open.

Firstly, there is the matter of what would have happened, had Rommel successfully conquered all of Egypt and the taken over British Mandate Palestine. SA planners and task forces had indeed already been preparing for this. Key to this were plans about the faith of any Jewish populations they would get hold of across these areas. For the population in the Yishuv, the Jewish-populated parts of British-occupied Palestine, a successful German conquest would have meant that the "Final Solution", the planned mass extermination of all Jews, had arrived there too. This was even though Rommel was said to have adhered to agreed procedures for the treatment of prisoners of war. Unlike Hitler's other generals, Rommel was also said to have harboured no personal hatred towards Jews. Evidence for this was apparently the fact that he did not order any separation between black and white prisoners in line with racist Third Reich ideology, and that he also did not segregate Jewish POWs from the non-Jewish ones.[167] On the other hand, according to historian Ralf Georg Reuth, it is unlikely that Rommel, as a high-ranking officer close to Hitler's Führer-command, was unaware of the ongoing mass-murders of Jews under German orders.[168]

What is one to make of the fact that following the German capture of Tripoli, German troops were ordered not to buy anything from the Jewish population that lived there, or the fact that Jewish Libyans were forced by Rommel's troops to clear minefields?[169] After Rommel and his troops withdrew to Tunisia following their defeat in Egypt, the German deployment command set up labour camps. This resulted in the murder of 2,500 Tunisian Jews within six months of the German occupation, assisted by members of the *Wehrmacht*.[170] The German *Einsatzkommando* under SS-Obersturmbandführer Walter Rauff was fully prepared and ready to commit further atrocities, if they were given the chance. He

---

[167] See: Haus der Geschichte, Baden-Würtemberg (2008)
[168] Reuth (2005), p. 35
[169] Paterson (2011)
[170] Mirror (2007)

was the same Hitler-loyal commander who had previously tested the "efficiency" of systems employed to mass murder of Sinti and Roma people in Eastern Europe.[171] The air raids of the Axis forces on Haifa and Tel Aviv in 1940 should also not be discounted in any assessment of Rommel's status as a "hero".[172] Further questions need to be asked about murders, forced relocations and victimisation of Cyrenaican Jews, especially from the area around Benghazi, where Italian and German Nazis had worked hand in hand.[173]

As far as Rommel's alleged good or noble character is concerned, his actions in Italy in 1943 and his previous role during the First World War in the extremely brutal Twelfth Battle of Isonzo must also be considered.[174] Reuth noted the following about Rommel:

> *He understood neither National Socialism nor the resistance to it. In that respect, he is like millions of other Germans. The tragedy of the Germans is reflected in the prototype of the field marshal (Rommel). He followed the Führer, who restored the self-belief of a humiliated nation in the midst of disaster, and while he was at it, he believed he was doing his duty.*[175]

The same could probably be said about the 100,000 troops that were deployed under Rommel's command, including my great-uncle Alfred. Alfred appears to have returned from the front before the end of the war, following the defeats in North Africa. Then, in February 1943, he married Charlotte Matschkewitz (1919-1956).

Alfred's and Gerhard's other brother, Bruno, remained in Munich throughout the war. In 1943 he and his family had to move from Adalbertstraße in central Munich's Maxvorstadt district to the outskirts

---

[171] Fanizadeh (2021) on Dan Diner (2021).
[172] ibid
[173] see Roumani (2020)
[174] Schreiber (1996), and Haus der Geschichte, Baden-Württemberg (2008), p.13
[175] Reuth (2006), p.198

of the town to the district of Planegg, due to damage caused by air raids.[176] A year later a far worse tragedy struck the family.

In June 1944, Bruno Lewandowski and his wife Erna would lose their only daughter, Erika, in another air raid. The attack is said to have begun when Erika was on her way to school. Although the young teenager and her companions rushed to an air-raid shelter belonging to a friend's family for their safety, neither she nor any of the other children she was with survived the bombing. According to my aunt Gerda, the loss of their only daughter had driven the parents into madness. Bruno himself wrote these words to his brother Willy:

Planegg 1944

Dear Willy!

Erna is not able to write to you, and so I want to pass on the terrible news that has affected us. Our beloved Erikachen, all of our happiness, was killed during an air raid on Munich on 13th of June. You can't imagine our grief and pain! Erikachen had travelled with me to Munich on 13th of June and then to the secondary school on Bergstrasse. The air raid came at 9.20 am. Erikachen and 3 other friends had to go to the air-raid shelter of a fellow pupil near the school at Jakob-Klar-Str. 10. This air raid shelter was very well-equipped. (But) there was a bomb that penetrated all 4 floors and into the air-raid shelter and only then went on to explode, killing all 19 people inside, including the 4 schoolchildren. We dug the whole day, the following night and the following day, still hoping to discover someone alive. Unfortunately, it was in vain! These and the following hours were the most terrible of my life. Erikachen was then laid out in the Nordfriedhof (North Cemetery) in huge mourning and was buried in the Planegg Cemetery opposite her (maternal) grandparents with great honour and huge attendance from friends and relatives. There (in Planegg), according to God's

---

[176] Letter to "Tanzher" in the possession of Philipp Lewandowski, 1 Sept. 1943

unfathomable decree, our very favourite (girl) now rests close to us. Erna has completely collapsed. I can write no more for today. Many greetings.

Bruno

We have sent you an obituary, but since posting printed matters are forbidden, it was returned to us yesterday.[177]

I don't know where the fourth brother of Gerhard, Bruno, and Alfred held out during the war. However, Wilhelm Lewandowski most probably also lived in Munich.

---

[177] Private letter in the possession of Philipp Lewandowski.

9

From Auschwitz-Birkenau to New York

It may very well have been David Lewandowski's marriage to Luise, a Christian German woman, that spared the worst for the Munich side of the Lewandowskis during the Hitler years, with the one exception of my grandfather. But on the Berlin side of the family it was different. The bitter and dark shadows of the Third Reich's "Final Solution" was unforgiving here.

My great-grandfather's brother Max Lewandowski (1852-1912, 5612-5672) and his wife Johanna Chaja (née Caspar) had lived as Jews and kept Jewish traditions. Their children grew up with both a Jewish and a German identity. Their daughter Elli (born 1891, 5651) married the Jewish-German Max Elkeles (born 1888, 5651), owner of a Berlin fabric and clothing shop by the name of "Stoffhaus Les." Elli was thus a cousin of my grandfather Gerhard and his brothers and was also involved in the family's textile business.[178] Elli and Max Elkeles had two children, Karla (born 1927, 5687) and Gerd (born 1923, 5683). The family lived "like all our relatives and acquaintances"

---

[178] Gundel, K. Reborn (1986), pp. 6-7, retranslated

in the Berlin-Schöneberg district until their flat, was confiscated or rather stolen for "housing needs" of the SS.[179] Part of this knowledge stems from a memoir that Karla had written after the war, when she also took on her new name Kay Gundel. She called the unpublished memoir "Reborn." It contains not only her recollections of Berlin, but also the story of her remarkable survival during the Shoah. She wrote, that before the rise of the Third Reich she had enjoyed a comfortable life in Berlin:

> "We enjoyed the finer things in life, a penchant for art, music and the "good things." We had a large, comfortable flat, the windows overlooked the beautiful street full of chestnut trees and the rooms were full of heavy antique furniture, with oil paintings and hand-woven Persian carpets. We had silver cutlery and crystal glasses and beautiful porcelain crockery for celebrations.[180]"

Kay wrote that the extended Berlin Lewandowski family looked after each other. "My mother used to send my uncles and aunts a fat, freshly slaughtered chicken for Shabbat."[181] Sunday afternoons were reserved for visits to the wider family. She wrote about an exciting childhood in Berlin and her passion for the piano. Then things took an increasingly bad turn. Karla recalled how fellow school-students harassed her with racist and antisemitic remarks referring to her amongst others as a "dirty Jewess," and she remembered that Jews weren't allowed to sit in certain areas in Berlin. She wrote that increasingly the hatred of Jews was propagated in newspapers and on the radio. Eventually the situation became so intolerable that she was forced to change schools. Only when she started to attend a school for Jewish children, did she have some reprieve from being constantly harassed.[182]

---

[179] The address was Berchtesgarnderstraße 38, see Gundel (1986), p .6-7
[180] Gundel (1986)
[181] Ibid.
[182] i ibid. p. 11f

She wrote that her family had quite wrongly assumed that the German enthusiasm for National Socialism would eventually fade. This believe was the cause of them remaining in Berlin during the time when emigration would have still been relatively easy. In 1942, after prolonged illness, probably cancer, Karla's mother Elli passed away. In spite of the persecution of Jews being in full swing by that time, they still had the opportunity to bury Elli. Kay wrote, that due to her mother's premature death she was probably spared the fate the rest of the family had to face soon and, unlike those in the family who were soon to be murdered, she was still given a dignified resting place.

Following the death of her mother, Karla was deported to Terezín (Theresienstadt) on 22 August 1942, alongside her father Max. According to Karla's memoirs, the Gestapo initially intended to arrest only her father, but Karla begged the Nazis that she should be taken alongside her dad. In the end she succeeded in her endeavour, unlike her brother "Gerd" who tried the same, but was refused. Staying behind, he would still find himself arrested only a few weeks later and was transported directly to Auschwitz (probably Auschwitz-Birkenau), where the Nazis ended his life murderously on 9 December 1942 (5703) at the age of just 19 years.[183]

Meanwhile Karla (the later Kay) described a year of hunger, unhygienic living conditions and a severe bout of scarlet fever. It was here that father and daughter grew close. Kay wrote how her father was initially housed in a completely overcrowded room in one of the houses of the garrison prison. He was however able to save himself by getting employment as a guard. Those who had such employment got a little more than others.

Theresienstadt was the "showcase camp" of the Third Reich, in which the Nazis aimed to demonstrate "how humane and good" the living conditions for Jews allegedly were inside camps. But it was a charade.

Karla was also able to get a job as a carer for small children in the camp's children's home. She wrote about her experiences in great detail,

---

[183] born 30 May 1923, information from MyHeritage.com

including the visit of the International Red Cross on 23 June 1943. In the words of Karla:

> *In mid-fall a podium was suddenly under construction…, and one day like magic, an orchestra was in rehearsal… (and) the order passed through … that the entire ghetto would undergo a massive cleaning… SS-men and camp officials scurried from building-to-building checking and rechecking that all was in immaculate order. …Only a certain number of the ghetto inmates were selected to be out in the ghetto's streets, and they were issued new, clean and pressed clothes. The rest of us were locked away inside. The very worst --the starved, sunken eyes and hollow cheeks, bones lightly covered with flesh -- were shut away in other rooms far away from windows. … Clean and laughing children played in the festive pavilion, tasty food was served in gigantic heaping portions, and nowhere amongst the serving barrels and tables was thin coffee and dry buns.*

A few lines later, Kay continued:

> *It was all so phoney, a terrible charade, but only we, locked behind the windows, knew the real game the Nazis were playing. … Look here, I silently screamed. Don't leave thinking they care for us. It is Hell here. They are killing us, working us to death, starving us. They are using us up and throwing us away!* [184]

Having passed the Red Cross inspection, those imprisoned in Theresienstadt had largely "fulfilled their purpose" for the Nazis. There was no reason for them to remain in the camp, unless they could be exploited further. Accordingly, Karla and Max were deported to the extermination camp Auschwitz-Birkenau on 10 October 1943. Karla's account of how she fell asleep on her father's shoulder during the

---

[184] Ibid. p. 88

excruciating and long train journey in an overcrowded cattle wagon makes tragic reading, when she writes about the eventual opening of the doors amid the shouting of the German SS personnel in Auschwitz-Birkenau. There Karla was separated from her father within minutes. It was, as she would later learn, her very last sight of her beloved father.

Her father's murder was "officially" recorded on 6 October 1944 (5705). However, Karla believed her father to have been gassed and burnt soon after her arrival. Older prisoners who had been interned in Auschwitz-Birkenau for some time had assured her that all older people would usually be murdered immediately. The stench of the incinerators left her in no doubt.

After ten depressing days searching for her father in Auschwitz-Birkenau, Karla was selected from amongst the many women interned in the camp for further exploitative work purposes. She soon found herself in the Merzdorf (now Marciszów) subcamp of the Gross-Rosen concentration camp. Here she was assigned the new task of the monitoring of several spools of spinning machines for hours every day. "Standing… it was the only thing I did. Standing at the machine, standing twice each day for the long roll calls, standing in line for food, standing in line for toilets", she wrote, referring to the entire place as nothing but a sealed tomb.[185]

If the data from Auschwitz regarding the date of Kay's father recorded death, and he really "survived" Auschwitz-Birkenau for a full year after his arrival and had Kay been aware of this, her story may have taken a very different turn (for she may have tried to take measures to remain in the camp). As she later wrote, after her arrival in Auschwitz she desired for nothing more than to find her father. In this regard, she had contacted inmates from the men's camps, and before she was taken to Merzdorf in order to find out more. Perhaps Max, her father, did likewise. It is not impossible that he found out that his Karla had been taken away to another camp. Was it the hope

---

[185] ibid. p. 113

of a reunion that kept him alive? Such thoughts are speculative, but they allow us to understand that each person here was dealing with tragic individual fates, people who all had feelings, their own hopes and stories to tell.

When Karla had eventually been liberated by Soviet troops at the end of the war, she was found to be very weak and barely alive due to her starved out condition. With the help of the Russian liberators, she slowly recovered and then set to return to Berlin, full of hope that she might find other survivors of her family. What she found, however, was a city lying in ruins and not a single family member. She was now unable to imagine any future for herself in Germany and decided in 1947 to leave Germany and to emigrate to the USA, where she settled in New Jersey and married Walter S. Gundel (1921-2011/5681-5771),whose original full name was Gundelfinger, a Jewish refugee from Ulm in 1948.

Walter Gundel had initially fled with his family to Tel Aviv, but in 1941, after Italian bombing raids on Tel Aviv, the family decided to continue their flight and to travel on to the USA, via Egypt.

Walter and Karla, renamed as Kay, had three children, Steven, Susan and Linda, who in turn had their own children.[186] Kay passed away after a long life in 2001 in her adopted new homeland. It was only 20 years later, that I came across their children at the beginning of the 2020 coronavirus pandemic, which led to a long overdue reunion of some of the descendants of Minna and Jacob Lewandowski via a video conference.

But Karla was one of the "lucky" ones in the family. Others were not as fortunate. Arthur Lewandowski, Kay Gundel's uncle (Elli Elkeles brother) was deported from Berlin to Theresienstadt together with his wife Käte (born 1882 as Bärnkopf in Ostrovo) and his sister Betti Crohn (born 1889 as Betti Lewandowski).[187]

---

[186] Karla Kay Elkeles 6 Jun 1927 (5687), d. Berlin-15.3.2001 (5761)), see also Walter Gundel, The Record (2011). According to this, the names of the children are Steven, Linda and Susan

[187] Betti Crohn (1889-1943 / 5649-5703)

As chance would have it, Arthur and Käte met Max and Karla (Kay) in Theresienstadt. However, this tragic reunion was the last "lucky" occurrence for this side of the family, because, like Max, they were all later murdered in Auschwitz.[188]

But at the same time, there exists another incredible escape:

Kay's cousin Lola Crohn, the daughter of the above mentioned Betti Crohn and Leopold Crohn (1874-1922/5634-5682). Lola (later Jones, 1919-1999/5679-5759) managed to escape Germany on the SS Manhattan on 22 March 1939.

Allegedly, her mother Betti had received warnings from acquaintances within the German military advising her to flee. The ship carrying Lola from Hamburg was the same ship on which many children from the Jewish Kindertransport were taken to Great Britain. Lola, however, was no child, but already 20 years of age. Her mother Betti had probably made preparations to emigrate during a trip to the United States a few years earlier in 1937.[189] Lola's son, Frank Jones, thinks it is possible that Betti met with relatives on that trip with whom she discussed her preparations.[190] Researchers from the Stolperstein Foundation discovered that Betti had actually paid half of the exit fee for herself also. She probably was unable to come to more money, apparently by selling what valuables she possessed. As already stated, having saved her daughter, Betti was murdered in Auschwitz four years later (1943) at the age of 54.[191]

---

[188] I use Auschwitz here as standing for both Auschwitz and Auschwitz-Birkenau, both being death camps in close proximity to each other. Betti Crohn was transported on transport 35 from Berlin to the Auschwitz Birkenau extermination camp on 6 March 1943. Arthur and Käte Lewandowski were transported on Transport I/35 from Berlin to Theresienstadt on 31 July 1942 and are both believed to have been murdered in Auschwitz. (Source: Berlin's Memorial Book of Jewish Victims of National Socialism, Freie Universität Berlin, Central Institute for Social Science Research, Edition Hentrich, Berlin 1995).

[189] Betti Crohn was born as Betti Lewandowski, and was the daughter of Max/Marcus and "Chaja" Johanna Lewandowski (1857-1920)

[190] Personal correspondence, by e-mail. Frank and I have undertaken DNA-tests that prove shared close ancestry.

[191] Howard Jones details of his son, Frank Jones.

In New York, Lola met and married Howard E. Jones (1904-1984), a Black American human rights activist born in New York. Lola and Howard had four children.[192] According to Frank Jones, curiously, as if it was something insignificant or perhaps dangerous, or perhaps more likely very painful, his mother never mentioned her past, nor that she was Jewish.

On the 30th of June 2025 Lola and Betti were given the honour of Stolpersteine. They were placed at Winterfeldtstraße 90, in the Schöneberg district of Berlin. The house in which they lived no longer stands and was replaced by a post-war housing block. Nearby stood however period houses from the 19th century that together with the splendid fountain spring dominated Victoria-Luise Square gave an impression of a former exquisite, modern and well off area.

Various members of the wider Lewandowski family gathered together for the Stolperstein revelation, Frank Jones, one of Lola's son, her grandchild Elisabeth and her great-grandchild Beckett, as well as my cousin and her daughter, Claudia and Johanna Gross, and Phillip Lewandowski and his partner.

As part of the presentation, Frank Jones read a dedication of his grandmother as if she was to tell those present herself about her life, from the I perspective. I have asked Frank to share this with me for the English edition of Soll sein Schulem. The reading was constructed around a photo album that Lola had carried with her to New York.

I was born to a prosperous German/Jewish family of Lewandowski. I had a happy life with my parents Marcus Lewandowski and

---

[192] The date of arrival is explained by an application for naturalisation for US citizenship in 1939, which was found in the New York National Archives. *https://catalog.archives.gov/id/6218697*. According to Frank Jones, the children of Howard E Jones and Lola are: Ronald Jones (Berea, Kentucky), Frank Jones (Sorrento, Florida), Jennifer Jones (West Melbourne, Florida) and Alan Jones (Sorrento, Florida). Frank Jones wrote me that on his paternal grandfather's side, the family had never been enslaved in America, but that they were farmers on their own land. Other ancestors on the grandmother's side, possibly his great-grandfather, were however most likely enslaved persons of African background. Source: personal correspondence.

Johanna Casper along with my two brothers Arthur and James and my sister Elli. My family was very important to all of us. I was very close to my sister Elli. We had our picture taken when we were young women, we looked so pretty in our fine dresses. Then I met a wonderful man Leopold Crohn and we were married this very day, June 30, 1911. We had this wonderful picture taken of us at a photographer's studio in our finest cloth, we were so happy. A year later in 1912, I lost my dear father Marcus. Eight years later, February 1919, after WW1 we were blessed with our wonderful daughter, Lola. We were so happy. Lola was the most beautiful daughter one could hope for. In 1922, when Lola was only three years old, I lost both my dear mother Johanna and also Leopold, who had been taken sick after a long period of suffering. As a widow I raised Lola on my own in the company of my loving family. We enjoyed so many happy days in the country and at the seashore. Lola and I spent happy times with Elli and her husband Max and their children Kaye and Gerhard. Lola grew up enjoying a happy childhood with her family and friends. Lola and I loved the winter and the snow. Lola and I would take a sled out to play in the snow. I loved dressing in my finest cloth and going to the country. However, in 1933 the political climate in Germany changed and a dark cloud came over the Jewish community and our beloved country. The Nazis seizure of power was very bad. Because of that in April, 1937, I went to New York to secure a way for my daughter Lola to escape the horrors of what was happening to our happy home in Germany. Then in March 1939, the saddest day of my life, I had to say good-bye to my beautiful daughter Lola as she left to start a new life in New York. As for me, I lost my dear sister Elli due to illness in 1942. My brother James escaped to South America but my brother Arthur was not so lucky and was arrested and like me was murdered in Auschwitz. I was forced out of our home that you stand in front of today and had to move to share an apartment. On March 5, 1943, the Gestapo arrested me. But before I tell you about

> *the last days of my life, I want to tell you, as I told my daughter many times before, "Don't give up, you can do it,"*[193]

Elisabeth and Frank Jones then read the report of a woman who was collected and transported to Auschwitz alongside Betti. It included a collection from her home by the SS, who escorted her on the way to an assembly camp in Grosse Hamburger Strasse, after which they were taken to the Jewish Home for the Elderly from March 5 to March 6, 1943. On March 6th they were driven in trucks to the Putlitzstrasse Railway Freight Station:

> *"There we were loaded into freight cars. (...) In the room at the assembly camp in Berlin, it was only possible to stand due to the overpopulation of the house with people of all ages both sick and healthy. This room was terribly overcrowded. I would also say that there was a lack of washing facilities and the condition of the toilets was very poor. As to the food supply, I can say that I didn't receive any provisions on Friday, March 5. Only on March 6, before boarding the transport, we received a pre-prepared packet with 3 sandwiches spread with margarine. I don't recall anymore whether these sandwiches had some sausage or anything else edible in them. In this assembly camp in Berlin there was no medical care whatsoever. (...) When I was arrested on March 5, I was neither abused nor verbally harassed. However, on March 6, when we were being loaded onto the train at the Putlitzstrasse railway station, an SS man struck me on my back with a stick, and this was apparently because I didn't get into the freight car fast enough. (...) We only knew that we were being taken to the East, but we did not know where the transport was headed for. Among us prisoners there was talk about us being taken to some ghetto. We then arrived in Auschwitz. There, we were*

---

[193] Frank Jones added, that this was the advise his mother Lola gave him, and that he believed this advise to come from Betti.

unloaded and separated into lines of men, women and children. SS women spread a blanket in front of us and we had to put our jewellery, handbags, and all our belongings on it. Afterwards, most of the prisoners, mainly women and children, were loaded onto trucks and driven away. At first, we did not know where these people had been taken. At the selection of the prisoners in Auschwitz I was assigned to a working unit like many others. When we were in the camp in Auschwitz, I learned that those women and children, who, as I mentioned, were driven away on a truck, were murdered in the gas chamber…"

After finishing the account of Betti's life, Elisabeth read a bit on Lola, Betti's daughter. This included information that she had received letters from Betto via the Red Cross, which eventually stopped. They also revealed that Howard had been Lola's English teacher, with whom she fall in love. Howard was studying law at the time. After bringing up all her children, Lola would enrol in college and complete an Associate's Degree. Frank Jones told me that his mother's final days were hastened through an unnecessary operation. A hospital had managed to mix up medical records. On that basis a large surgery was performed for a condition she did not have but was another patient's condition. As Lola the refugee who escaped the Nazis, lay in her final days heavily incapacitated due to the grave hospital error, Frank and others became embroiled in a huge legal claim, which eventually was settled just before Lola slipped away.

Zol Zayn Shulem I: Zores

Photos from Lola Crohn's Photo Album, with thanks to Frank Jones.

10

Escape to All Corners of the World

Sometimes people ask me (and other relatives), if we are related to the composer of Jewish liturgy, Louis Lewandowski. As far as I know, we are not, but there was another professional musician in the family, not as well-known as Louis. His name was Walter Lewandowski, and he was another member of the wider Berlin family who was able to escape the mass murders, because he had managed to leave Germany early. Born in Berlin in 1887, Walter Lewandowski was one of the two sons of Adolph Lewandowski and Amalie (née Ephraim, 1853). His brother Eugen had already passed away in 1923.[194]

An entry in the Lexicon of Persecuted Musicians during the Third Reich (2017) reveals that Walter lost his father shortly after his "confirmation."[195] As his father was buried in the Jewish cemetery in Weißensee,

---

[194] Adolph Lewandowski(1853-1903), was the brother of my great-grandfather David. Amalie Lewandowski (née Ephraim 1853-?)

[195] Fetthauer, Sophie (2017), Walter Lewandowski, in Maurer Zenck, Petersen & Fetthauer (eds.) (2017) also in Lexikon verfolgter Musiker und Musikerinnen der NS-Zeit, University of Hamburg: https://www.lexm.uni-hamburg.de/object/lexm_lexmperson_00003365 (retrieved on 20/11/2023).

I assume that the term confirmation refers to a bar mitzvah (his mother's maiden name, Ephraim, although not definitive, also suggests a Jewish background). After graduating from a grammar school and completing an apprenticeship, he worked in wholesales before serving the German Reich during the First World War. In 1917, he began to radically turn his life around and worked as a pianist and illustrator in Berlin's silent film cinemas. When silent film made way for talking films, he was forced to make his living through musical entertainment in Berlin's bars instead. The German Lexicon of Persecuted Musicians also states that he regularly performed at the "Berlin Tonkünstlerheim" between 1917 and 1933 and writes:

> *According to his own statements, he had a pronounced ability to play by heart and play music by ear. He also composed various dances.*[196]

After his career as a musician came to a premature end with the rise of National Socialism and the Third Reich, Walter continued to work for various insurance companies until 1938, before he also lost these positions. After several unsuccessful attempts to emigrate with his fiancée Auguste Miloslawski (born in 1899) to Manchukuo, he and Auguste, now his wife, finally managed to escape to Shanghai instead in 1939, possibly via Italy.

At almost the same time in March 1939, Walter's sister-in-law Hertha (born 1886/5646 as Hertha Michaelis), the widow of his brother Eugen Lewandowski, committed suicide, aged 52 years.[197] It is difficult

---

[196] ibid. "Auf zum Tanz, Walzer, für Klavier," Berlin-Charlottenburg: A. Fritsche (1920).

[197] The date of Hertha's death is 10 March 1939. She was buried in the grave in which her husband Eugen was also buried at the Berlin Jewish cemetery, Weißensee, grave 100360. Berlin Memorial Book of Jewish Victims of National Socialism, Freie Universität Berlin, Central Institute for Social Science Research, Edition Hentrich, Berlin 1995. The Document on the "suicide" is available in Arolsen https://collections.arolsen-archives.org/archive/11244122/?p=1&s=Lewandow ski%20 Herta&doc_id=11244122

to say to what extent and whether the two events, Walter's departure and the suicide, are connected.

Auguste's mother, Flora Miloslawsky (1866-1944 /5626-5704) née Grünthal), now left behind in Berlin on her own, was deported to Theresienstadt in 1943. There she died within a year at the age of 78. It can be assumed that the conditions there facilitated or caused her death directly.

Although Shanghai may have initially been a good and safe place for Walter and Auguste to flee too, not least because many other refugees from Austria and Germany had also fled there, the couple was later transferred to the ghetto in Hongkew in 1943, set up by the Japanese occupiers. Surprisingly, Walter and Auguste declined an offer to settle in Australia after the end of the Second World War.

It was not until 1949 that they finally agreed to leave China, shortly before the Chinese Communists took power. On 27 May 1949, Walter, now 62 years old, and Auguste, 59 years old, arrived in San Francisco. A later entry connects them to Detroit. I have not been able to discover anything further about their continued stay in the USA (so far).

There is a third person from the Berlin side of the Lewandowski family who also managed to escape Third Reich Germany. James Lewandowski (born 1885-19?) may even have been the first amongst the extended Berlin family to manage to leave Germany.[198] James was another son of Max and Johanna Lewandowski (his sister being Elli Elkeles nee Lewandowski). He initially endured imprisonment in the Sachenshausen concentration camp near Berlin. The archivist at the Sachsenhausen Memorial informed me that James Lewandowski was probably arrested after or during the November pogrom (Reichskristallnacht) of 1938, which is consistent with Kay Gundel's memoir. According to her recollection, the arrest is said to have taken place on 10 or 11 November 1938.[199] After his release, James fled to

---

[198] Hebrew date of James is 5645-?
[199] Gundel (1986), p. 18

Lima, Peru, together with his wife and children. Kay Gundel had the following to say about his departure:

> With some luck at least for my family, my aunt and uncle still had their own passports, so my aunt immediately went to work arranging for emigration papers and boat passage to Chile. Within four to six weeks after Uncle James' arrest, the passport and papers were approved, and Uncle James was released from Sachsenhausen. It was not long after on the eighth day of Hanukkah, when all the candles burned on the menorah, that the family was reunited briefly at our apartment. We spent a quiet night together, knowing, we're saying a final goodbye. A few days later they were gone.[200]

James' and Johanna's (1889-1980/5644-5740, née Bergmann) children were Max (1914-1993/5674-5753) and Margaret (b. 1926/5686-?), and they lived in Peru, the USA and Chile.[201] Margaret's family (Cherry) eventually adopted the Christian faith, while Max remained loyal and committed to Judaism. In the 1970s, he carried out his own research to locate relatives and survivors of the family and as part of that search he visited my family in Munich. His daughter Jeanette, granddaughter of James Lewandowski and great-granddaughter of Jacob Lewandowski, worked for many years in the Jewish community in Santiago.

Georg Wolff, the son of Ernestine Wolff and Louis Wolff Georg, was not fortunate enough to be able to flee.[202] He was deported from Berlin in 1942 and consequently murdered in Trawniki. The liquidation of the Trawniki SS-training and labour camp, ordered by Himmler

---

[200] Ibid. James was released on the seventh day of Hanukkah, 23 December 1938, research by the Brandenburg Memorials Foundation / Sachsenhausen Memorial and Museum, based on information from the Russian State Archives, Moscow, by email 18 August 2020.

[201] Margaret Cherry's children were Patricia, Albert and Debbie. Patricia Schwabe (died 2002), had two children, Nicole and Davey Schwabe.

[202] Ernestine Wolff, née Lewandowski and sister of my great-grandfather David

under the cover name "Operation Harvest Festival", was one of the most perverse and brutal low points in the murders committed under National Socialism. Victims not only had to dig their own graves under the deceptive pretence that they were merely creating trenches, but the subsequent executions were accompanied by the playing of loud music played from loudspeakers. To cover up all traces of their murderous deeds, the firing squads that had killed the Jews were also shot afterwards. The bodies of all those murdered were then burned, to try to hide any evidence.[203] The "Aktion Erntefest" was seen as revenge for Jewish uprisings in camps, including the uprising of the Jews in Treblinka (see later).

Whether Helene Neumann (1904-1942), who died in Auschwitz-Birkenau, was Georg's sister remains unclear.[204]

---

[203] Transport from Berlin to Trawniki, Lublin, Poland 02/04/1942.
[204] Yad Vashem lists that Helene Neumann, born in 1904, as a saleswoman. She stayed in Caserne Dossin (Malines-Mechelen) in Belgium and was then deported to Auschwitz Birkenau on 15 February 1942. USHMM also lists her in the Antwerp Jewish register with the date of birth 24.4.1904.

Zol Zayn Shulem I: Zores

Za'ar

All masters of every stripe are rubbish. And all slaves of every stripe are noble and exalted... Once you cease to be a master, once you throw off your master's yoke, you are no longer human rubbish, you are just a human being, and all the things it adds up to. So too with the slaves. Once they are no longer slaves, once they are free they are no longer noble and exalted. They are just human beings.

Jamaica Kinkaid in A small Place

Za'ar anachnu makirim otcha
Za'ar sot anachnu ba Olam,
Am israel ba olam
Le Kol Adam

Pity, we know you.
suffering, that is us on earth, kol the
Jewish people worldwide
To all human beings

Ha Zipur ha Ham a Jehudi
ha zipur ha za'ar
Sawalnu Ba Mitzraim
Abednu Arzenu
Lergschu Otanu la Olam
Za'at sot anachnu ba Olam

The history of the Jewish people
is the history of suffering
We suffered in Egypt
and lost our country.
They chased us into the world
Suffering that is what we are in the world.

Chipasnu Chofesh
at ha sof shel ha Za'ar
Matzanu Oiehvut
u-Mawet U-zaa'r
Ba Kol ha Olam

We sought freedom,
the end of sorrow
We found hostility
and death and suffering,
in the whole world.

Hargu Otanu
Kimat kol ha Beit Israel Nafal
Sheh igia Yom Shichrur
le za'ar ba Galut

They murdered us!
Almost the entire House of Israel fell
May the Day of Freedom come,
from suffering in exile.

Poem by Daniel Zylbersztajn-Lewandowski from 1996 (Zaar)

11

"They Only Came to Murder"

"What we experienced back then – no film or words can convey that."[205]

Wolf Zylbersztajn

The Germans entered the town of Szczekociny on 3 September, and their first "greeting" was the murder of 46 Szczekocin and Żarki Jews. As soon as they (began to) march, they torched a total of about 70 per cent of the city. During the first two weeks, around 20 September 1939, when the German army reached the banks of the Vistula, those who left the city gradually returned to Szczekociny. To their misfortune, they came across rubble everywhere, their belongings, their long ploughing, had turned to ashes.[206]

Zwi Grajpner

---

[205] After my father. He kept saying that often.
[206] Szwajcer (2010), p. 218, own translation.

"They Only Came to Murder"

On Rosh Hashanah in September 1939 (5699), neither apple slices with honey nor prayers for the new Jewish year could cheer up the Jewish community of Szczekociny. It was the day of the invasion of German troops. In 1959, my uncle Abraham tried to remember the attack and invasion of the Germans 20 years earlier in *Pinkes Szczekocin*, the survivors' book of memories:

> *On Friday, 1 September 1939, nobody thought about the destruction that would come to the city. Friday evening, everyone sat mesmerised in front of the radio and the first reports about the war. Among other things, we heard that the tunnel under Sędziszów had been bombed.*[207]

According to my father, the family did not have their own radio, but a few restaurants did. In this way, neighbours informed themselves about the situation, including a speech by the "*Verbrecher*" (criminal) Hitler![208]

> *It was a bit dicey at the time. But I thought maybe it wouldn't be quite so dangerous. So, we went back home, and went to sleep, thinking, well, maybe everything will calm down.*[209]

My uncle went on:

> *I slept through the night from Friday to Saturday and was still lying in my bed when fellow Jews came round on Shabbat morning and told us to grab shovels and start to dig trenches. I joined the others on the road that led to Dębowiec, where we worked together until 5 pm. When we returned to the city, there was an atmosphere of optimism. Various people had arrived from nearby towns (most of*

---

[207] Sędziszów is situated about 20 kilometres south-east of Szczekociny
[208] Zylbersztajn, Wolf (2001), Cassette I, 8:20, Verbrecher (German and Yiddish) a criminal
[209] Ibid.

them from Żarki) and told us about the first victims of the war.[210] *Nevertheless, they didn't want to believe that we were facing such a huge holocaust (as it came to be), the precedent for which is unique in history.*[211] *At the end of August, there were already major debates (between us) whether the Germans would attack Szczekociny too, bringing about a tense situation. Many thought it impossible that Germany would be able to break through the fortifications of western Poland. But that did not make most of us feel safe.*[212]

It was on Wednesday, our market day, when mobilisation posters were put up everywhere. Panic broke out amongst the population, as if the war had already arrived. This panic lasted until Friday morning, 1 September. Although the news on Polish radio did not inform citizens about the (actual) start of the war, we already had reliable information by 07.00 a.m. that the Sędziszów-Miechów tunnel had been bombed by a German plane at 04.00 a.m.. From the very beginning, a stream of people and goods moved through the centre of Szczekociny and continued further to the East. On the same Friday, our community issued an order that all men between the ages of 16 and 60 should come the next day, it was Shabbat, to help dig trenches (again).[213] *The order also stipulated that everyone should bring their own tools to work. On the initiative of the leadership of the Jewish community, all Jews were asked to pray together on Shabbat in order to be ready for work at the appointed time.*[214]

My father also remembered the stream of people from the neighbouring towns and villages moving through Szczekociny in the same way

---

[210] Zarki, 50 kilometres west of Szczekociny
[211] Szwajcer *(2010), p. 245,* own translation
[212] Szwajcer (2010), 177f., own translation
[213] Lacking further details, it is here assumed to be another Saturday of digging fortifications.
[214] Ibid.

my uncle had reported it. He said that various people had spoken of the German invasion and of murders taking place, but he noted also that:

...everything was still fine where we were. We went to bed the same day. Then we got up in the morning (Saturday) and (saw) that things were indeed happening.[215]

My uncle stated:

All night long, various people drove through the city, in carts and horses and cars. (The people carried) sunken and worried expressions on their faces. They all made their way towards Kielce.

I got home late after midnight. Before I heard a knock on the door. I don't remember exactly who was knocking (but) I could hear a man's voice telling me that everyone had left town. He asked me why I was still at home. So we hurriedly packed our things together and moved into the basement of the house of (our relative) Bluma Zelma. My parents and the whole family then travelled to the village of Chlewice, 13 kilometres away, at around 8.00 in the morning. Only I, my brother Wolf and Dawid stayed behind. That (day) was Sunday, the 3rd of September 1939.[216]

The family decided that the eldest of the brothers, Moisze, should immediately head East together with his cousins, aunt and uncle (Orla, my grandfather Herszik's sister, and her husband Awrum Schwarzboim) to try to find safety in Communist Russia. He was to join a speedily arranged escape transport that his uncle had helped to organise. With the help of a hired bus, they basically intended to flee in the opposite direction from which the German troops were advancing. My uncle Moisze was certainly not yet aware that he would later end up at the

---

[215] Zylbersztajn Wolf (2001), 8:40
[216] Szwajcer (2010)

Asian city of Yangiyul in Uzbekistan, an area of the USSR to which the Soviets had assigned Jews, or that others from Szczekociny would soon end up in Siberia. Nor could anyone guess that they and Uncle Awrum Szwarcbojm, who was travelling on the same bus, would be living in the Promised Land in Israel many years later. At that time, their only concern was to get to safety. Here is Awrum Szwarcbojm's daughter Cela's account, my father's cousin, remembering the hastily organised escape:

Typical bus in Poland around the end of the 1930s. Picture Polish National Archive.

On the day of the outbreak of the Second World War, Awrum Szwarcbojm, my uncle, who had been suspicious of the Nazis' intentions towards Jews, once again took on the initiative. He pushed aside the interests of his own family and thought about the entire (Jewish) community. (Therefore) he accepted the offer of a local bus driver who wanted to take Jews out of the city if he could get enough (money to pay for the) petrol. Awrum filled the bus (with people) until no more could fit on it (almost 100 people) and ordered his own family to board empty-handed and without luggage in order to make as much room as possible. Even today, Jehudi "Jadzia" Cukerman remembers how her terrified mother waved 'goodbye' to the overloaded bus, and when it later drove past her house, how she threatened to throw herself under the wheels of the bus.[217]

---

[217] Szwajcer (2010), p. 12, own translation

Others, like the Bornstein family, escaped into the neighbouring forest. This was not the only advice people received. For example, people were advised to close their windows with tape due to rumours that the Germans might employ tear gas.[218]

On the second day of the war, Prince Jozef Poniatowski's Polish Eighth Uhlan Cavalry Regiment tried their best to face the German attackers, but their soldiers on horseback were no match for the Germans, whose soldiers were protected inside rolling metal fortresses.

The inhabitants of Szczekociny experienced this attempted defence through the fact that fewer refugees but increasing numbers of defeated Polish troops now crossed the town. My uncle Abraham recounted this in the book of remembrance *Pinkes Szczekocin* written after the Shoah with words that illustrate the confusion of the time:

> *I stayed hidden and didn't want to move. Around 9 o'clock I went to the market. Polish artillery units with light cannons had just arrived. A group of soldiers with several cannons were reinforcing their trenches.*
>
> *They kept a firing their guns for about half an hour. Because the soldiers were very hungry, they asked us to bring them bread and water. There were several people at the market who also brought the soldiers food and buckets of water for the horses. We also enquired about the situation. They replied that we should run away because the German army was already inside the town. After they said this, they immediately left the town themselves. People who were still at the market also left the market (-area) to (try to) hide somewhere.*[219]

It was this sight of devastation and chaos that made Leon Zelman's mother decide that she had to flee with her two children there and then and on her own initiative from Szczekociny to Lodz, where she knew

---

[218] B-94 The Spirit of the Survivor
[219] Szwajcer (2010)

relatives. But when she reached the Lodz with great difficulty about two weeks later, the Germans were already there and one of her relatives, who was a socialist Jewish politician, had already been murdered, hanged by the German occupying force.[220] This was the beginning of Leon Zelman's own survival story, which included internment in Auschwitz.

Back to the moment of the German invasion in Szczekociny and the vivid descriptions of my uncle Abraham, may the memory of his name be a blessing.

> *At around 11.00 a.m. several aeroplanes appeared, which circled in the sky above the area (Szczekociny). They soon disappeared again without anything happening. But two hours later they returned. Before I could take a good look around, I heard loud explosions and black smoke coming out of Chaim Guterman's house. I was residing right by the market at the time, in Berisz Cukernik's house. I quickly ran to my place, but the house (where I had lived) was (also) on fire. I ran back to the market where more houses were on fire.*[221]

According to Leon Zelman's memoirs, these fires were the result of the air raids. Artillery and gunfire were to follow.[222] My uncle continued to give his detailed account:

> *I was beside myself. I ran aimlessly back and forth. Suddenly I found myself near the church when a bomb fell (again) – this time (it exploded) onto Majer Dowid Manela's house. After that I didn't see anyone on the street. As I ran further along Senatorska Street, I noticed that the mayor of Chruzik was standing in his house. When I asked him where he was going, he told me to come in. He told me there that many people were hiding in the bakery.*

---

[220] Zelman (1995) pp. 39-45
[221] Szwajcer (2010), p. 246
[222] Zelman (1995), p. 35 f.

Of course, I also went there and met many Jewish and Christian friends (but) didn't really look around and when we heard yet another bomb hit, everyone quickly jumped out of the bakery and ran off aimlessly.

I (myself) ran along Senatorska Street and went to Szmuel Rusin's house, where I again met many Jewish fellow citizens, including Jechiel Rycht and his family, as well as Dowid Płatkewicz and others. I stayed in that cellar with Szmuel Rusin until one o'clock in the morning. During the whole time, shots could still be heard. Nobody dared, to even stick their head outside. There was nowhere I could have run to.

After one o'clock it (finally) became quieter. The shootings stopped. Only then Jechiel Rycht's brother-in-law and Dowid Płatkewicz were sent out to learn if it was safe to leave and to decide what to do next.

He then soon returned and told us that he had encountered the first German patrol. They had spoken to him and announced that he did not need to be afraid. The Germans had (already) occupied the whole of Szczekociny. After these words of "reassurance", everyone left this cellar. All wanted to know if their home was still standing.

As we walked a few steps towards the church, we saw that the whole town was in flames. Mojsze Jankew Fajwisz was the first to try to save things from his shop. I wanted to know what had happened to our house and went there with what remained of my strength.

The sight that presented itself to me there will never fade from my mind. I had the impression that I had landed in actual hell. The whole marketplace was ablaze with flames.

Several German patrols were already on site, but they (also) told us not to be afraid. However, there were already several dead bodies lying on the pavements. They were people who had been hit by shrapnel: Aj Got's (Gotlib) child, Szlojme Sztybelman and others whose names I can no longer remember were lying there. Awrum Danciker's wife ran with her child in her arms and was killed, but her child survived.

> *I stayed at the market all night and poured water into the cellar of our shop. In the morning, I went back into town and looked for a place where I could rest. As fate would have it, the area around Kryman's shop remained intact. My uncle Awrumcie Szwarcbojm had lived there. I went into the house and was delighted to find the entire building undamaged and without fire damage. I was so exhausted that I fell into a deep sleep still wearing my clothes. I only woke up when I heard loud gunfire on Monday afternoon around 4.00 pm. As it turned out, the Germans had started their work again, firing dum-dum rockets into every building that was still intact. I almost didn't manage to get out of the now burning house alive and went across the market square to the cellar of Jankew Szlojme Honig's house, where I found Dowid Płatkewicz with his wife Pesl. I stayed there until Tuesday afternoon. As I was leaving, I encountered a German who ordered me over with the words "Come here!." I immediately raised my hands in the air and approached him, trembling. There were also some people there – Jews and Christians. The German ordered everyone to raise their hands and took us in this position to Berisz Cukernik's house, where we found more people standing with their arms raised and their faces to the wall.*
>
> *The German then removed my watch from my arm. He hit anyone who dared to lower their arms a little with the butt of his rifle. Everyone had to remain in this position in spite of the severe pain. With our hands raised and turned towards the wall, we stood motionless for five hours without a break. We were a group of several hundred people.*[223]

Finally, the sad news came from the neighbouring village that Abraham and Wolf's grandmother (my paternal great-grandmother) had been shot by Germans in her hiding place in the neighbouring village of Leluv (Lelow). I suspect that this could be Sura, the maternal grandmother of my father,

---

[223] Szwajcer (2010), p. 246f., own translation

"They Only Came to Murder"

because it was where Szyfra my grandmother was from. The Germans are said to have discovered the old woman hiding in a cellar together with other relatives, two uncles and an aunt, and shot them, all were harmless unarmed civilians.[224] According to Leon Zelman's memoirs, not only were Jewish people executed, but he states, that by the entire family of a Christian Polish girl named Basia, with whom Zelman was in love and who was the first girl he had ever kissed, was murdered during the German invasion.[225] As if losing his love was not enough, Zelman also lost his father, shot by German machine gun bullets.[226]

Years later, when my father tried to comprehend what happened at this most traumatic and difficult time, he usually emphasized that he did not understand it. What crime they all supposedly had committed, to deserve this? He reiterated that he had not even met a German person in his life before the war.

What he and others had experienced in Szczekociny was extraordinary "special treatment." This was because a Polish soldier had thrown a grenade onto a German tank from a tree near the town and successfully hit it. What happened to Szczekociny was therefore an act of aimless revenge. The first bomb, according to *Pinkes Szczekocin*, fell on one of the town's most loved buildings, Rab Kopl Koplowicz's old mill.[227] His mill had made the businessman and entrepreneur a rich man and before the war it was used as a meeting place for various Zionist groups, among other things. The dreams that were once forged there thus ended during that night for most, just a few handfuls would see beloved Eretz Yisrael eventually, after first losing everything, they knew, enduring tremendous pain and suffering.

It should be noted here that the acts of destruction and the burning down of the houses the German troops committed were probably one of the reasons why no photos or even paintings of my family from the

---

[224] Zylbersztajn, Wolf (2001), Cassette I, 13:50
[225] Zelman (1995), p. 29
[226] Ibid. p. 39
[227] Rab Kopf Koplowitz, died 1929

period before the Second World War survived. What was preserved may have fallen victim to later looting or may have been confiscated from people during the later selections or destroyed alongside the lives of the family members to whom these objects belonged.[228] One hopes, that maybe over the years something else will turn up, unexpectedly.

But my uncle's brilliant account of the first hours and days of the German invasion is not yet finished. Here he is remembering being forced to stand against a wall, and learning the reason for his and the others arrest:

> *Later, we were instructed (by the Germans) to stand in rows and (they) led us from place under the bridge to a special shed that was hastily being cleared for a new purpose. On the way there, I came to notice several bodies lying in the streets. I recognised the dead remains of Henech Iczele's son among them.*
>
> *The Germans finally led us into (this) shed and explained that we were to die by death of fire as penitents for the grenade thrown at the German army...*[229]
>
> *The tension amongst us inside the shed soon reached its peak. Christians bid farewell of their lives with the sign of the cross and wept. Jews prayed and sang psalms and asked the Eternal One for help. It lasted a long time – three long hours. Everyone felt that she or he had been condemned to die.*
>
> *When the shed door suddenly opened and a German soldier approached us, all (our) hearts froze. Everyone stood still.*

---

[228] Itzyk Mendel Bornstein was a little luckier. Twenty years after the war, he even discovered a book about the life of the Jewish scholar Rabbi Jedaijah ben Abraham Bedersi, with the entry. "For God is the land and its fullness" The book belonged to Joseph Hanoch Bornstein. In addition, after Bornstein's death, a class photo was found showing him as a schoolboy.

[229] And further: "*What they meant was that in the village of Tęgobórz (three kilometres from Szczekociny) a Polish soldier had climbed a tree. When the first German patrol arrived, he threw a grenade that blew up the tank and its soldiers. It was because of this that the Germans had decided to take revenge (in this way).*" in Szwajcer (2010)

The German soldier ordered everyone to stand again in a line and (then) began to write down all our names. He told us that we (who were now "saved") would be shot if something like this grenade throwing ever recurred.

It is difficult to describe the joy that overwhelmed us at that time. Jews and Christians threw themselves into each other's arms and kissed each other. We were set free.

But now I was again confronted with the initial problem of where I should go. I decided to go back to the cellar of Jankew Szlojme Honik, where there were) several other Jewish families. There was no bread to eat, but instead we raided the many jars of jam that were stored in the cellar.

On Thursday morning, we suddenly heard loud shouting, coming from the direction of the market. I went up to the roof of our house with a few people, and we saw gangs of Christians breaking into Jewish cellars and pulling out sacks of various goods that had been hidden there by others. With deep pain (in our) hearts, we went back to the cellar and spent a sleepless night there. Only the next day, on Friday morning, when things became calmer and the shootings ceased, did I (allow myself to) leave the cellar again… Gradually, Jews who had fled the city (also) began to return.

I walked towards the house of Efroim Kryman. A terrible thing awaited me there: the son of Shames Josl Majer was trying to pull the half-burnt (lifeless) body of his son out of the house.[230] He asked me if I could help him to load the burnt body onto a cart. Of course, I honoured his request and went with him to the cemetery and assisted him with the burial.

He told me that the Germans had taken Jews as prisoners and then threw them into fires, where the (people) burned to (their) deaths.[231]

---

[230] Shames – Synagogue servant
[231] in Szwajcer (2010), own translation

Finally, my uncle Abraham began to report what happened next in the now occupied town:

> *"Life" began to normalise (somewhat) afterwards. The Jewish population began to search for (suitable) accommodation, because many of their houses had been destroyed. Due to the lack of space, several families were (often) forced to move into one single house together…*
>
> *In the meantime, a new ethnic German man, Johann Pluta, was appointed mayor. He had come to Szczekociny (only) a few months before the outbreak of the war and had worked as an electrical engineer for Trawiński. After he took office, he ordered all residents, Jews and Christians alike, to hand over their radios. He also ordered all Jewish possessions to be handed over to him within 24 hours. He promised that anyone who still owned anything after that, would be shot. This caused great chaos.*
>
> *Things were carried to (Pluta) without a pause. When the scheduled 24 hours had passed, Christian (groups) armed with metal rods began to break into the cellars of Jewish merchants to pull out (left behind and still hidden) goods. In the cellar of Lejzer Blat, several haberdashery items and various goods from other merchants were extracted (in that way).*
>
> *As it turned out later, (this new) mayor and his exclusively Christian councillors made this decision on their own initiative. As far as the German orders were concerned, it applied only to the seizure of radios.*[232]

What my uncle did not write was that the ghettoisation of the Jews of Poland was the very first step towards their murder according to the plans of SS Obengruppenführer (senior group lieutenant) Reinhard Heydrich. This plan began as soon as three weeks after the invasion of

---

[232] ibid

Poland by German troops. Jews were initially and temporarily to be contained in towns with a railway station or that were close to railway stations. This was in preparation for their onward transportation to the places where they could later be murdered.[233]

According to my father, after the invasion many bodies of dead people were scattered all over the streets. He recognised some among them.[234]

Eventually news spread about the fate of the city's rabbi Szlojme Sztybelman spread. Rabbi Szlojme had tried to rescue the Torah scroll from inside the burning synagogue of the town. When German troops noticed this, they shot and wounded him, but the Rabbi was still able to carry the Holy Scriptures to safety. Three weeks later, however, Sztybelman succumbed to his wounds, possibly due to a lack of medical care. His son Ephraim Sztybelman, who would later survive Auschwitz-Birkenau, said that shortly after the war began, his father was the second victim in his family since the Germans had arrived. Mojsze, his sister's son, a small defenceless boy of kindergarten age, had already been brutally beaten to the ground by Germans and died from the injuries inflicted upon him.[235]

The first enslavements of Jewish people for forced work, which would continue for several years, also began soon. The first order was to search for valuables such as gold, furs or other valuables amongst the burnt-out houses. During this period, however, people were also continuously being murdered, my father reported. They could be arbitrarily strangled or shot by the German occupiers and their helpers, most notably by a particular German Sturmbannführer, whose surname my father could still remember 60 years later – Stümmler:[236]

---

[233] Arad (1992), p. 2
[234] Zylbersztajn, Wolf (2001). Cassette I
[235] Szwajcer (2010), p 224-235, own translation
[236] Surmbannführer – rank equivalent to a major in various Third Reich paramilitary organisations

> *Stümmler always came into the ghetto and shot about randomly. I was with my colleague. I looked out of the window and I saw that he killed two people, he just shot, spat and shot. He was such a Verbrecher (yid. criminal).*[237]

He also remembered another man who went by the name of Stückel (Stückl?). One of Stückel's first "heroic deeds" after his arrival was to brutally murder the son of the town's Jewish butcher by kicking the boy's skull with his boots. Like many other Germans mentioned by my father, Stückel was, he said, not an SS-man, but a member of the German factory defence unit referred to as the *Werkschutz*. This unit was supposed to monitor the German forced labour camps in Poland. These people were often a mixture of so-called Volksdeutsche (ethnic Germans, born outside Germany), Ukrainians and some Germans from Germany.[238] In general, the initially still open labour camps were controlled by various forces, including members of the German Wehrmacht and the SS.[239] When my father gave testimony to the Shoah Foundation, the interviewer asked him what function he thought the labour camp guards had. His short answer was as follows:

> *Yes, in order to murder! If they caught a Jew, they shot him. That's it! They shot a lot of people.*[240]

Zwi Grajpner, another survivor of the Shoah from Szczekociny, remembered the man they called Pluta, whom he also described in clear words: a real executioner!

> *Pluta quite often broke into Jewish houses, where he carried out searches and beat everyone present at the same time. And when he*

---

[237] Zylbersztajn, Wolf (2001). Cassette I, 18:50
[238] Karay (2004), p. 12
[239] Karay (2004), p. 20
[240] Zylbersztajn, Wolf (2001), Cassette I, 19:30

was in that kind of a mood, he didn't limit himself to "dry" work, but left some victims behind, as "souvenirs".[241]

Grajpner also remembered that my grandfather Herszik had been one of the 14 men who were ordered to form a so-called *Judenrat* (Jewish council) together with his own father, Zwi Jeszajahu Grajpner.[242] Pluta later dismissed some members of the *Judenrat* on grounds of "differences", presumably because they failed to agree to some of what he wanted.[243]

My father's parents had already returned to Szczekociny a few days after the Germans had marched into the town. Because the house had burnt down, the family was forced to rent a room in a house that had not been damaged by fire. It belonged to a Christian Pole. Just as my uncle Abraham had told me, my father reported that the family moved in together with cousins, with a total of eleven people in one room.[244] Such cramped conditions soon led to widespread outbreaks of disease. The Jewish Council therefore advised some families to move to the neighbouring villages if possible. My father himself soon also changed living quarters again, together with his closest relatives, and occupied a room opposite the previous house, again rented out by a Christian Pole. This meant that the core family of my father now lived by themselves.

Confident that by now they must have had survived the worst, my grandfather Herszik went back to work. In the cellar under his burnt-out

---

[241] Szwajcer (2010), p.218f.
[242] Szwajcer (2010), p.218f. And my uncle Abraham said: "*A commander's office was set up, which began with the introduction of the German "order." Among other things, they demanded ... a detailed list of all the Jews (who lived in) Szczekociny. (...) In Szczekociny (only) about 1,500 Jews remained (others had left). A Jewish council was organised, which held its meetings in Szmuel Rusin's house. We lived with his father's cousin, Herszel Zelma. (As I said), life slowly began to normalise again, i.e. "normal life" under the wartime conditions of the Nazi regime.*" Own translation
[243] Ibid.
[244] Zylbersztajn, Wolf (2001), Cassette I 13:30

shop and house, which Abraham had saved, unburnt leather remnants could be cut into leather goods or be sold.[245]

My uncle Abraham wrote the following about the first weeks under German occupation and he too remembered the arrival of Pluta:

> *On Rosh Hashanah and Yom Kippur we prayed in Herszl Drezner's mill. The bakery of Mojsze and Wolf Ickowicz was restored, and bread baking had begun again. Furthermore, the Jewish population was in search of sources of income. Gradually we got used to this "new" life. As the saying goes: "If you get used to trouble, you can live happily with it." We got used to the fact that the Judenrat assigned a hundred Jewish people to various jobs every day.*
>
> *This "happiness" lasted about a month in total. Then a Volksdeutscher from Upper Silesia who was known among the Jews through the timber trade as Johann Pluta – may his cursed name be forgotten – arrived. And with his presence in the town, the real extermination of the Jewish people of Szczekociny began.*[246]

My own father Wolf said about Johann Pluta: *"He was a sehr schlechter Hund (Yid. /German – a very bad dog)! He had a brother-in-law, who ordered us to work – to clean up, houses that were broken. We had to clean up every day and he beat us – it wasn't good."*[247]

Abraham explained further:

> *Pluta was, as I said, immediately appointed city-mayor and took over the mills and sawmill of Herszl Drezner and the sawmill of Mojsze Wolf Goldszmit shortly after taking office. Goldszmit was killed on the third day of the war.*

---

[245] Ibid. 12:30
[246] Szwajcer (2010): Statement of my uncle Abraham Zylbersztajn, own translation
[247] Zylbersztajn, Wolf (2001), Cassette I 13:55

"They Only Came to Murder"

Chaim Dowid Drezner was ordered to leave the mill immediately, as were the two children of Mojsze Wolf Goldszmit. After Pluta came to power, the torment intensified. He gave the order to demolish the remaining walls of Jewish houses. He forced the Judenrat to provide two hundred people every day for this purpose. His brother-in-law also became his superior and mercilessly beat anyone who got in his way.

The work was very hard, and at the end of the day we were lined up and asked to sing and dance. With sadistic glee, exhausted Jews were ordered to walk on their hands. The Polish Christians of the town watched this perverse spectacle and applauded.[248]

The historic synagogue was also to be demolished during the liquidation of Jewish houses. The entire tiled roof was ordered to be undecked. And while the mayor removed the four pillars of the synagogue, in the end he still considered it a waste to demolish such a well-built synagogue and ordered the work to be stopped. It seems to have moved his conscience because he had instructed me to build a new roof. So the synagogue was more or less preserved and turned into a granary. The building exists to this day as a remnant of the former Jewish pride. However, the old Jewish cemetery, next to the synagogue, was completely destroyed and turned into a pile of rubble.

At the same time, the living conditions of the Jews worsened. Some took on risky journeys to Częstochowa to get various foodstuffs in order to survive. When Pluta learnt about this, he rose up earlier than usual to catch these people out, beat them severely and rob them of their goods.

The consequence thereof was the spread of a massive famine, which also triggered dispute between the members of the Jewish community. Some of the Jewish population accused the Judenrat of not being interested in their situation. This was exactly as the

---

[248] I think my uncle would have expected horror and indignation by his Christian neighbours instead. Original states "wild" rather than perverse.

occupiers intended. They wanted the Jews to argue among themselves and forget their miserable situation for a while.

A kitchen was erected in Chaim Josef Szwarcbojm's tannery, where eight hundred people were served every day. It was depressing to see how once wealthy people came every day with heir pot and had to queue only to get a little bit of soup.

Even this miserable "life" did not last long. New decrees were issued every day to further worsen the situation…

Both the mayor and the police tried to inflict as much pain and suffering upon the Jews as possible. They seemed to be in a kind of competition with each other to see who could be meaner and who could be better to brutalise the vulnerable Jewish population.

The situation became so unbearable that Rabbi Lejbl Goldberg and Isroel Fromer "succumbed to poverty", if one interprets this description correctly, either starving to death or succumbing to illness in a desolate state. The housing situation also deteriorated. More families had to move into small rooms.

To be able to sustain themselves in this life of poverty, the Jewish population sold all they had left from their previous life and yet even so there remained hunger everywhere. At the end of 1939, a decree was issued that all Jews were to wear white armbands with a Magen David (Star of David) and that every window, where Jews lived, was also to be marked.

Meanwhile, winter had spread in full horror. It was a year of immense rainfall and violent storms. One family's house was flooded. The mother died, but, miraculously, all the children survived.

Another decree followed. Within but one single day, all Jews were ordered to leave their homes and move to a delineated ghetto. The Christian population living in the streets where the ghetto was to be located did, however, not have to leave their homes. Szczekociny was almost the first town in which this regulation came into force, whereas in nearby towns such as Żarnowiec, Wolbrom, Lelów, Włoszczowa this had not yet happened.

This decree was immediately followed by the announcement that Jews were not allowed to leave the ghetto without authorisation. Failure to comply was punishable by death. A (new) separate Jewish police force was set up to ensure that all orders were carried out correctly.

With the hermetic closure of the ghetto came new challenges. Despite the imminent danger, Jews literally risked their lives to find something to eat so as not to starve. Often such desperate people did not return, because they were caught by Germans or betrayed by farmers they had trusted and were simply shot. This is what happened to Lejzer Krzeszower and his wife – may God avenge their blood. They travelled to the nearby village of Goleniowy to try to buy some poultry there. The farmers from this village immediately informed the German gendarmerie. Both were shot on their way back to Szczekociny.

A second such tragic fate befell the son of Josef Fefe (Ferleger, from the oil mill). On the way to Tęgoborz, he came across a Gestapo officer. That officer saw him, he escaped and hid in a toilet. The Gestapo pursued him and shot at the building. His soul slipped from his body there in the depth of the stinking faeces.[249] *The Gestapo then rushed to his father's house and demanded to shoot him too. But he miraculously escaped his fate.*

Similarly, two butchers, Awrum Siódmak and the grandson of Szmuel Rusin, were accused of unauthorised slaughter. They were arrested and held in prison for a fortnight. After spending two weeks there in the worst, most inhumane conditions, they were taken to Lelowska Street for their execution. The Gestapo ordered them to step into a specially prepared ditch (and) they shot them there.

In general, the murder of Jews took on the character of mass annihilation. There was never a day on which a Jewish person was not murdered. Even those who had left the ghetto with expressed

---

[249] freely translated.

permissions were not spared. Two young men, Jankew Miodowa and Kalmen Mangl – may God avenge their blood – were sent to Jędrzejów by the Judenrat. They received a special exit permit from the gendarmerie. On the way, however, they were met by a Gestapo officer who shot and buried them there.

In June 1940, the president of the Judenrat, Mojsze Jankew Fajwisz, fell ill and died. The situation became worse from day to day. The work became even more difficult. We began to break stones.[250]

This continued until the summer of 1942, when in June Abraham was unexpectedly taken away from the family. Once again, he was able to describe what happened in his own words:

Suddenly there was a (serious) change in our lives. I remember it as if it had happened only yesterday: On the 5th of June 1942, I was working with fifty Szczekociny Jews on paving a road when suddenly the military police from Skarżysko-Kamienna arrived and took us all to Skarżysko to the munitions factory. When we arrived there, we were divided into two groups. One group of 25 people was ordered to another place, and we never saw each other again. This was the beginning of a new chapter in our problems.

In the first few weeks, everything was still bearable. This was before the deportation of everyone. My father Herszl Zylbersztajn – may God avenge his blood – was a member of the Jewish Council and was able to bring food for everyone there (to Skarżysko-Kamienna). This "idyll" only lasted until 1 September 1942, when the deportations began. People from Szczekociny would be deported to Treblinka for the first time. And from that point on, I lost more and more.

The Germans issued a decree – and people set off to search towns and villages and forests to bring Jews back. Those who did

---

[250] Szwajcer (2010), own translation

the searching were the "good" non-Jews, our recent neighbours. They tried to find as many Jews as possible. A bottle of vodka or a kilo of salt was the agreed price paid for each Jewish head. They went to great lengths to collect as many bottles of vodka or kilos of salt as was possible. They then took the bottles and crossed themselves "piously." They drank the vodka and didn't choke on it, as if it was a totally normal thing.

With a bitter conscience, they thought about how they could find any hiding Jew or a hidden Jewish child.[251]

My uncle did not continue to elaborate what these drunk men would do next, as if it was self-all too well known.

---

[251] Szwajcer (2010). p. 8, own translation

12

And the Heavens Did Not Open

Stone in memory of the victims from Szczekociny at the Treblinka Memorial. Photo DZL.

Of my colleagues, that I've had. Not one of them is left.[252]

Wolf Zylbersztajn

---

[252] Zylbersztajn, Wolf (2001), Cassette II 6:00

And the Heavens Did Not Open

My father and his family endured these dreadful living conditions for two years. But after meetings between German government members of the Third Reich and various experts on different methods of mass murder, the Hitler regime introduced their plan of mass extermination, nicknamed *die Endlösung* or the Final Solution, on 20 January 1942.

It was all about the methods employed. Initial mass shootings of completely defenceless civilians, for example under the personal supervision of SS Reichsführer Heinrich Himmler in Minsk, had turned German "warriors" into psychological wrecks. Therefore, the murders had to be methodically organised in such a way that it was not too emotionally upsetting for these heroes. In addition, the victims could also be deceived as to what was awaiting them, all the better.

The Final Solution was the plan to murder all those whom the National Socialists regarded as a "dangerous race of sub-humans" and who allegedly threatened the very existence of all Germans. Those who represented a "devilish race" in the eyes of German Nazis, were totally ordinary children, men, women and elderly people of Jewish faith. They were to be murdered using the same methods of efficient murder previously trialled on other "undesirables". These were people with mental and physical disabilities who the Nazis assigned to euthanasia programmes as well as Soviet war-prisoners, who were murdered by the Germans with gas. In Himmler's words, a "hidden, never recorded and never to be recorded murder" was to be carried out.[253] Those who had to implement these murders for the German state were sworn to absolute secrecy by the SS leadership.[254] This intention to murder all Jewish people also reached my family.

Despite the attempts to keep the murders a secret and despite the lack of radio equipment, the Zylbersztajns had heard about murders and deportations of Jewish people in the surrounding villages by September 1942, mainly through people from elsewhere who had been ordered to

---

[253] See Arad (1999), pp.7-13
[254] Arad (1999) p. 18

join them in the Jewish ghetto of Szczekociny. One such person now living with my father's family was, my father remembered, his 97-year-old great-aunt, "whose brains were still bright and with better eyesight than my mother."[255] Despite the rumours, nobody in Szczekociny believed that the terrible things that other people reported could happen in their own town. After all, what had they done to deserve that?

Rabbi Pinchas Trajan, the last Chazan and Mohel of Szczekociny, z "l. With the kind permission of Y. Bornstein.

However, they were mistaken. Shortly before Yom Kippur 5703 (21 September 1942), they received the disturbing news that the entire Jewish population of all the small towns in the immediate vicinity of Szczekociny had been deported by the Germans.

The now very high likelihood that such German action was awaiting Szczekociny led to the decision of the family that Szyfra, my father's mother, together with my father's 12-year-old brother Fiszl, should take some food and water and hide in the nearby forest while the rest of the family would stay behind in the ghetto. But as it was, the cold in the

---

[255] frequent story of my dad

And the Heavens Did Not Open

forest and the uncertainty drove the two of them back to unite with the others only a few hours later.

The first sign that bad things were to come announced itself at the synagogue. Henoch Trajan, the son of the last Chazan and mohel of Szczekociny, told it like this:

> *I always have the image of my father in my eyes, may G-d avenge his blood, dressed in white silk crabs, smock and white socks on the eve of Yom Kippur. How profound was the faith and deep humility of this great man?*
>
> *What a wonderful time it was when he blessed us children with his silver-white beard and the biblical figure of the patriarch before he went as messenger of the faithful to perform the Kol Nidre! Unfortunately, as fate would have it, in 1942, on the very eve of Yom Kippur in the evening when the Jewish community of Szczekociny was preparing for the prayer of Kol Nidre with sincere fervour and broken hearts, a group of German murderers turned up to kill them.*

My father Wolf Zylbersztajn recounting his memories to a team from the USC Shoah Foundation at his home. Here is the moment when describes how Germans separated his mother and his little brother from him. The memory of this moment caused him great pain.

> *Then my father, may G-d avenge his blood, took the Torah scroll to himself with fervent Hasidism and wrapped himself in silence and said: "Light rises for the righteous" – and so, as he uttered these words, the murderous hand of a German with a revolver aimed at him. In that way my father fell with the Torah scroll in his arms and sanctified the name of the Lord and his people on the eve of the holy Yom Kippur – and the heavens did not open!*[256]

The German order for all Jews of Szczekociny to gather in the central square of the ghetto was also announced on Yom Kippur. It set in motion the infamous and notorious Selektionen. Herszik, my father's father, hoped he could escape the worse, as he knew a German officer who had something to do with horses. His name was Reihmann. According to my father, my grandfather had made Reihmann shafts for riding boots or even entire boots without asking or being able to ask for payment in return.

> *"My father thought that if something happened, maybe he (Reihmann) could be of help to us to a certain degree."*[257]

The following description of the day stands for much that would follow: The Hasidic Rabbi Reb Jechiel Rycht was ordered by the Germans officers on the ground to come to German local headquarters, now based in Julian Ciechanowski's little castle. Rycht was a member of the Judenrat at the time, in the same way my grandfather Herszik was. *"He (Rycht) went to the small castle accompanied by the young social worker Jehuda (Julek) Rafałowicz, who was head of Ha-Noar ha-Zioni. When the two reached the stairs leading to the palace, they were both shot on the spot not a word uttered."*[258]

---

[256] Szwajcer (2010), p. 118, own translation
[257] Zylbersztajn, Wolf (2001), Cassette I 22:50
[258] Szwajcer (2010), p 78, own translation

And the Heavens Did Not Open

Recalling this day during the Shoah Foundation interview, my father clutched his fist against his head, seemingly still tormented after all those years, his facial expressions revealing pain that overcame him. Speaking in a broken and angry voice while shaking his head, he stared into the distance. It was as if he was reliving the scene before his eyes right at that moment. I have never heard him like this before or since.

I'll never forget that! He was such a beautiful boy. Eleven years old, or twelve. My mum – he stood with us. He was such a lovely jingele, such a beautiful boy.[259]

He shook his head again as if he still couldn't believe what had happened back then.

So, this Reihmann pulled us out. My father and me. But my mother with the…

Here he was just for a moment no longer able to speak. He meant to say boy, but he stares into the emptiness of the room. He then gathered himself, and continued:

– he said – No! He didn't take her out.[260]

Pointing his index finger accusingly, he said:

I can never forget him (Reihmann)!
  He (my father's brother Fiszl) was such an innocent child, only eleven or twelve years old. He hasn't done anything to anyone! Verbrecher arrived and murdered him!
  What did he do? He didn't do anything to anyone, didn't he? And another thing! We didn't know any Germans. I've never seen

---

[259] Zylbersztajn, Wolf (2001), Cassette I, 25:30-26:40,
[260] ibid

> *any Germans in my life! Who are these people? We haven't taken and eaten their bread; we've never seen any Germans. We've never seen anything. How was it that such fremde (foreign) Verbrecher came to the scene?*
>
> *… if someone goes to a bank and he commits a break-in – maybe he's in debt – he says he's in trouble, you give him the money, then he leaves, then he goes away again.*
>
> *But they didn't want money, they just wanted to murder!*
>
> *What were those Germans to me? What were they looking for in Poland? Did they come for a holiday? What were they looking for? Why did they kill?*
>
> *I always asked myself that during the war – why did they (do this)?*[261]

My father's expression was consumed with pain at that moment.

But over his lifetime I can't say that that I could observe any feelings of guilt in him concerning his survival, a frequent state of mind observed amongst people like him, which psychologists referred to as *survivor's guilt*. Those who were to blame for the terrible crimes he had witnessed, were collectively Germans. He was totally clear about that in his mind. Having survived he would defy the Germans and live as long as he could as a form of revenge.[262]

---

[261] Ibid (my father left the do this out, leaving the sentence incomplete)
[262] Survivor's Guilt see Krystal (1968), Niederland (1961) and (1981)

13

Treblinka

**The memorial in Treblinka at the stopping point of
the deportation trains. Photo DZL.**

The moment that my father's mother and little brother were ordered away with the majority of the Jews of Szczekociny was the last my father would see of them. Their journey was destined for Treblinka and took place in densely crowded "Umsiedlersonderzügen" – special resettlement trains, inside of which nobody had enough space to move. They were stuffy and stank of sweat, excrement and urine. This they had to endure only to be murdered at the trains' final "destination." The train transports, which left from the Jedrzjow district between 16 and 25 September 1942 counted a total of some 6000 people from Jedrejow, 1000 from Sedziszow, 5000 people from Wloszczowa, 3000 people from Wodzislaw and 1500 people from Szczekociny.[263] Amongst them were, needless to say, members of my family, such as my grandmother Szyfra and my uncle Fiszl Zylbersztajn and my 97-year-old great-aunt and most likely others.

I assume that the very old great-aunt may have lost her life already on her way to Treblinka, or she may have been shot straight away upon arrival as a "useless" old person at a designated ditch behind a façade masquerading as a first aid centre. A report by the Polish underground about the transports in the Polish Radom district states that 20-30 percent of the transported were dead by the time they arrived in Treblinka, as the Jewish people inside were forced to travel without any drinking water and in some cases without sufficient oxygen. Especially during the hot summer months, many people are said to have succumbed to the extreme conditions inside the wagons.[264] At the death camp, which had been completed only months earlier, a total of between 700,000 to 900,000 people were murdered. Those lucky to still live after their torturous train journey were commanded to hand over whatever few valbles they had taken with them. After that they were ordered to undress.

Part of the model of the Treblinka extermination camp in the Treblinka Memorial Museum, where between 700,000 and 900,000 people died. Photo DZL.

---

[263] Arad (1999), p. 394
[264] Informations Bulletin, 5 January 1942 see Arad (1999), p. 354 and Arad (1999), p. 63-64.

Already naked, women had their hair shorn off before they had to queue in a purpose built passageway cynically referred to by the Germans as *"Himmelstrasse"* (gateway to heaven) in order to reach the "shower rooms." These shower rooms were in fact disguised gas chambers. As the victims walked towards their deaths, they would be watched and harassed by SS personnel with dogs. Ukrainian assistants such as a man known by the nickname "Ivan the Terrible" were even reported to have shoved swords between the legs of defenceless women or violently severe their bodies otherwise, by cutting off ears and noses of victims, whose looks they didn't like. "Ivan the Terrible" was also reported to have raped women. There was great haste imposed upon the victims, intended to deprive them of sufficient time to engage in any contemplation regarding their expected faith and in order to drive and increase the "Mordproduktion" – murder production rate (what a terrible term). A trio of Jewish amateur musicians was frequently forced by the SS to play music in the background of these scenes, in order to drown out the screams of the victims. That comfort was so important to the German and Ukrainian guards that later, after the arrival of large transports with victims from Warsaw, the trio was enlarged to a ten-piece orchestra.[265] Yechiel Reichman, who survived forced labour in Treblinka, described an incident that could have involved my grandmother Szyfra. Reichman's job was that of a "hairdresser" forced to shave women heads before they had to queue up for their later execution in the showers of death.

> *I look at the victims – I can't believe my eyes. Each woman sits next to a hairdresser. A young woman sits down in front of me. My hands freeze and I can't move my fingers... My colleague next to me is shouting at me.*

---

[265] Arad (1999) p. 231 The identity of this man is not clear, but after the Israeli Supreme Court case against John Ivan Demjanjuk, he is said to have been a certain Ivan Marchenko, according to SS men who later received the death penalty from the Soviets. See New York Times (1993).

"Don't forget, you're finished – the killers are watching you", and "You're working too slowly!" I move the fingers of my dirty hand and cut off the woman's hair, throwing it into a suitcase. The woman stands up. Another woman sits down. She takes my hand and wants to kiss it and says: "I beg you – tell me, what are they going to do to us? Is it the end for us?" She cries and asks me if dying is long and hard. Will we be killed by gas or by electric shock? I don't answer her. I'm not able to tell her the truth and comfort her. The whole conversation only lasts a few seconds, the time it takes to cut off her hair. I turn my head away because I'm ashamed to look her in the eye. The murderers standing next to us shout: "Cut faster!" One victim after another comes and the scissors cut the hair without stopping. You can hear crying and screaming everywhere, and we had to watch it all and remain silent.[266]

Shower tile with a Star of David pattern. Museum of the memorial site Treblinka, Photo DZL.

Further eyewitness accounts are listed in Ytzhak Arad's study of the death-camp Treblinka. The Yad Vashem historian lists many of the tragic and disturbing and brutal details, all of which allowed me to

---

[266] Arad (1999), p. 212 retranslated into English from German by author

comprehend the probable final moments of life of my grandmother and uncle, a little boy still, in particular.

The "shower rooms", that were the gas chambers in Treblinka, could only be opened from the outside. They were four square metres in size and 2.60 metres height. They finished with tiles to make them look like a real shower room. Some of those tiles perversely had patterns of Stars of Davids on them, and a Star of David was also placed above the entrance to the murder facility, as if to say this is the pathway reserved for Jews. Inside the gas chambers were real shower heads. But as soon as the doors of the chambers were hermetically sealed, diesel exhaust fumes rather than water streamed out of the shower heads into a completely dark room full of panicking people.[267] Through this meticulously calculated method, transports of up to 6000 people could be "processed" in but a few hours. The lifeless corpses of the victims would then be disposed in a huge pit behind the death chambers.[268]

The art of fakery was everything in Treblinka , including a pretend railway station. Furthermore, the entire murder camp had been deliberately erected in one of Poland's most remote regions. The gas chambers and the mass graves inside the camp were concealed from view from all areas of the rest of the camp. The overall aim of such concealment was to suggest that Jewish people were only being sent to labour camps in the East, although that too would have been already a crime. Poles (non-Jewish) who lived near the camp, however, were well informed about what took place in Treblinka, because some of the locals had been hired to help with the construction of the death-camp. Between 2 September and mid-November 1942 alone, 438,000 people were murdered in Treblinka. The murders worked so well that they had to be modified in August 1942, when the pits full of corpses began to "overflow" and more and more dead bodies were visibly scattering across

---

[267] I October 1942, after the murder of my family members, somewhat larger "shower rooms" would be opened in order to be able to kill even more people, even more "efficiently".

[268] Arad (1999), pp. 37-43

the camp, defeating the intended concealment that the purpose of this place was murder.

All confiscated possessions of those condemned to die were carefully sorted and organised in German methodological fashion. Gold teeth were one of the looted objects removed from inside the mouths of the murdered. According to one slave labourer who was forced to complete this gruesome task, two whole suitcases containing some 18 kg of gold teeth were regularly collected each week.[269] Hundreds of trainloads of shoes, clothes and other items left the camp every week also.

Between April and July 1943, all the bodies that had been thrown and buried into the large pits of Treblinka were ordered to be cremated. The intention was the eradication and elimination of any trace that could hint to the crimes committed and to literally cover up what had taken place here.[270] Abraham Goldfarb, a survivor of Treblinka, testified how, when being ordered to bury bodies, the forced workers sometimes hid complete (unburned) skeletons with messages sealed inside bottles in which the crimes had been written down, in the hope that one day future generations would come across them.[271] If the murders could not be stopped, they at least tried to ensure that the truth about this place could one day be discovered. It was a particular form of defiance. Soon the pressure of the spirit of rebellion could no longer be contained:

Although terrible and detailed eyewitness reports from Treblinka and similar locations were passed on to the British government via the Polish government in exile, London, did nothing to put an end to the killings, for example through targeted bombings. It remains a stain on the later earned reputation as liberators of places such as Bergen Belsen. The enslaved and forced labourers at the camp increasingly came to understand that it was their duty to try and do something about the killings themselves. On 3 August 1943, they finally rebelled against

---

[269] Arad (1999), S. 37-43
[270] Ibid. p. 177
[271] Ibid. p. 176

the camp leadership in an uprising. Although only about a hundred people survived this attempt, it must be considered a success because the uprising led to the German perpetrators eventually giving up their murderous activities on this site.

But let's jump back to the scene of the selection in Szczekociny that later led up to the deportation.

My father described Reihmann as a "radikaler *Verbrecher*." This was not only because Reihmann hadn't saved his mother and his youngest brother, but also because, according to his testimony, Reihmann was often walking around with a hammer with which he was randomly hitting people over the head.[272]

For the rest of his life, my father could not understand and rationalise all of this, not for want of trying. There are some things that go beyond rationality, and unfounded and brutal hatred of people may very well be one of them. When he recorded his testimony for the Shoah Foundation, my father was already 82 years old, and he spoke about the events with such vivid memories, as if they had happened the week before. Part of that memory was his description of Reihmann. The Nazi and sadist became a symbol of the injustices inflicted upon him. It is true, If Reihmann had not sent my father's little brother to Treblinka, he may very well have perished later in the Shoah. In the eyes of the perverse ideology of the Nazis children and women, as well as anyone considered unfit for hard labour, had no right to continue living. On the other hand, there may have been a slim chance that my father's mother and his brother Fiszl might have been able to survive. As Felicja Karay, the historian and survivor of one of my father's next sites of horror, Skarżysko-Kamienna, would point out, there were both women and children inside that work camp, and children were being looked after and protected by the adults, as well as they could.[273]

After the gruesome selection process, there was no doubt what was in store for my father. Just witnessing what happened to the town's

---

[272] Zylbersztajn, Wolf (2001), Cassette I
[273] Karay (2004), p .127

master baker was enough to understand it. You see, my father said that amid the turmoil and confusion, one of the town's bakers had wrapped himself in his tallit and was praying to the Allmighty. After all, it was Yom Kippur, so this God-fearing man prayed amid the crowd, atoning for all wrongs he may have committed. For that alone, some German, seeing this, pulled him out of the crowd and simply shot him on the spot.

Another rather heroic baker was reported on in *Pinkes Szczekocin*. The report tells us what occurred as he and the others were led to the station where the trains that should transport them to Treblinka were waiting :

> *Icze Majer, a baker, may God avenge his blood, shouted: 'Why do we let ourselves be slaughtered like cattle…? I'm not moving from the place' – and there, under the bridge, on the road to Sędziszów-Treblinka, he was shot and fell like a sawn tree wrapped in a cloth.*[274]

Mordche1 Wisznicki, who was known to everyone in Szczekociny as "Mordche Brajtbord (broadbeard; he did actually have a broad beard!) and who always studied in the prayer house, is even said to have slapped one of the Gestapo officers during the deportation in Szczekociny, when the officer called on him to walk faster. The memorial book *Pinkes Szczekocin* also reports on the *Agudat Israel* activist Reb Shmai Madalinsk, who is said to have proclaimed the following words leading a group: "Be ready for the martyrdom of sanctifying the name of the Lord, G-d will pay for our forgotten death! Jews, arm yourselves: We are grandchildren and great-grandchildren of a nation of holy martyrs!"[275]

Perhaps my father had also heard this speech. He had vowed to himself never to give up and, as a fearless fighter, to "go all the way" and risk everything, if it came down to it. He emphasised that again and again.

---

[274] Szwajcer (2010), p, p. 83 Own translation
[275] Szwajcer (2010), p 84f. own translation

At this juncture, I would like to take a short break, if you forgive the unusual stylistic interruption, but after all I am the one who is writing this all up. I urgently must take a breath, for I am totally overcome with tears of sadness. This happened frequently whilst I was writing this book-series, with a feeling of deep emptiness.

> *Liebe Bubele Szyfra, Z"L, Vetter Fiszl, Z"L, ich veys vos is geschehn mit Eich, wie die Deitschn ham geharget Eich. Ich werd dem gedenken fur mein ganzes Leben und werd schreiben a Sefer von dem woz sich hat zugetragen.*

(Dear Granny Szyfra, Z "L, Cousin Fiszl, Z "L, I know what happened to you, how the Germans have murdered. I pledge to remember this for the rest of my life and will write a book about all of it.)

The Oven

> *A candle of light is burning*
> *Lit for the burning of life*
> *A candle of light I am*
>
> Daniel Zylbersztajn-Lewandowski, English original, August 1996

The chaos that had been created on the day of the selection was just the beginning of a journey through a world of immense brutality lasting several years. At the *Umschlagplatz* (germ. transit centre), the atrocities were endless. My father remembered a (married) couple standing next to his family with two small children of kindergarten age, with whom my father was playing. "They took them in order to send them to their deaths," he ended the story.[276]

People who could no longer walk well, such as the elderly, were asked to get onto a horse-drawn carriage (including my father's great-aunt).

---

[276] Zylbersztajn, Wolf (2001), Cassette I

This carriage brought them to Sędziszów, the "nearest" well connected railway station, about 20 kilometres from Szczekociny. According to eyewitness accounts, more murders took place there, particularly of those who could no longer walk. On the next day, trains transported all of the approximately 1,500 people waiting there to Treblinka.[277]

Sędziszów railway station, the place where people from Szczekociny were loaded to Treblinka, including my grandmother, my uncle and other family members. Photo DZL.

Amongst those condemned to be murdered, the Germans sought out 30 craftsmen for further exploitative tasks. They were looking for manual workers like tailors, plumbers, builders, engineers and leather workers and the like. My father, his other brother Dawid and his father managed to be counted amongst these. In return, they were now allowed to stay behind in the eerily deserted ghetto. Could they sleep that night? Isroel Ber Cukerman, is one of these men who survived the Shoah, and he remembered the morning after the selection:

The following day at 05.00 we were sent to unload brick wagons. I hoped I would still find some traces of our loved ones, but

---

[277] Arad (1999), p. 394

unfortunately all the living had been sent to Treblinka at night. We only came across the dead bodies of men, women and children, who were scattered all over the area. We buried them all later.[278]

Cukerman went on to report that the Werkschutz Officers had shot people at random for their entertainment until the train had arrived. Fortunately for him, his wife and daughter had managed to escape during the long journey to the railway station.[279]

Still not satisfied with their humiliation and destruction of Jewish people, the Nazi mayor Pluta now instructed my father to make insoles for Polish firefighters' boots from one of the Torah scrolls. And, my father reported, the lives of the survivors were by no means guaranteed. Even among the very few who had been spared as labourers, more people were murdered.[280]

Abraham, my father's brother, who was still an enslaved forced labourer in Skarżysko-Kamienna, sent a Polish woman to Szczekociny, 120 kilometres away, so that she could ask my grandfather for shoes. Good shoes were probably essential for Abraham's survival, whatever work he was forced to do in that camp. My grandfather and father promptly cut the leather for the uppers and asked a shoemaker to make the shoes accordingly and, my father told me, "they hid a few dollars" in them.[281] The woman messenger was also paid and through her help the shoes actually reached my uncle.

In Skarżysko-Kamienna labour camp the Jewish enslaved forced labourers received neither pay nor a wage, unlike German, Polish and ethnic German workers. This meant that the Jews in the camp had to try get hold of food and other necessities of life on the "black market", for example from Poles of the Christian faith who worked there. Whatever

---

[278] Szwajcer (2010), p. 200, own translation
[279] ibd
[280] Zylbersztajn, Wolf (2001), Cassette II, 9:00
[281] Ibid, 9:30

the forced labourers possessed, money, or even a gold tooth, or other possessions served as "currency." Whilst this exploited the Jewish people in the camp even further, it was possible to establish contact with the world outside the camp via non-Jewish police officers. Some people in the camp, such as the Jewish elite in Werk C, even managed to maintain these contacts for the entire duration of the camp's existence.[282]

The small group of workers that included my grandfather Herszik and my father were able to stay in the empty Szczekociny ghetto for another four months. Then they too were finally ordered to leave Szczekociny. It was December 1942 or January 1943, in the depth of the Polish winter.[283]

The group was picked up by horse-drawn carriages and taken on a 70-kilometre journey to another fenced-in ghetto in Radomsko, north of Szczekociny.

In Radomsko they were sent to a neighbourhood full of abandoned houses. According to my father, there were many Jewish people hidden in the surrounding woods. To lure them out of the woods, the German made fake announcements that Jews would be safe in Radomsko. Some believed it and returned.

According to the memories of my uncle his other brother Dawid was also in Radomsko. Dawid had previously been in Libnitcze and had to perform forced labour there.[284] This time it would only take two weeks before another so-called *Aussiedlungsaktion* (resettlement operation) took place. It was announced by a group of Werkschutz officers and assisted by Ukrainian accomplices of the Nazis. As in Szczekociny before, the procedure caused great chaos. Mothers had to give up their children, family members were separated. I remember my father often telling me that women were tearing their hair out because this.

Some 200 people were selected out of the crowd, some of them in exchange for bribes. My father described the situation with the following

---

[282] Karay (2004), p. 24 and Strigler (2019)
[283] Zylbersztajn, Wolf (2001), Cassette II, 11:00
[284] Zylbersztajn, Wolf (2001), Cassette II, 4:50

words: *"I was going to play all (my) cards, all or nothing. I've never been afraid!!"* My father told me that it was a moment between the fate of continued life or certain death.[285] He offered the little money he had to a Werkschutz guard, who took the money and instructed him to go to the group of the selected "*Fachmänner*" (skilled workmen). But then my father suddenly saw that his father was still standing on the "wrong" side, he quickly repeated the bribing attempt with another *Werkschutz* guard. When someone within the crowd shouted that my father's father didn't belong there, my father reacted promptly and gave the snitch an unmistakable warning to shut up instantly or he himself would no longer be on this side of the selection.[286] Those who were not chosen were ordered to board the backs of lorries in which they too were driven to the Treblinka extermination camp. The "saved" were taken to the Skarżysko-Kamienna SS labour camp, precisely the place where Abraham, my father's brother, had already been for months. In the jargon of Third Reich terminology, they ended up in the *Judenzwangsarbeiterlager Hasag Skarżysko-Kamienna* or in English the Hasag Skarżysko-Kamienna Forced labour camp for Jews. I prefer to use the word Jewish enslaved forced workers, because the workers' lives were totally in the hands of the SS and their affiliates. It wasn't just forced labour. The people working had a lower status, their lives like those of enslaved people were disposable at whim of those who claimed to own them (the SS and other Germans).

According to research of Felecja Karay, who was herself a survivor of Skarżysko-Kamienna, bribes were a deliberate mechanism to exploit Jewish people beyond all measure. And yet that forced labour assignment to Skarżysko-Kamienna provided a glimmer of hope of a future and continued life unknown, at least not immediate death.[287]

---

[285] Ibid. Loosely translated into English by author
[286] Zylbersztajn, Wolf (2001), Cassette II 16:00
[287] Karay (2004), p. 34

14

Skarżysko-Kamienna

In the Skarżysko-Kamienna camp
in a forest there, not far from the city, fenced in with barbed wire
Oy, I'm locked in there, I have no one left.
And when I die, no one will shed a tear for me.

The father gone, like an old stain. And the mother there
It's over, it's over…
Remember that,
I don't want to live any more,
for to whom do you belong, and who is yours, who?

It's only at work that I can often forget myself, like when I was a child,
When I still hoped. But when I come back, the barrack is bare and empty,
Then I feel so heavy in my heart
In the camp of Skarżysko
Oy my good God, when I think of it
Oy, my arms and legs are shaking, if only I had never got to know Skarżysko

Well-known song from the camp period. As quoted in Strigler (2017).
p. 388f., in die Fabrikn von Toyd. Translated from the Yiddish by Karay.
The author of the song is unknown.

In this so-called branch of the Hasag company, the practice of human slave labour was employed to the greatest extent. It did so, by driving the Jewish population, all of whom were Polish citizens, out of their homes with the help of the SS and forcing the workers to the Kamienna factory. Here they were exploited to the point of being bled white, driven to work at an immense pace by threats, beatings and under the most inhumane conditions until they literally collapsed to their deaths into the pits – and from those German industrialists, German corporate directors made their profits, these gentlemen literally capitalised on the blood of the workers.[288]

Hans Frey, the Hell Kamienna, 1949

Scene from a hall of hell in Skarżysko-Kamienna, photo: archive.

The song of the Skarżysko-Kamienna camp was not only from the camp carrying the same name. It also actually comes from the very part where, as far as I know, my father had to experience what many labelled

---

[288] Frey (1949), p. 4, translated by author.

hell on earth. The song was premiered at one of the many concert shows that the Jewish "commandant" was able to organise there with others. *Werk C* (Werk C) in Skarżysko-Kamienna was the most brutal factory area of the entire camp but was also the only place where such artistic "luxury" existed. It is obvious that such shows could breathe a little life and hope into the "half-dead" people who listened to them, some of whom had to carry out life-threatening tasks under the worst conditions every single day. It perhaps allowed them to forget where they were, if even just for a moment. Although the melody of this song is no longer known, the lines were immortalised by Mordechai Strigler and they perfectly capture the situation in which my father and his brothers and many of the others found themselves.

The factories of Skarżysko-Kamienna, of which some buildings survived until this day, were divided into factories A, B and C when they were repurposed by the Leipzig-based company Hugo Schneider Action Gemeinschaft, in short Hasag for their exploitative operations.

Company boss Paul Budin during a visit to Skarżysko-Kamienna. Picture from Frey, 1949.

Hasag was an industry showcase of the Third Reich. The perimeters of its industrial opertions in Skarżysko-Kamienna extended over an area of at least three kilometres. The camps for the enslaved forced labourers were located in their midst. Even before the war, Skarżysko-Kamienna had been home to a Polish ammunition plant, originally built in 1923 in the middle of a forested area, so that it was more hidden from aerial reconnaissance and thus also more protected from air raids. In 1940, after the violent occupation of Poland by Germany, the entire plant had been taken over by the Germans and was passed on to Hasag. In the same way, Hasag operated factories in the neighbouring Polish towns of Częstochowa and Kielce. Behind all of that stood the fact that Hasag had been licensed by the leadership of the German Third Reich to manufacture ammunition in Poland. Its operations were gigantic, encompassing a total of 3.5 million square metres work-space.[289]

Mesko administration building in one of the buildings in Skarżysko-Kamienna that was once taken over by Hasag AG. Photo DZL.

The beginnings of the company were rather innocent. Hasag was originally a petrol lamp manufacturer founded in 1863 under the name of

---

[289] Karay (2004)

"Häckel und Schneider." In 1899, the company became "Hugo Schneider A.G." – A.G. for Aktiengesellschaft, meant that it became share-controlled company. Abbreviated, it simply became known as Hasag and around 1900 employed some 1,000 workers with an annual turnover of around five million marks.[290] Up to this point, the development of the company, perhaps correlates with the success of the Lewandowski Family's corsets and lingerie operations. As for Hasag, due to the global economic crisis, the company began to experience difficulties and decided to switch its production to a more lucrative business endeavour: munitions manufacturing. It led to the German bank houses Dresdner Bank and Allgemeine Deutsche Kreditanstalt becoming the majority shareholders of Hasag.[291] With the arrival of the new company boss Paul Budin in 1931, Hasag's turn for the better was sealed. At the start of the German Third Reich it was becoming part of the armaments' industry for the German Wehrmacht with great success. The company soon achieved an annual turnover of an incredible 22 million Reichsmarks.[292]

In contrast to what happened to Jewish companies, including the Lewandowskis under National Socialism, this rapid growth of Hasag should be emphasised. Here is an example of a "German company" that was able to leave the depression of the 1920s behind and flourished during the Hitler years. In contrast, Jewish businesses like those of the Lewandowskis and of many others with Jewish or part-Jewish owners, were exploited, boycotted or even Aryanised during the Hitler years and their owners had to flee or were persecuted and eventually murdered.

Hasag, increased its workforce between 1932 and 1938 from 1,500 people to 14,000 people. The historian Martin Schnellenberg reported that the company was able to increase its turnover almost tenfold and soon approached a record 100 million Reichsmark.[293]

---

[290] Value, according to the year 1900, Frey (1949), p. 4
[291] Klein (2009), p. 13 and Martin Schnellenberg, „Die Schnellaktion Panzerfaust", in Dachauer Hefte 21/2005, p. 241
[292] ibid.
[293] Ibid.

As this chapter will show, Hasag not only expanded, but threw all business ethics overboard. It became haughty and arrogant and literally evolved into a business that was not afraid to be tainted with brutal and daily murder.

Hasag was content to employ Jewish enslaved people whose rights to security and life the management deliberately negated. This was not without irony, as the leadership of the Third Reich, according to classic conspiracy theories, accused Jewish companies of being "malevolent and dangerous for Germany", as Goebbels once put it.[294]

It was therefore no wonder that both Budin and Hasag's plant manager, SS-Standartenführer Dalski, agreed over what the fate of Jews should be. Dalski had already eagerly helped organise the November pogroms in 1938. He and other like-minded people put much effort into the operation in Skarżysko-Kamienna. Frey tells us that "SS men who could not be given tasks anywhere else due to their complete lack of professional skills, but who, in line with the Nazi ideological and stereotypical concepts of an apparent 'racial' order and who were of a firm stature and were quick tempered, could succeed in finding employment with Hasag.[295] All members of Hasag's Skarżysko-Kamienna general directorate, directors, foremen and supervisors, counting in total some 25 to 30 people, were selected in line the aforementioned criteria."[296]

> *"You were specially selected for this work", wrote Hasag's management to a worker transferred to Skarżysko-Kamienna on 19 June 1942: "Your transfer to Kamienna expresses our fullest trust in you, including with regard to your human traits and traits of your character. Hasag aims to rely on employees (in Skarżysko-Kamienna) who understand the need to demonstrate a leadership that is characterised by iron discipline and modesty at all times. Any advantages you enjoy in Kamienna must not become a reason*

---

[294] Joseph Goebbels: "Joseph Goebbels: Vom Kaiserhof zur Reichskanzlei, Munich 1934", quoted in Luh (2022)
[295] Frey (1949), p. 5
[296] Frey (1949), p. 5

to become arrogant or ungrateful for even a minute. You must never forget that you should display your German knowledge in the most beautiful form at all times and in every situation. Heil Hitler!"[297]

Later war trials documents revealed that after tests, Hasag's leaders showed themselves to be psychologically "normal."[298]

This fusion between German companies and the German National Socialist state became even clearer in Budin's case. In 1942, he was honoured with the War Cross of Merit First Class for his "operational achievements for the National Socialist armaments industry."[299]

From 1940 onwards, artillery and infantry cartridges, flag projectiles and various explosive devices, including torpedoes and bazookas, would all be manufactured in the former Polish ammunition factory at Skarżysko-Kamienna.

By March 1942, Hasag selected its first 2,000 enslaved Jewish people on the market square of Skarżysko-Kamienna and then forced them to work in the ammunition factories. During this "recruitment", Jews were led to believe that they would have a better life, or a "life" at all, if they worked in the factories. In the words of the head of the SS Economic Administration Office Oswald Pohl, in October 1942 the aim was Arbeit – labour, *"that should be exhausting in the true sense of the word, in order to achieve maximum performance."*[300] In May 1942 the workforce of the German "master-race" in control of the camp, counted a total of 119 "German" men, 29 "German" women and 71 so-called "ethnic Germans."[301]

The Jewish population originally living in Skarżysko-Kamienna suffered the same fate as all other Jewish populations in the wider area. This included obsessive and murderous behaviour displayed by some Germans, including by a certain Leo Metz, a member of the local criminal

---

[297] Ibid. p. 95, translation into English by author
[298] Frey (1949), p. 79
[299] Klein (2009), p. 13
[300] Martin Schnellenberg, die Schnellaktion Panzerfaust in Dachauer Hefte (2005), p. 239
[301] Kray (2004), p. 24

investigation department of the German administration. Amongst the victims were many Jewish women and girls, who frequently became victims of sexual crimes committed against them by the Germans. Eventually the entire Jewish population of the town was ordered into a ghetto.[302] In 1937, two years before the Nazi invasion of 1939, the Jewish population of Skarżysko-Kamienna counted some 2,800 Jewish people out of a total regional population of 19,000.[303] In 1942, after the town's Jewish ghetto was dissolved, a total of 2,500 people out of the 2800 were deported to Treblinka, where they were murdered upon arrival. Pregnant women, children and the sick were murdered on the spot during the ghetto evacuation. Only 500 people were selected to work in the factories.[304] Initially Polish resistance remained strong until it was laid bare, leading to the execution of some 350-400 people in 1940.[305] Nevertheless, other underground organisations managed to continue operating undercover despite the occupation, including subunits of the Polish *Morwa* underground army.[306]

In her book, *Death Comes in Yellow*, Felicja Karay documented how the establishment of the labour camp for Jews in the summer of 1942 ran against the National Socialist policy of the Final Solution. The industrialists preferred to profit from the "freely" available manpower rather than to serve the Masterplan of the total execution of the Jews.[307] Karay emphasised that it was *not* the lack of availability of Polish wage labourers – there were plenty of them in the area – that led to the recruitment of Jewish enslaved people, but that Germans wanted to profit deliberately from free slave labour.

Poles who had previously worked in the munition factory were increasingly transferred to labour camps inside the German Reich's home territory, so that they could take on the vacated positions of German men

---

[302] Gibaszewski (2015), p. 15
[303] Ibid. S. 18
[304] Ibid. S.22
[305] Ibid.
[306] Ibid. S. 16
[307] "Free," since the SS paid a daily fee for the forced labourers in concentration camps. Six Reichsmark for skilled labourers and four Reichsmark for unskilled labourers

recruited into in the military. In his research, Gibazewski cited financial hardship, blackmail and simply fear as other additional reasons why non-Jewish Poles would take up labour "offers" in Germany.[308]

Was Skarżysko-Kamienna just a workplace like any other? Karay poses that question differently, when she suggested that Skarżysko-Kamienna was not actually a labour camp but an extermination camp. She argued that the conditions there were not designed to cherish and protect the lives of the Jewish enslaved workers whatsoever. It was only towards the end, in spring of 1944, when millions of Jewish people had already been murdered, which meant that there was no longer a continued "supply" of, or, as the German operations managers called them, "*Austauschjuden*" – "Exchange Jews" – available, that the Hasag administration was forced to improve the conditions inside the camp.

It is worth examining some figures here. By the summer of 1943 alone, 17,210 Jewish people would arrive in Skarżysko-Kamienna. Within the first 15 months, 10,802 of these would be dead, either because they were murdered directly or because they were murdered indirectly, the later meaning murder by virtue of the living and working conditions. By the time the camp had been dissolved in the summer of 1944, 25,000 Jewish people had passed through the Skarżysko-Kamienna "labour camp", 20,000 of whom had died due to maltreatment, torture and beatings, or from the inadequate hygienic conditions and denied medical care. Others had been murdered directly or shot and thereafter had been buried and burned. Such were the real "splendid achievements" of Hasag in Skarżysko-Kamienna – a German company *par excellence* of which the Reich was so proud.

My father and all the other Jewish people in this industrial undertaking were, it is hard to believe, the private property of the Hasag company. However terrifying this may sound, this actually had one little advantage. It also meant that these enslaved people escaped the direct control of the SS, who had supplied these Jewish people to Hasag on loan.[309]

---

[308] Ibid. S. 16
[309] According to a report issued by General Commandant Anton Ipfling on 15 October

In January 1943, ownership of all the Polish factories transferred solely to Hasag AG, as prior to that time they had been managed in trust for the Reich. As already hinted at, they had to persuade the German leadership focused on the Final Solution to continue to serve Hasag's operational and industrial needs and interests regarding the supply of lucrative Jewish enslaved labourers. In a meeting with the Reich's leadership, Lieutenant General Maximilian Schindler referred to the "indispensability" of Jewish skilled labourers with racial undertones:"[310] "The workers are stronger than the Polish, in the best physical condition and would be considered Maccabees", he said.[311] He did not talk about the fact that these enslaved Maccabees metamorphosed into walking skeletons in the factories. These are the facts as to why Hasag became one of the most important companies in the German armaments industry at the time, owning it to their "indispensable" Jewish work force.

It was not only in Skarżysko-Kamienna that weapons were manufactured by foreign workers and forced labourers. Up to a quarter of all German weapons in the Third Reich were manufactured by French, Polish, Russian and other workers, some of whom were forced labourers and prisoners.[312] At Hasag, the number of enslaved and forced labourers amounted to 60 percent of the total "workforce" in 1943.[313] At the end of the Second World War, more than 40,000 of the company's 64,000 employees were foreign concentration camp prisoners, more than in any other private German company during the Second World War.[314]

In the camp itself, the forced labourers were controlled by Jewish policemen, and another group, Werkschutz guards. The latter were

---

1942, 4361 Jewish forced labourers were interned in Skarzisko-Kammiena, 2,590 men and 1,771 women, in July 1943 there were 6,408 Jewish people inside the camp Karay (2004), p. 44 and p. 49.

[310] 31 May 1943, Maximilian Schindler has no known connection to Oskar Schindler!
[311] Karay, p. 49
[312] Ibid. p. 240
[313] Klein (2009), p. 13
[314] Haikal (2002), p. 81 and Klein (2009), p. 12, see also Arad (1999), p. 46.

largely responsible for the decisions over life and death or for implementing execution orders. The Werkschutz guards, most of whom were of Ukrainian or of ethnic German descent, forced the Jews in the factory to comply with German orders.

The Jewish sourced police and Werkschutz officers carried similar responsibilities but within living quarters. The SS itself was responsible for monitoring ammunition and internal security. They were also responsible for all confiscations of Jewish property. According to Krzysztof Gibaszewski's research, the factories had a military police station manned by around 50-60 people, including a small criminal investigation team of ten men, a special commando unit, made up out of 50 people, 100-150 Werkschutz Guards and company guards, as well as around 20 people from the German Railway Security Force.[315]

Hasag was obliged to inform the SS about any escapees and about any acts of sabotage and breaches of German racial laws. All property stolen from Jewish people was to be handed over to the SS. Hasag paid the SS to be able use the enslaved people.[316] Jewish forced labourers did not receive any pay. For every day of the work of a male, the SS in Radom were paid five zlotys and four zlotys for the labour of a woman – a bargain![317]

The camp population organised themselves in a hierarchy based on influence, status, and resources they had managed to smuggle in. Germans were at the top of the hierarchy, Poles and Ukrainians in the middle, and Jews at the bottom.

The position of the Jews suited the German leadership. Karay wrote, that it was important for Poles to be able to take out their frustrations on Jews. Ukrainians, Poles and Germans, despite all their differences, could agree on who was to be regarded as the lowest in the pecking order, to be exploited physically, financially and sexually, without any shame:. The Jews![318]

---

[315] Gibaszewski (2015), p. 14
[316] ibid.p. 45
[317] Karay (2004), p. 44
[318] ibid

15

The Cushion from Heaven

Remaining railway tracks next to the supposed place where people arrived in Skarżysko-Kamienna *according to historian* Krzysztof Gibaszewski *today Photo DZL.*

When my father arrived in January 1943 in Skarżysko-Kamienna the industrial complex must have looked bleak and austere. It was the middle of the Polish winter, and the living quarters must have been particularly smelly and filthy during that time.

Immediately after he and the others were destined to become property of Hasag on loan from the SS, a tremendous and important decision was made over their faith. The question that would make a huge difference in their treatment was which of the three factories, Werk A, B or C, they would be assigned to, and moreover if they would be given the chance at all to become an enslaved labourer, rather than being ordered to be shot straight away.[319]

Some of the arrivals were instantly declared unfit for labour, due to age, either for being too young or old, or due to being too weak or ill. This meant that to the Nazis they were deemed to be economically useless. A firing squad would end their lives without any delay.

Menachem Frajkorn, who, like my father, came from Szczekociny and had also ended up in Skarżysko-Kamienna, described this moment in the following words:

> *Those who had the good fortune to enrol as skilled workers in the metal industry stayed at Werk A. Most of them would survive, while those who did not work as skilled workers were sent to Werk C, of whom only few survived.*[320]

Zwi Grajpner, who was also taken to Skarżysko-Kamienna, described Werk C as a certain death factory:

> *Of the several thousand Jews who were there (in the Rodomsky interim camp), two hundred and fifty survived, including twenty Szczekocynians, and they were miraculously sent to factories A, B and C in Skarżysko. Only those who had the "pleasure" of being sent to factories A and B survived, because no one left Werk C alive.*[321]

---

[319] Werk, German factory / Works
[320] Szwajcer (2010), p. 240, translation by the author.
[321] Szwajcer (2010), S. 218f., translation by the author

My father confirmed this:

Werk C was not for living. (When) they used to shoot from Werk A, they were also brought to us (to Werk C). They were always brought to us from Werk A for transfer. (At the place) where we were was a large area just for the purpose of killing.[322]

This is where my father indicated he had been, not in Werk A, but probably in Werk C. You, the reader, already know how it will turn out. I wouldn't be writing these lines if my father hadn't survived despite the assignment to Werk C.

And it was not just my father who was in Werk C, but his father and his brother Dawid were also sent to this factory of death. His other brother, Abraham, however, seems to have been in Werk A.

Felix Krebs, a German overseer who can only be described as a passionate sadist, was the authority over Werk C. According to witnesses, he enjoyed forcing a married Jewish couple to hang each other in front of everyone after a failed escape.

Werk C produced explosives for the German military using tetryl and picric acid.[323] Those who handled these substances awaited a slow and agonising death. There was no occupational safety in place, nor were there any washing facilities to wash off any of the corrosive acid. People who were forced to work with these substances were often near death within a few months. Many described them as appearing yellowish. Their death was caused by external and internal corrosions, burns and lung and heart damage. The average period somebody could survive the daily handling of these substances was no more than two months.[324] People who worked with tetryl and picric acid had the status of a damned untouchable caste within the camp and were nicknamed "prikiner." But

---

[322] Zylbersztajn, Wolf (2001), Cassette III 08:00
[323] Karay (2004), p. 44. p. 15 Tetryl is short for 2,4,6-trinitrophenylmethylnitramine
[324] Ibid. p. 12

others at Werk C did not necessarily last longer than the prikiner. Karay estimated the general survival time of others, provided they had no extra resources or contacts at their disposal, at just one additional month longer, three months in total.[325]

In addition Werk C with its adjoining forest was, as my father reported, also the site for all major and regular executions. Those condemned to be murdered were sent to the "firing range" of Werk C in front of the forest that opened up behind it. They were stripped of their clothes and often shot and buried defencelessly while standing in a grave that had been dug before their eyes. According to Gibaszewski, there were in fact numerous death pits in the forest.[326] Mordechai Strigler reported that the pits dug became so full of corpses that the earth beneath the corpses rose upwards after some time. Metaphorically, it could perhaps be described as their spirits moving the earth upwards in a final act of defiance to shame their executioners.

Logistically Werk C was connected to the vast railway network. Small groups of Jewish enslaved labourers had often to load and unload heavy goods weighing several tonnes there. My father held that job for a short while at the beginning of his time there.

Factories A and B manufactured mines and projectiles and were each scenes of immense brutality and horror. In charge of Werk B was a German former member of the Foreign Legion named Willy Seidel, who, according to survivors' testimony, would rush around armed with a horsewhip.[327] Rarely sober, he was described by those who witnessed him as a habitual groper and cruel sexual predator as well as murderer, who did not even shy away from murdering babies.

Perhaps it was the same man my father described under the nickname "Zack Zack:"

---

[325] Ibid.
[326] Information provided in a personal interview on site August 2022
[327] Ibid. p. 15 Dreck, German dirt, schnell, German fast

The Cushion from Heaven

> *"He was such a Verbrecher, when somebody committed suicide, he said, get rid of him, get rid of the Dreck, get rid of it, get rid of it! That's how he spoke, schnell, schnell!"*[328]

The description could fit Seidel, but other Hasag overseers also owned and used whips, belts, knots and straps in order to command "respect."[329] Some of these Germans were reported to regularly tie the enslaved forced labourers to chairs in order to beat them without receiving any resistance from their victims.[330]

Anyone who wanted to survive in Werk C or the other factories had to know their way around its cruel system. Above all, one needed access to money to survive. I think that my uncle Abraham was already acquainted with the local circumstances before his father and his two brothers had arrived, and thus he may have been able to advise them very early on, and pass on vital information. The fact that my grandfather had been forced by the Germans occupiers to serve on the Judenrat of Szczekociny, the Nazi enforced Jewish Council, may also have helped. Such previous status could lead to certain "privileges" amongst those who served Werk C.

All decisions as to who was deserving or not were made by Fela Markowiczowa, the all-powerful Jewish commandant, who with the gift of a social talent knew how to play the German guards. The enslaved Jewish population called her simply the Commandata. Markowiczowa was from a Jewish family from Skarżysko. This is why she was able to use her relationship with the immediate outside world successfully to her own advantage in a clever, diplomatic but also unscrupulous manner. With the assistance of Polish non-Jewish labourers, she was further able to smuggle all sorts of goods into the camp. Those who were close to

---

[328] Wolf Zylbersztajn, Shoah Foundation Testimony. There was also a guard by the name of Raczak, see footnotes ch. 20.
[329] Zylbersztajn (2001) Cassette V, 7:20
[330] Ibid. p. 53f and p. 72

her or could pay for their privileges were allocated better jobs through her and were even able to have their own more private living quarters, cook their own food and even do their own laundry.

In her book "*Death Comes in Yellow*", Karay summarised the hierarchy amongst Jewish people in the camp into five classes: "Prominente", who were involved with the internal administration and police, "Court Employees" who performed lower-level functions within the internal order, "Money Barons", a small group of people who had access to some money, the "Proletariat" to which most of the others belonged, and last but not least, "Musslmänner", people who had been written off as walking dead.[331]

What privileges did my father his brother and grandfather have? Did they have a better place to work and sleep inside the area of this Factory of Death?

In Karay's analysis of the camp, I discovered the mentioning of a Jewish policeman called Zylbersztajn who supposedly worked in Hall 13. Unfortunately, she didn't reveal this man's first name. A Zylbersztajn being a policeman? I calmed down when I found that Zylbersztajn had been a "man of relief" to the people in the camp.[332] "Good Jewish policemen," as Karay described this Zylbersztajn, were few and far between. Whether he was one of the three Zylbersztajn brothers or even their father – my grandfather – will remain unknown, unless further testimonies emerge. No such position was ever mentioned by Abraham, or my father and the surname Zylbersztajn was by no means rare in Poland in all its spelling variations, similar to the English surname of Smith.[333] On the other hand, if it had been one of the brothers or my grandfather, this fact would most probably have contributed to their survival.

It was, however, most likely that access to money helped my father, his brothers and his father, and I will share here a story about this from my father's recollections and testimony:

---

[331] Karay (2004) p. 99
[332] Ibid, p 178 probably based on the testimony of Helena Zorska, given as YV, 033/1797.
[333] See witness Zylberstein, Frey 1949, p. 66

The Cushion from Heaven

When my father and his father arrived with the others in Skarżysko-Kamienna they were ordered to hand over all their possessions in a small room. The Nazis were after gold, money and other valuables. But my father was a rebel. He did exactly the opposite of what he had been ordered, and that momentary defiance quite possibly determined his and the others later fortunes.

When my father found himself in the room, he saw lots of money lying around, which others had already given up and left behind as ordered, he also spotted a small cushion. My father had already learnt to appreciate the lifesaving power of money in the Radomsky interim camp when he was able to bribe Germans and thus save himself and his father from the crowd. It is also possible that my father already understood that money was important in the camp because of his brother's (Abraham) request for boots some months earlier. He must have observed also that people were allowed to take some seemingly worthless items with them. Seeing these vast amounts of money beside him, perhaps in a moment where the guards attention was elsewhere, my father didn't hesitate and grabbed several note bundles towards him in a flash alongside the cushion, tore a small hole in it, and pushed the banknotes deep inside it.[334]

My father stated that despite the real risk of being instantly taken out and shot if he had been caught, he felt no concern or fear. With that cushion under his arm, he proceeded to leave the room, the danger being far from over. When one of the inspectors patted down the cushion my father feared for the worst, but in the haste with many more people to be checked the inspector failed to spot anything unusual and allowed my father to take the cushion with him. In his statement to the Shoah Foundation, my father referred to this cushion as "the cushion from heaven".[335] The cushion's contents would soon guarantee improved conditions for his brothers, his father and himself. The money they now possessed could be used to buy easier places of work, better

---

[334] Wolf Zylbersztajn, Interview 51541, 21 February 2001
[335] ibid

accommodation, and more food than the others had, it meant nothing but life and survival itself in the camp.

My father recalled an additional stroke of luck when he had "found" money a second time in the camp. He had noticed that one man was always very careful with his cap. When he once saw it hanging unattended in the cloakroom, he quickly examined it and discovered a huge fortune inside. Again, fully in survival mode and thus without thinking twice, my father grabbed it. This time the owner of the cap soon enough realised that the money he had hidden inside was no longer there, and he immediately called for the guards. These ordered a search of the entire work-unit. Hiding the money under his belt and as he said, pulling in his stomach, he was lucky to once again escape certain death and was not caught. His life literally depended on an opportune moment, quick thinking and a string of luck. What provided some more assurances of survival was possibly also a catastrophic loss and step closer to death for the now seemingly penniless other man.

Needless to say, if you owned anything valuable in Skarżysko-Kamienna, you also had to be able to guard and hide it well and also not attract much attention. Somehow my father managed it, having two brothers and his father in this hostile world may have helped to lessen the risk and distribute the resources, but the danger of loss, confiscation or theft was still constant and omnipresent. There were informers about who were always on the lookout to find any hidden away valuables. In addition, Werkschutz and German guards often organised raids and strip searches. Newly arrived people who seemed to be doing too "well" in the eyes of others were the ones most at risk in the hacking order.[336]

In October 1943, suspicions and lust to profit even further from the already subjugated led to a huge raid in which around 800 Jewish enslaved labourers were ordered to hand over whatever valuable possessions they had. According to Karay, confiscations of this type were not officially documented by the camp administration. Karay described it

---

[336] Karay (2004), p.39

The Cushion from Heaven

as theft in the name of production.[337] And there was more. The aforementioned raid was concluded on the following day with mass murder, the execution of 195 people by firing squad.[338]

When I visited the site of the former Hasag factories in Skarżysko-Kamienna, Krzysztof Gibaszewski, who led me through what is left of the area, pointed to a large courtyard behind a fence next to a forest where the living quarters had probably once been located. There were cars parked there today. As I looked up at the surrounding trees I wondered whether my father had once looked at these too. This was as close as I was able to get to feeling the presence of my father's past experiences. Nothing more but old buildings and a gaze into leafy trees. Moreover, the moment I spent there appeared to be too short. I longed to connect, contemplate, maybe stay for 15 minutes or hours, however long it took me. But we had to walk on. In fact, Krzysztof was worried that our presence could be alerting security. Even if we could have stayed there longer, it is likely that it would not have made a huge difference, though perhaps my need was more of a contemplative necessity. From this place, it was but a 15 to 20-minute walk to the actual Werk C. An old guard's house next to a car park suggested that the people forced to work here, possibly my father and grandfather too, might have walked past it. There was nothing more than attempts to imagine the past and think about lost relatives and history, and that that deep desire to get as close to the past as I could. But I would be disappointed and not only here. What I desired was simply impossible.

Where exactly my father and grandfather slept in the camp, I could not find out. What my father did mention was that there was a bunk bed for six people opposite him. Elsewhere, he spoke of a mixed-gender barrack with around 1,000 people, where a certain woman by the name of Milet would have examined him, following his arrival.[339]

---

[337] ibid.
[338] ibid.
[339] Karay reports only of one Szmuel Milet, p. 232.

The accommodations for the enslaved population was sparing and unhygienic. The latrine near the forest was frequently overflowing. Some had dug a trench alongside their barrack so that they could relieve themselves more quickly. Those who were affected by the handling of tetryl and picric acid had to relieve themselves far more often than others. Yet anyone who ventured outside at night could put their life at risk. Some Jewish policemen and Werkschutz personnel were overeager to benefit from extra rewards: They randomly shot innocent people to claim that they had caught the victims on the run. As a result some preferred to relieve themselves in their food bowls or in the corners of their rooms instead.[340]

"Washrooms" were partially covered in faeces, and often lacked running water.[341]

FA forced labourer tries to save something from the soup bucket. Photo from Frey 1949.

---

[340] according to Karay (2004) and Strigler (2017)
[341] Ibid.

There was only a bit straw on the beds or boards to make sleeping more comfortable, sometimes not even that . Only those with connections, privileges, or money could think of "luxuries" such as mattresses, pillows and blankets.[342] According to Strigler, the conditions in the accommodation facilities were a "boiling *tohuwabohu*" worse than those in Majdanek concentration camp, which had been after all an extermination camp.[343] None of the living quarters were fitted with a heating, sufficient light, chairs, tables or hot water (the latter was only available in Werk B).[344]

As said, money meant not only being able to buy yourself a better job-assignment or place to sleep, but also the opportunity to get hold of food smuggled into the camp.

No one could survive for long on the starvation rations of thin water soup, 150 grams of black bread and "coffee" distributed to the enslaved labourers. These rations were part of the deliberate plan of slowly killing the enslaved workforce.[345]

Karay wrote that the soup at noon was the same as that in the evening. Those who were clever or could pay for the favour, or got on well with their superiors, got into the queue a little later, because then they could count on a few pieces of potato or meat from the bottom of the pot.[346] Again and again, despite all their efforts, many people were unable to get hold of any food at all. The hunger of the people was further exploited to humiliate. To the amusement of those who held all the power over the Jewish enslaved, the soup pots would sometimes be turned over, and spilled over the ground.

The starving desperately hurried to lick the filthy soil for scraps of food – to those who hated them as an apparent inferior race, this served as further evidence that Jews were supposedly less human and beneath them.

---

[342] Karay (2004) p. 77
[343] Strigler (2017), p. 89
[344] ibid.
[345] Ibid. p. 104f.
[346] Ibid. p. 77

To further understand the conditions under which people like my father had to live the following description from Felicija Karay is helpful:

Food was available in two ways, through official channels and unofficial channels. Official responsibility lay with the Hasag supplies department (BeWi) in Kielce. From there, the supplies would be delivered to the Konsumlagerhaus (storage), which was administered by the German administrative group "Schlicht." In theory, there were enough provisions for the calculated minimum caloric values for forced labourers. However, Hasag's administration did not distribute this itself.

The bakery and kitchen were not located inside the camp, but in the factory area. Although dark rye flour was supplied for the bread of the Jewish forced labourers, most of the flour was stolen by the Polish and German kitchen and bakery bosses, which the Poles then processed into loaves of bread and sold to the Jewish forced labourers.[347] *The "Jewish bread" was then baked from the leftover flour and potato flakes, which was produced in a special mill in Werk B.*

The same flakes were used for the forced labourers' "soup." Twice a week, a little barley, carrot peel or horse meat was added, and twice a week it was prepared with sugar.[348] *This was the so-called "sweet soup." The soup for Polish labourers was also made from potato flakes, but here more nutritious ingredients were often added in, at the expense of the Jewish rations. In total, the daily food ration for prisoners consisted of 230 grams of bread, 0.75 litres of soup twice*

---

[347] When Karay speaks of Poles, she means non-Jewish, Christian Poles. The fact that she did not describe Jewish people from Poland as Poles gives an insight into how Jewish people were neither seen as Poles, nor that they ultimately saw themselves as Poles, despite the centuries-long Jewish presence in Poland.

[348] Since horse meat is not kosher, and is one of the forbidden animal species, just like pork, this can be understood as further humiliation of Jewish people who had no choice.

a day, and "coffee" in the morning and evening. Every now and then there would be a spoonful of beetroot jam. Prisoners received no cutlery at all.[349]

Frey wrote that empty tins and similar items were used to consume food in, and prisoners often had to share them.[350]

It was not until the spring of 1944 that the limited food rations finally improved. This was done out of pure self-interest, because the camp management realised that there would be no more "Exchange Jews" to replace those who had been murdered or worked to death. The reason was that most of the Jews in Europe had already been mass murdered in the many extermination camps in the Nazi sphere of influence as part of the Final Solution.

But there was a tiny glimmer of hope of life for prisoners, even if only for those with the necessary resources like money or other valuables. After work, the entire camp turned into an open market, where people tried to sell everything they could to get their hands on vital money or valuables. The items sold included utensils made in the camp, such as knives and spoons, food and fabrics. The money could then be used to purchase food or other necessary items. If you ran out of money or lost your contacts, your luck ran out too – it meant a speedily approaching premature death.

I am sure that my grandfather, my uncles and my father did not have endless resources, despite their luck with "finding" money. However, they were resourceful and skilled craftsmen. They may have been able to make things from scraps and smuggled items that could be sold on the black market in the camp, such as shoes and the like. Karay, for example, wrote of a shoemaker who had been executed because he had secretly stolen a leather strap from the factory in order to try to make shoes out of it.[351] Others turned diused tin cans into useful objects such as knives,

---

[349] Karay (2004), p. 77 retranslated from German by author
[350] Frey 1949, p. 11
[351] Karay (2004), p. 103

scissors, combs and other tools.[352] One of the most treasured items my father owned was a razor blade.

My father told me that his father also had a razor blade (perhaps it was however the same one) and that they shaved each other before roll calls to look younger, healthier and better groomed. What a father-son ritual that was! Boris Kazik Weinberg, who survived the hell of Treblinka as a forced labourer, wrote similar things about the roll calls and the "selections" that took place:

> *The selection symbolised a constant danger that hung over our heads like a drawn sword. Never, not even in the best of times, did we shave as often as we did in Treblinka.... Some powdered their faces, or squeezed their cheeks until they were rosy... All this to stay alive for a few more days, maybe weeks, who knows.*[353]

Many years later, when in 2011 I visited my then terminally ill father in his flat, a month before he died, I was only allowed to go into the flat after he had submitted himself to a lengthy preparation procedure. Part of this procedure was fixing the toupee he wore and shaving himself thoroughly. Fully consumed by the viscous cancer that eventually killed him, it was important to him "that he still looked good," in other words, that he looked better than he actually was.

Cheating appearance was not the only trick in the unwritten survival-guide for Skarżysko-Kamienna. My uncle reported that there existed a network for Jews from Szczekociny in Skarżysko-Kamienna.[354] These "Landmanschaften" communities of people from particular communities or cities, helped each other out, where they could. Karay wrote, that family members also tried to find ways to see each other in the camp. I know from my father that he and his father and brother Dawid

---

[352] Ibid.
[353] Arad (1999), p. 97f
[354] Szwajcer (2010), p.257

visited their other brother Abraham once a week in the "bath" of Werk A to talk to him. According to my visit to Buchenwald in 2022 and the explanations given by Pamela Castillo Feuchtmann, an educator there, this was probably one of the latrines which usually, no guards dared to enter (out of fear of diseases).

16

I Still Looked Good

Recalling his memories in Skarżysko-Kamienna, my father repeated one thing above all, claiming it to be fundamental for his survival: "I still looked good, with strong boots and a jacket."

This can only be understood in the context of the situation on the ground. Hasag in Skarżysko-Kamienna issued no clothing to those it forced to work in its factories. The clothing people wore and with which the people entered Skarżysko-Kamienna was therefore all they had. The winter of 1943 is said to have been one of the harshest and coldest for years. Many lacked sufficient protection from the extreme weather and were forced to wrap themselves in scraps of cloth and paper to stay warm.[355]

Karay also wrote that the daily struggle for survival was about looking neither too strong nor too poor. Those who looked "too strong" or "too good" compared to others would attract unwanted attention, because this meant that the person concerned must surely have some resources that could be taken away, or that they would be assigned to the heaviest work tasks. In the same way, if any woman was too good-looking, she could easily become the target of sexual advances, especially

---

[355] Karay (2004), p. 78

by guards with absolute power over them. Those who looked too weak and too unkempt, on the other hand, risked being considered useless and to be singled out during selections.[356] Sometimes such caution was still not enough if an overseer had a bad day and desired to spill blood.

Part of the former factory A, where my uncle Abraham worked.
The electrical transformer was added after the war, I was told. Photo DZL.

How the order of suitability for work functioned was something my father was taught on his very first day following his arrival to Skarżysko-Kamienna during one of the frequent roll calls. It was principally during these that the "weak" were "weeded out" from amongst the "strong." On that first day, my father remembered, some ten people had been randomly selected by Werkschutz personnel.

"*They took them to one side and shot them with a machine gun. We were forced to watch*", my father remembered.[357] On that occasion, my father didn't quite understand why these people had been murdered.

---

[356] Ibid. p. 79
[357] Zylbersztajn, Wolf (2001), Cassette II 23:00

He assumed that they were executed because somebody had run away. Their act was a murderous and bloodthirsty exploitation of the power over them, intended to intimidate the others not to try the same.[358]

Indeed, there were sometimes attempts to escape into the forest. Those who managed to run away, however, often placed their fate into the hands of partisans. According to the Polish historian K. Gibaszewski it was a mere lottery if such escapees were able to survive. Either those found by partisans were helped and absorbed, or they were shot, so that these fugitives could not reveal to anyone, and above to Germans, that they had encountered partisans. Occasionally they were left unhurt but without further assistance. It all depended on whoever the refugees came across on any day.[359]

My father also remembered his first day at work in Skarżysko-Kamienna. It began with waking up at 05:00 in the morning, a hurried run to the washroom and consuming his morning meal and "morning coffee".[360] A single work shift could last at least ten hours. Frey wrote that it could often stretch to 14, 18 or even more hours on certain days.[361] My father recalled having been sent to a three-storey building where he was supposed to work under a Polish foreman called Ogrodowczyk.[362]

My father's first task was to push alongside other enslaved labourers an old and groaning cart loaded with heavy shell casings (probably 15.2 cm diameter) on rusty rails "up a long hilly track" to a location where the foundry for explosives was situated.[363] If I identified the correct place, the shells would have been the heaviest that Hasag produced.[364]

---

[358] Zylbersztajn, Wolf, Interview 51541, 21 February 2001 and Karay (2004), p. 78
[359] Personal statement, August 2022
[360] Work started at 05:00 according to Karay (2004), p. 89.
[361] Frey (1949), p. 11
[362] Name in accordance to oral testimony
[363] Zylbersztajn, Wolf (2001), Cassette II 24:00
[364] "*The large (shells) with a diameter of 15 and 15.2 cm, weighed 57 kilos. They were referred to as calves due to their slender shape. The empty shells (Hülsen) were transported from Werk A on a special railway line that led to Werk C.* Strigler (2017), p. 193

I Still Looked Good

Following descriptions of Strigler, the rusty vehicle would be pushed by a total of four people and often got stuck.[365] My father labelled the people who helped to push this cart alongside himself as "Muselmänner."

"They looked like Muslmänner! There was already no flesh left (on them.)"[366]

Muselmänner, previously mentioned as one of the five classes of people in the camps of Skarżysko-Kamienna, is a term that was often used in Auschwitz and some other camps to describe people who were but walking skeletons, and who, in the hours before their death, fell into a cramped and contracted position, apparently like "praying Muslims."

When the men spotted my father, they spoke to him in Yiddish:

They said: "Oy Yid, Yid (Oh fellow Jew, fellow Jew), once we looked good too!" That's when I understood, that it was bad, that it was my likely end[367]

My father referred to the immediate foreman and supervisor of this group as "the brigadier" and recalled his name as Fiett.[368] Like most supervisors, Brigadier Fiett carried a club to admonish and coerce his slave labourers. My father said that the brigadier watched him, probably recognising that he was a new arrival. He ordered my father to push the cart. After a while, he addressed my father with the following sentence in Polish, which my father vividly recalled many decades later: *"Sprzedaj moje buty! (Sell me your boots)!"*[369]

He added that he did not want the boots for free, but that my father should sell them to him! My father immediately understood that this

---

[365] Strigler (2017), p. 145
[366] Zylbersztajn, Wolf (2001), Cassette II 25:00, own tranlation
[367] Zylbersztajn, Wolf (2001). Cassette II 26:00, own translation
[368] Oral testimony
[369] Zylbersztajn, Wolf (2001), Cassette II 26:00

was not a well-intentioned offer: *"I took a look at the people and looked at myself, and I understood, it was now over."*[370]

Such situations in which new arrivals found themselves were mentioned by Karay. She wrote that newly arrived workers were the most vulnerable in the camp, as they were not yet familiar with it. In addition, people who had already been in the camp for some time attempted to exploit or steal from the new arrivals. Karay also reported that newly arrived women were being checked out as potential "cousins." Karay explained that women and older girls were frequently offered to enter relationships by better-off forced male labourers. Through such "relationships" and their sexual exploitation, women who owned nothing could acquire small degrees of protection. Although only heterosexual relationships were reported by Karay, there were must have been also some, perhaps more hidden, of a different kind.

As far as my father was concerned, he owned boots that this Brigadier Fiett obviously had his eyes on. It is probable that these boots had been specially made for my father by my grandfather, so I assume that they were indeed of exceptional quality.

My father's interpretation of the situation, that the offer to sell his boots could be the beginning of the end for him, was by no means misplaced. Who would sell their boots in the middle of an extremely cold January? If he had no more boots, what then? Maybe he also had money hidden in them. Thus my father concluded that there was only one way out of the situation. He had to stand his ground. The answer that he gave Brigadier Fiett is reminiscent of a scene from Mordechai Strigler's novel, in which the protagonist Mechele (synonymous for the author himself) defended himself boldly against harassing attacks from the (catholic) Poles in the camp.[371] And that is precisely what my father did:

---

[370] ibid
[371] Strigler (2019), p. 67-77

I was not exactly bright, but neither was I afraid. I possessed a vocabulary of a few vulgar words (and) I told him: If I hit you, you'll lose your blood! So come on, hit me! I'm not afraid of you, you won't do to me what you did to them![372]

Addressing the interviewer from the Shoah Foundation, he continued: *"And I can say, it helped – Mazel Sachen!"*[373]

My father could not believe that the man backed down. It was self-respect, reluctance to give in, and a daring attitude that earned him the respect of his superior, who was in a clear position of power. In a change of tune, Fiett even ordered my father to let the others push the cart.[374] But according to my father, that was easier said than done. *"The others weren't able to do anything anymore,"* my father commented.[375]

In Strigler's novel too, the protagonist Michele pushes a cart up a hill, possibly at the very same place my father had been describing.

What was most fascinating about this situation that my father remembered, is the fact that the men working alongside the fictional Michele, impersonating Striglers experiences of Skarżysko-Kamienna, had also told him, that he still looked good. Were they the same men? Unlike my father, Mechele, however, got into an argument with his fellow workers because they failed to teach him how to load the sharp aluminium grenades without cutting his fingers and making them bloody.[376]

My father pushed these heavy grenades for about a week, he said. After that, he was suddenly assigned to another job. This was due to a contact from his father and possibly in return for something. His new job was now to work with a grenade press, a "relief" and one of the many individual factors in his survival.

---

[372] Zylbersztajn, Wolf (2001), Cassette II 26:40, own translation
[373] Ibid. Mazel Sachen – yid. Lucky Things!
[374] Ibid.
[375] Ibid.
[376] Strigler (2017), p. 145-151

In Strigler's book "*In den Fabriken des Todes*" (*In the Factories of Death*), I think I even discovered the hall in "Werk C" where my father and grandfather may have been forced to work. Here is his word by word description:

Each shell had to be stamped on a special machine, before it was filled. This was done in a special hall where a group of Jews worked. This hall was the lightest (workplace). Only people who enjoyed great protection worked there. It was also the only department in the whole factory with a foreman who was Jewish[377]

My own father remembered the place in these words:

It was upstairs. It was a large room, and the grenades were stamped there. The grenades were placed on a large table. I was a bit of a professional. They had these pens, made of iron. You had to make the date, knock out the date and year, and so on.[378]

My father always said that he was "nimble." In the factories of Skarżysko-Kamienna, this was one of the most important attributes. Frey said that the number of shells that were to be completed during each shift was increased from 1000 shells, as it had been before the war, to 5500 for the Jewish enslaved labourers working on starvation rations. This was nothing else but a literally murderous pace, with an emphasis on the word murder. And not only here. All tasks in the entire camp were to be carried out according to this "norm", as the Germans there called it.

Workers who were too slow, were harassed, beaten, tortured or murdered. This includes those who were old, unwell, weak or injured. Here are testimonies that report how enslaved labourers who were not working satisfactorily were forced by a sadistic overseer to mount burning hot

---

[377] Strigler (2017), p. 194
[378] Zylbersztajn, Wolf (2001), Cassette II 27:00

industrial containers until they succumbed to the severe, agonising burns that these inevitably caused.[379] One German factory foreman, Alfred Wagner, who worked in the "shoe department", had figured that he could dispossess forced labourers of the little valuables they carried. If he didn't get his way with the workers, he ordered his enslaved workers to jump into ice water or into containers full of acid and then proceeded to "scrub them down" using a wire brush. He would finish their treatment off with salt and soap rubbed in "to promote healing." Not surprisingly, many of his victims died during or after his "treatment." It was plain murder in the most sadistic way.[380] Felicija Karay reported countless other such hellish details in her book committed by many others.[381]

The confrontation with brigadier Fiett, his subsequent change of workplace, and the money he found and smuggled into the camp were not the only "Mazel Sachen" that occurred to my father and contributed to his survival. One story in particular was recounted by my father several times when I was a child and young man. It goes like this: Late one evening, being bored, he threw some corks, which were used to seal the grenades, against a small round window of one of the factories. To his great misfortune, a *Werkschutz* Guard had witnessed the activity and went on to confront my father.

On the following day, my father was taken to a supervisor at Werk A. He was a "*Volksdeutscher*", my father added.[382] As my father left his workplace to be taken to this supervisor, his father (my grandfather) was sure he had seen his son for the last time alive. But on that morning the supervisor must have had a good day and for whatever reason wasn't minded to give an order for the execution of my father. Potentially, he also judged my father to be of still good potential use for more work, my father's offence perhaps too miniscule even to a man with the power

---

[379] Ibid. f. and Frey (1949), p. 17
[380] From the documents of the Kamienna criminal trial, see Karay (2004), p. 92f and Frey (1949), p. 66
[381] Ibid. 92-97
[382] Volksdeutscher, an ethnic German from an area outside of Germany.

over life and death. He therefore decided that my father be brought back to his place of work instead, perhaps with a warning. The words my grandfather uttered when he spotted my father alive upon his return, my father never forgot: *"You have returned from heaven."*

17

The View from the Past

In February 2020, Imran Manzoor, a long-time friend, who organised at the time guided tours on the history of the Shoah in Poland, told me, that a college in Swindon in the South-West of England had asked him, if I could give them another lecture on the history of my father and mother for a group students aged 16 and 17 in line with their study of the holocaust.[383]

Imran is a British citizen born in Yorkshire of Pakistani-Muslim family background. His wife is Polish. He is a psychotherapist and psychoanalyst, who has been organising tours of Nazi murder sites, in particular Auschwitz for many years.

Many people he meets on these tours mistakenly hold him to be Jewish, which is why I particularly mention his background here, so it can break down stereotypes and assumptions.

Imran's own story is fascinating. For a while, he led a project that aimed to take radicalised Islamists to Auschwitz. There Imran showed them where the ideology of hatred, particularly hatred of Jewish people, led. Interestingly, I first met him after he had signed up to a seminar on

---

[383] Part of this chapter appeared in English here: Zylbersztajn, Daniel (2020). I was there, Medium, 21.4.2020

conflict-transformation work between Jewish Israelis and Palestinians with Israeli citizenship in the Jewish-Palestinian peace village *Wahat-Al-Salam – Neve Shalom*. But that is another story.

Swindon, a town in the south-west of England, was difficult to reach for the few elderly survivors and witnesses of the Shoah who were still alive and who mostly lived in the wider area around London. This is why the school was happy that I, who was the son of a survivor, would make myself available as the next best thing. As said, this was already the second time I had travelled to Swindon, as Imran had invited me some years earlier. Like the last time, my presentation would follow weeks of learning of their students on the Shoah and would be followed by a trip to Poland (on that occasion in 2020, I understand they just about managed literally just before lockdowns set in motion).

During the presentation, I intended to show the students a few photos of the Hasag Skarżysko-Kamienna labour camp. I mainly came across pictures of the ruins that remain today.

But what I was actually looking for was a picture giving an impression of the camp as it was during the Second World War. Continuing to search, I came across a newspaper article in Polish entitled "The Monstrous Secrets of the Skarżysko Factory" by the Polish journalist Tomasz Trepka. The report was accompanied by a black and white photo of what looked like some workers in one of the halls.[384]

The longer I examined this photo, the clearer it became: one of the faces of the persons on it was familiar to me in some way. There was a momentary hesitation. A man was standing there who was younger than I had ever seen him in my entire life. Could it be true, indeed, was it possible, that the familiar looking person was nobody else but my own father?

It was. My father was standing on the far left of the picture.

He appears with a serious look and gazes, as I read it, almost dismissively into the camera. Beside him was another surprise: The person

---

[384] Trepka (2016).

standing next to my father was my grandfather, Herszik. According to my father's testimony to the Shoah Foundation, my grandfather hadn't worked with the machine he is depicted with in the picture at all, but in another room sorting papers. It can be assumed that he was perhaps brought in for the purpose of this photo, or that he had also worked there from time to time.

The image of my grandfather was only the second picture of him that I have ever seen. The only other photo of him was also taken during the war years, with my father always emphasising that it did not portray his father well. On the picture, my father is about 24 years of age and my grandfather is in his early 40s. Both are standing behind the worktable that my father had described earlier. A large lathe can be seen on the worktable. Next to it lie other mechanical instruments and tools.

My father Wolf on the far left, next to his father, Herszl "Herszik," in Skarżysko-Kamienna.

What cannot be appreciated on the photo is the noise which most likely was surrounding the people in the picture. Adam Neuman-Nowicki, a survivor from the Hasag factories of Skarżysko-Kamienna who had also worked in a grenade pressing facility, mentioned however the noise, although the room he spoke of may or may not have been the same as the one in which my father worked:

> *My first visit to the Hasag factory left a great impression on me. Huge halls, the deafening noise of the presses, and huge machines and red-hot wrappings caught by forced labourers in mid-air, appearing like dwarves next to the gigantic furnaces.*[385]

Historians of Poland and the Shoah told me that I was extremely fortunate to have come across this photo. There are only a few photos of the Hasag factory of Skarżysko-Kamienna that have survived the war years, and finding one with my dad on it was like winning the lottery.

The discovery of this photo was one of the most special moments in my life. My father had never mentioned that anyone had ever taken photos of him and the others there. Indeed, such an occurrence may have been such a trivial event that he had long forgotten about it. Rediscovering the image in 2020 encouraged me to continue to write this book. It felt like a sign. And to do so was my act of resistance against amnesia and denial. If it had appeared during my father's lifetime, it would probably have reawakened many priceless recollections of the place in my father.

Amongst the many memories my father did share of his time in the labour camps, were also stories about resistance. It is known that the factories of Skarżysko-Kamienna were were places were workers engaged in sabotage acts. According to Toamasz Trepka's article, up to 40 per cent of the explosives made in Skarżysko-Kamienna were deliberately manufactured with faults or with water sealed inside them to render the gunpowder unusable, no longer exploding due to the locked in humidity. It should be noted, however, that Karay claimed that unexploded munitions were not caused by sabotage acts of Jewish forced labourers.[386] Who is right here? Karay's words contradict the testimony of my uncle,

---

[385] See Neuman-Nowicki's (1998), own translation
[386] Karay (2004), p. 96

things that he told me and which I remember. According to my uncle's stories, the workers would occasionally leave out the detonators from the munitions.

Karay also mentioned smuggling of weapons to the Polish underground.[387] Conversely, newspapers, money and other items were smuggled into the camp, as well as news such as on the Warsaw Uprising in August 1944 and the German defeat in Stalingrad in February 1943, for example.

After my father had been working in Skarżysko-Kamienna for three months, a starved forced labourer from Blashov approached him. He asked: "*Jingel (boy), how long have you been here?*"

When my father answered, "Three months", the man pronounced the following oracular statement:

"*You will survive this, for if you have endured three months, you will survive this!*"

Whilst I wouldn't be writing this book, if he hadn't, the truth is, he almost didn't survive. Once, during a roll call, my father and others were asked if they wanted to change to a different work-station based in Werk A because, apparently, they were looking for volunteers there. As Werk A was considered a place of lighter work, and because his brother Abraham was there, my father volunteered, only to be surprised to be pushed back into line by the guards. The initial disappointment soon turned into considerable relief, because the offer was just a macabre bloodthirsty trick. This was because any volunteers who were not pushed back as my father was, were taken away and instantly shot. "I still looked good," my father rationalised once again, as to why he had been pushed back in line.

---

[387] ibid. p. 117

18

Typhus

In 1943 the heavens would soon open again inside the factories of Skarzisko-Kamienna, yet would no longer be so "friendly." Typhus was a widespread disease passed on by lice that affected everyone housed in the camp. It is closely linked to the lack of hygienic conditions. Until 1949, there was no effective way to fight typhus, although optimal care for patients was deemed to help. Without any other treatment, typhus could and can be fatal, especially for people from mid-age onwards.

Hygienic toilets, bedrooms, washing facilities and clean clothing go a long way towards prevention. However, none of this was available to the enslaved forced labourers in the Hasag camp of Skarzisko-Kamienna, not even warm water or soap (warm water was only available in the camp of Werk B).[388]

The way the Germans forced Jews in these camps to live was nothing but shameful, given the fact that Germany had such a cultural obsession with hygiene that the country even had opened a Hygiene Museum as early as 1912.[389] The facilitation of death of Jews through typhus was

---

[388] The aforementioned hot water in Werk B contributed to the health of the forced labourers there, apart from the fact that it was the workplace of another of the camp's sadistic overseers. Karay (2004), pp. 141-161

[389] The Deutsches Hygiene Museum is still located in Dresden today https://www.dhmd.de/ (retrieved 4 February 2022)

in fact an intentional and desired outcome for the National Socialists. Those who were too slow, too weak and sick or both, in effect those who could no longer be exploited, would be murdered, if an early death did not come of its own accord.

According to my father, those selected to be shot were not only people who were ill, but also people who were not dressed "neatly" enough and or did not stand straight enough or who appeared to be unkempt or somehow "bad looking" to those inspecting them. During their "selections", there was a constant search for sickly and run-down people to be taken to the firing range.

Although there was an infirmary inside the camp, it totally lacked the ability to care or provide any medical treatment. Strigler mentioned this infirmary in his book.[390] Whatever care one could receive was only provided through further exploitation of the people unfortunate enough to end up in this facility. Those without any means to pay for services, simply received no help. As a result dead bodies were lying about, and these would often be piled on top of each other in ditches at the edge of the nearby forest. As if this would not be indignity enough, my father recalled that guards were sometimes shooting into these lifeless bodies with contempt as if they wished to make sure they were all really dead.

As already mentioned, up until the point where Germans had murdered nearly all Jewish people they could get their hands on, Hasag was able to rely on so called "Austauschjuden" – Exchange Jews. The "recruitment" of Jews from the Polish Radom district, that included my father, his brothers and their father, was in fact, one of those Exchange Jew "deliveries." Not long after my father had arrived at the camp, a further shipment of Austauschjuden, this time from the concentration camp Majdanek reached Skarżysko-Kamienna. Karay emphasised the significance of this and other "deliveries:" They were covert and "not official" deliveries. This was because Hasag was desperate for new supplies of labourers, having worked the previous ones to death. So the

---

[390] Strigler (2017)

Majdanek Austauschjuden were a much-needed under-hand resupply, achieved through the payment of a considerable bribe to the camp commander of Majdanek.[391] Hasag had become to rely on the supply of an almost free of charge enslaved work force as an essential basis of their mode of production. When that became suddenly endangered, they were willing to pay the SS whatever they asked for, so that operations could continue. For the SS it was a great business, for they would profit further from Jewish people who otherwise would have been murdered in the extermination camp.

There were further challenges for Hasag. The 1943 uprisings of Treblinka, Bialystok and Sobibor made the situation more difficult for Hasag, because the Nazi leadership were now even more focused to drive the mass murders on. An example of this was the "harvest festival action" of Trawniki between the 3rd and 8th of November 1943. A total of some 43,000 people were murdered in this short span of time, one of them was incidentally Georg Wolff, the son of Ernestine Wolff, née Lewandowski from Berlin.

And still Hasag succeeded to obtain more resupply of workers for its operations. This included a consignment of Jewish people from Plaszow. But this would be one of the last such transports. As far as the people already in the camp were concerned, each new arrival worsened the already poor hygienic conditions, as there were now even more people in the already overcrowded units, spreading typhus unstoppably and fast.

When my father arrived in Skarżysko-Kamienna in the winter of 1942, there had already been a typhus outbreak ongoing which was reported to have claimed the lives of many people.[392] The first of the small group of people from my father's town of Szczekociny to succumb to the disease was a man called Awrum Fromer. My uncle Abraham remembered him:

---

[391] Karay (2004), p 57f
[392] Karay (2004) p. 101f

Suddenly he (Awrum) came down with typhus. Everyone was sure he would not walk out of the hospital alive. However, he was very lucky: he looked as bad as a Muselman and a candidate for the execution(s). But when they came for him, he managed to hide… and saved himself. He survived and lives now in America.[393]

Eventually, my father also fell ill in spring 1943. When he initially developed a high fever, my grandfather took care to hide him under the lowest bed in the living quarters and put some bread by his side. He did this instead of taking my father to the infirmary, where hardly anyone could be helped anyway. This is where he remained for several days, falling into such a high fever that he had delusions that made him believe he was in an opera, as he remembered years later. After a few days, not yet recovered, he was instructed by my grandfather to get up and straighten himself despite his weakness and return to his place of work. At work, my grandfather once again "hid my father in a corner" so that he could continue to rest and get better. Once again, my father described his survival at that time as "just luck."[394]

His own father, my grandfather, was less "fortunate." About ten days later, he showed the first symptoms of typhus. He soon not only suffered from delusions, but also developed full blown meningitis, and it did not take very long until his body gave up the fight. In his interview with the Shoah Foundation, my father reported that my grandfather's body was simply thrown onto an open wagon heading for the shooting range and its trenches, where it was disposed of. Thus, that is where the body of my grandfather, may his memory be a blessing, rests.

It is extraordinary how much the second verse of the song about about the factories of Skarżysko-Kamienna cited earlier on, described the actual experiences of my father and his brothers, when it said:

---

[393] Swajzer (2010), p. 257, own translation
[394] Zylbersztajn, Wolf (2001)

*The father gone,
like an old stain
and the mother there.
It's the end – it's over…* "[395]

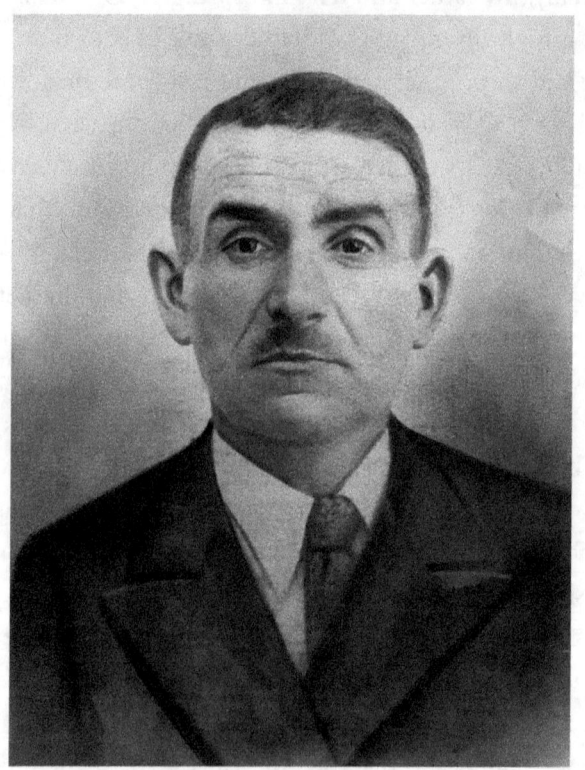

Herszik "Herszl" Zylbersztajn

---

[395] Strigler (2017), p. 388, own translation

19

Missing People, Questions and Answers

When I saw the testimony of my father for the Shoah Foundation for the first time, a year after his death, the part where my father spoke about his own father's death moved me. On previous visits to my parents, my requests to watch this testimony had been in vain, even though the Shoah Foundation had sent my parents a personal VHS copy (which still stands unwatched in my mother's cabinet at the time of writing). It was as if the video itself was a gruesome dead body in the drawer, that I was not supposed to see. One wonders, what my father would have said about my book, which now gives anyone who wishes more details about his life and that of his family and community than what he was able to leave behind.

It was the opportunity of a visit to Berlin in October 2012, shortly after starting my assignment for the German *taz* newspaper and the German Jewish weekly the *Jüdische Allgemeine*, that allowed me to watch the videoed testimony for the very first time. This was because Berlin had one of the few public access points for the Shoah Foundation archive (one also existed in London, but unlike the one in Berlin, it was rather far away from the city centre). That is how I ended up in the media room of a department at the Free University of Berlin, in front of a small monitor and with a set of shabby borrowed headphones, and how I finally began to watch the testimony that my father had left behind.[396]

There are many places during the interview where I wished for the interviewer to dig deeper. But there was a clash of purpose between my needs and those of the Shoah Foundation. The task of the foundation's interviewers was above all to collect information that would add evidence and verification to well-known events that occurred during the Shoah. The individual accounts of survivors often referred to stations, places, people and events that had also been mentioned by others. The more independent testimonies came together, the more robust was the evidence concerning certain events and places.

I am grateful to the Shoah Foundation for their great, important and essential initiative. What they recorded is better than nothing. Still, I had and continue to have many questions left unanswered during the interview.

To start with, there is a question to the foundation itself. Why on earth had they decided to interview my father in German, out of all languages? Indeed, my father spoke and understood German, but the language he had grown up with and in which he had experienced the Shoah emotionally, the language in which he could talk most fluently about it, was Yiddish. German in this context was clearly the language of the perpetrators. This was an oversight that may have been omitted due to pragmatic and convenient reasons, as the films were recorded in Munich, but they also show that there was a lack of understanding that the large majority of survivors, at least in Munich, actually came from Yiddish speaking backgrounds.

And then there was this scene in the recording when my father described how his father died of Typhus. My expectation was that the interviewer, it was Sabine Lessig, a psychotherapist and artist, would follow up on what my father had said. I was missing answers to many questions.

---

[396] Years later I was able to order my own copies.

Missing People, Questions and Answers

- What did the loss of his father mean at that moment?
- What did he discuss with his father before he died about the eventuality of him or anyone of the family dying?
- Were there plans for what would or should happen if someone in the family died?
- What were their assumptions about the rest of the family?
- What kind of person was my grandfather?
- What was going on in my father's head after his father died? Maybe he would have just said, "We never thought about anything like that, we were focussed on surviving day by day." Or he may have talked about promises and words of perseverance, discussions of what my father ought to do if he survived.
- The loss of a father and companion is something profound. Did my father say Kaddish, did he vow to avenge the loss, or promise himself to survive with even greater determination?
- What happened after he suddenly no longer lived with his father and had to go to work on his own? Had he shed a tear, or was crying no longer possible?
- How did he tell his brothers about the passing of their father and how did they react, what did they say to each other?

There will never be answers to all of these questions. People like me must learn to live with these voids.

Since the Shoah Foundation was mainly concerned with the establishment, confirmation and verification of facts and the personal journey of survivors through the Shoah, questions like those I posed may have been less important. But these points were and are essential for relatives and descendants. They seem to show us that each individual came from a family, with their own experiences of loss.

Of course, it didn't help that my parents hid the recording in a drawer and never gave me the opportunity to watch during my father's lifetime. Nor did I have the presence of mind to try to watch it, before he had died. Had I seen the video before my father's death, I may have been able to follow up on the testimony and fill in the gaps with further answers from my father.

Whatever could have been asked about the moment of my grandfather's death, my father and his father were certainly extremely close to each other. They slept next to each other, worked next to each other and suffered from the same illnesses. Until my grandfather's death, they had suffered the same fate, witnessed the same loss of my grandmother, after all my father's mother and my grandfather's wife and others, and they witnessed together brutal inhuman abuse and murder.

Besides the little that is known about my grandfather, I also lack entirely a description of my father's mother. Was that overlooked, or perhaps not investigated on purpose?

My father always said that he could remember everything in the most minute detail, that he could see everything in front of his eyes and that he regularly dreamt about what happened. Is it possible that his mother was absent from his memories, too painful to access and talk about? It was instead the memory of his younger brother Fiszl, that came to the forefront and for whom, perhaps, the memory and the pain of the loss became symbol of all the losses he experienced, including that of his mother.

Why had I never been told more? I had lived with my father for decades, thought a lot about the Shoah and talked to my father regularly about it.

The answer is that even if I had asked my father more questions, and I did try that many times, there were often no answers given. My father lost himself too quickly in "heavy thoughts" about this. I remember how he often avoided my questions, and didn't want to sit down with me for too long to discuss the past. He lacked the appreciation of my need to know the history of filling in the voids at least with some stories, of my desire to find out more about him, his – and therefore also of my – family. A "well, that's enough" often ended any attempt I made to put searching questions to him. The only exception was an interview with my father about the post-war period. It was 45-minutes long, and I was even allowed to record the conversation. But that interview too ended with the words "that's enough now."

During the Shoah Foundation interview, my father was also asked about his memories from before the Shoah, but he was far more focussed on the Shoah and wanted to pass on what the Germans had done to him and his family. The time before the Shoah? It was not sufficiently relevant.

The Shoah Foundation video was a unique opportunity to open the "Pandora's Box" of my father's closed off memories. My father understood this, as is evident by what he wore. He dressed elegantly in a grey jacket and a shirt. Not only that. My father was troubled by a cold on that day. Instead of postponing the interview, he was determined to give testimony without delay.

I wonder why the Shoah Foundation chose to make these recordings only over one day. I say that, because memories are usually fragmentary; after the statement on one day, there is a flow of further memories that get triggered by it. A visit a few days after the initial interview, perhaps even a phone call, could have ensured that these after-memories were also being recorded. The trauma inflicted onto our parents was often deeply buried. It required more time. Perhaps such a method was neither practical nor possible.

But at the same time, nothing in the world can make up for lost opportunities. My life and that of my family and descendants is poorer for that. It tells us less about the people who were murdered. It is a loss that cannot be put into words – an irreplaceable empty void.

20

Between Death and Happiness

I already wrote that the conditions in the Skarżysko-Kamienna camp improved in the spring of 1944 under revised management rules. Amongst the changes were increased food rations. Inspite of that, there were still terrible things taking place in the camp. Karay lists many strange incidents that my father had kept completely silent about. She reported public executions and deliberate violence inflicted upon the enslaved population. Karay also reported on rather difficult to imagine occurrences. An example was a competition and a prize for "the cleanest barrack" amidst it all, or that there were SS-informants who served as double-agents, assisting Jewish prisoners with aid from the Jewish Aid Council in Krakow.[397]

In the end Soviet troops moved ever closer to the area in which Skarżysko-Kamienna was located. As a result the entire work complex was ordered to be shut down. The same fate awaited most other work camps. Many Jewish enslaved labourers, now no longer needed, would be transported to Auschwitz-Birkenau extermination camp. But for those who were "SS property" like those hired by Hasag in Skarżysko-Kamienna, there were other plans: More exploitation!

---

[397] Karay (2004). p. 125f

Between Death and Happiness

During the Shoah Foundation interview, my father stated, that he left Skarżysko-Kamienna towards the end of August 1943, but incidentally, he got the year wrong. In fact, he stayed in Skarżysko-Kamienna for a whole year longer, until August 1944, just before the camp had been shut. We know this because of copies of my father's registration documents at Buchenwald Concentration Camp. It recorded the exact date of his arrival as the 5th of August 1944.[398]

When my father was subjected to another "selection", conducted by, as he remembered, a one-armed German officer prior to his departure from Skarżysko-Kamienna, he suspected that he was going to be sent to one of those extermination camps, people spoke about.[399]

In fact, the killings continued, though not in Auschwitz but in Skarżysko-Kamienna and that right after the selection. In addition, some 250 forced labourers tried to escape from Werk C in the night of 30 July 1944. They were soon tracked down, caught not far from the camp and executed. The 1,500 "chosen ones" for further exploitation, a group that included my father, could be considered "lucky" whilst they were being deported. Their destination was not Auschwitz, but Buchenwald and Częstochowa. A further 1000 people followed them in the month after.

Declared as still "fit for work," my father travelled to Buchenwald in an open train carriage. One of his brothers was also in the carriage with him, the other brother would follow later. His thoughts were gloomy, he said. "We'd all heard about Treblinka," he retold. It is probable he and others also knew of the murder operations from people who had

---

[398] His departure from Skarżysko-Kamienna occurred on 1 August 1944. According to information provided by the researchers of Schlieben-Berga Subcamp Memorial Site, this was also recorded in the records of other Buchenwald "prisoners", for example in the records of Peter Schwarz. What these dates also mean, is that it is hence impossible to estimate whether my grandfather died in 1944 or 1943. Hasag did not record the deaths of the forced labourers by name, and the Hasag files were all blown up before the end of the war in order to destroy as much evidence as possible.

[399] Karay mentions a one-armed commander at Werk C, his name was Friedrich Schulze, a former Wehrmacht officer whose nickname was Raczak (little arm) because of his prosthesis, Karay (2004), p. 212.

come to Skarżysko-Kamienna from death camps like Majdanek. and for a while at least, the destination of the journey remained uncertain.

The departures also brought the chapter of the Skarżysko-Kamienna Hasag murder factories to an end. The German factory management instructed the burning of many of the buried and now decomposing bodies before vacating the site. The intention was the destruction of any evidence that could reveal their odious crimes. Over the course of the camp's existence, some 20,000 people had been sent to the labour camp, 14,000 of whom, around seventy percent, perished there.[400] On 1 January 1945, large parts of the camp were ultimately dismantled, whilst many of the factory Buildings, including Werk C remained.

During his lifetime, my father hinted at best to some of the painful details of the camp life. Karay was braver and more generous in her book for the sake of truth. This included accounts on the sexual violence committed by the German administration, which included sex orgies, rape and murder.[401] She also reported on relationships and relationships of convenience between female and male enslaved forced workers, and even on the birth of children, some of whom had to be murdered by their mothers after they gave birth.[402] Pregnancy alone was in fact sufficient reason to murder any woman.

Karay reported that there were also real relationships in the mixed camp. Jewish people from the smaller towns like that of my father would

---

[400] ebd.
[401] Those guilty of these crimes included Fritz Bartenschläger, who was considered a leading these and, Kurt Krause, Otto Eisenschmidt, Paul Kiesling, Franz Schippers, Willi Seidel and Iwan Romano (an Ukrainian Volksdeutscher Werkschutz officer). An orgy and rape is described in the testimony of Szlomo Grinszpan, who reported how six unfortunate women were pulled out of the crowd after their arrival at roll call, ordered into a room, told to deliver food naked and who were consequently raped. *All but one woman were murdered the very next day.* The names of three of the victims were Cesia Kaplanski, Ewa Ernest and Bela Hercberg-Goldman. The names of the perpetrators were: Böttcher, Paul Feucht and Schippers. The names of the other victims were Gucia Michman, 19, Ruchama Eisenberg and Mania Silberman. According to the testimonies of Chaim Milchman and Srul Najman. In Karay (2004), p. 81
[402] Karay (2004), p.116

have been more reserved in this respect, but threw their conservative hesitations slowly overboard as time went on. I wondered whether my grandfather, my father or my uncles also may have had a girlfriend or "cousin" in the camp. But I assume that they probably did not, because they inherently didn't trust anyone anymore, and they also had each other for support.

Karay also reported on the existence of a crematorium located next to "*Werk C*", in a cordoned-off area of the nearby forest. Here, the mortal remains of up to 35,000 people escaped from the chimneys, most of whom had previously been gassed in lorries on the way to the crematorium.[403]

---

[403] Ibid. p.64.f (the victims were not just people who were former enslaved workers, but also others, including POWs)

21

68516 – Buchenwald

Entrance gate to the Buchenwald concentration camp, Buchenwald Memorial, 2022. Photo DZL.

Weimar
The silence of a democratic people's city. A blandly dressed people, half are residents, half are visitors of the big city.
That metropolis of your Bach, Schiller and Goethe –

What would these greats have made oft the fourth actors in their midst? A Karl-Otto Koch, Adolf Hitler or Björn Höcke?
Just a local bus journey away, human beings were imprisoned and tortured, they were starved and often they broke.

> *Today's Ukrainian flags and the LGBTQIA+ symbol alongside the town hall cannot distract from those blue and white striped uniforms of Buchenwald, soaked in sweat and blood, or the fact that the swastika in front of a red background once flew here.*
>
> *Not everyone wants to know this, but the dead-straight railway tracks, which still cut through this beautiful city, remind us even today (whilst we are admiring the culture of this town) of other things that are likewise parts of the possibilities of human potential: they talk about the infliction of suffering, of imprisonment and death and the fact that many observed and watched while they remained silent. All of that, in spite of the school and tradition of beautiful words and that wondrous music and the proud roots of democracy, that this city gave birth to.*

Hand-written note,
Daniel Zylbersztajn-Lewandowski, August 2022,
English version of original German, translated by the author.

The destination of the train my father had been ordered onto was the Buchenwald Concentration Camp. At the time that my father would arrive there, the camp would have been overcrowded, initially planned for 18,660 inmates, over 31,491 people had been accommodated in the camp by mid-August 1944. My uncle Abraham wrote concerning his arrival there that the main thoughts he had, as he arrived, concerned whether he could get something to eat, as he and the others had not eaten anything for a considerable time.

The short journey from the train ramp in Buchenwald to the so-called "Kleine Lager", a place at the far end of the camp where my father and his two brothers were to be housed, is said to have been accompanied by deliberate acts designed to humiliate the arrivals and put them in their place. The SS personnel were keen to demonstrate to any new arrivals that they were to be seen as the masters.[404] This meant that new arrivals were not only beaten, but that dogs could be set on them.[405] In addition, everything in the camp was designed to make life more difficult for the prisoners. For example, the camp had been deliberately erected on the side of a hill that was usually exposed to the winds. In spite of this, my father nevertheless reported some relief.

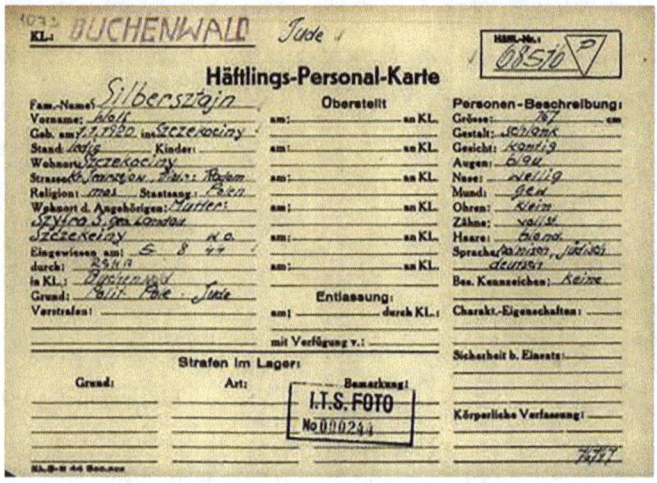

My father's registration card in Buchenwald.

Years later, my uncle judged that they were treated more like refugees inside Buchenwald. Nobody beat them or persecuted them, he said. The reason was that Buchenwald was not administered by the SS or the *Werkschutz*, but by a "camp administration" made up of other inmates.

---

[404] Pamela Castillo Feuchtmann, teacher for education and guided tours at the Buchenwald Memorial. Statement during my visit there, August 2022. "Kleine Lager" German for "Little Camp."

[405] Ibid.

According to surviving registration documents, at arrival my father possessed 400 Reichsmarks, 200 of which were taken from him on arrival.[406] Money was also taken from my uncle Abraham and his other brother, my uncle Dawid. Dawid even held 855 Reichsmarks at the beginning. They probably never saw that money again.[407] After the confiscations, the newly arrived had their hair shorn. Then they were sent to shower rooms, which spread immense worry and fear to everyone, because they could not be sure, if these were the often spoken about disguised gas chambers.

However, these were real showers, and they were probably only treated with an anti-lice agent. Somewhat relieved, they were handed out striped uniforms. *"It was wonderful,"* my father described the new

---

[406] 400 Reichsmark (1924-1945) corresponds to around 4,200 Euros (1998-2015). Source https://www.historicalstatistics.org/Currencyconverter.html (retrieved on 6 February 2022)

[407] This was the opinion of Jürgen Wolf, the director of the memorial site of KZ-Schlieben.

condition he found himself under, and he praised being without lice and with "sufficient food", "*a better soup with a bit of bread.*"[408]

My father was now assigned a prisoner number. Number 68516, his brother Abraham was given the number 68517 and the third of the brothers, Dawid, the number 68502.

The registration card of my father states that my father had "allegedly never been seriously ill." If this remark originated from my father, he must have concealed his battle with typhus. His date of birth was recorded as 1 January 1920, not his real date of birth.

They were to be accommodated in bottomless tents in which ten people had to lie on the ground side by side.[409] Whether my father, who had stood up courageously in Skarżysko-Kamienna to keep his boots, now had to wear wooden clogs like most others and walk with these over the uneven ground of the camp must remain an unanswered question.

But the supposed "paradise" that had followed the hell of Skarżysko-Kamienna also offered other opportunities: It was a place for the first chances of revenge after years of humiliations, beatings, torture and murder.

---

[408] Zylbersztajn, Wolf (2001)
[409] Pamela Castillo Feuchtmann Educator for education and guided tours In the Buchenwald Memorial. Statement during my visit there, August 2022.

According to my father, a "red-haired" member of the camp administration queried the new arrivals as to whether there were any people among their number who had mistreated and beaten them in the past.[410] These administrative guards were political prisoners with the task of the maintenance of order in the camps. My father recalled a number of such people who had mistreated them, and even remembered some names, "Tepperman" and "Krzepicki", amongst others.

Karay also mentioned these names. My father recalled that the red-haired man announced that anyone who had an appetite for it, was allowed to take revenge. This led to the execution of about 20 persons. "There were "gefährliche Menschen (dangerous / cruel people) among the Kapos", was how my father described it, by which he meant people who were sadists who had no regard for the lives of others.

This is the only time my father mentioned Kapos and Jewish guards in his recollections. In Skarżysko-Kamienna there were Jewish camp elders (responsible for the daily list of Jewish camp inmates), a Jewish police force and other similar functionaries.[411] In her book, Karay documented punitive measures taken by kapos "who had sold their souls to the devil", and whose methods included whippings and beatings that sometimes would only stop with the death of a victim. So it is perhaps no wonder that such tormentors were being dealt with, when and as the opportunity for raw justice arose. Not all Kapos and policemen however were targeted. According to Karay there were others who had tried to carry out their tasks with degrees of kindness and humanity by warning and even protecting people.[412]

My uncle could also remember the opportunity to take revenge in Buchenwald:

---

[410] Charles Kotowsky also spoke of a red-haired leader of Block 66 named Gustaw, allegedly from Lviv. He also mentions him as part of a gang of thugs who made it their business to kill "bad apples." See Kotkowky, Charles, Memoirs of a Survivor.
[411] Karay (2004) p. 85
[412] ebd.

> *Once there was an appeal to us in which the older people in the barracks asked us who had treated us badly in Skarżysko. At first, we were afraid to say anything, but after the question had been repeated multiple times, we got bolder and pointed to the Kapo from the camp who had beaten us bloody for every small thing. The elders ordered him and other Kapos to be taken away. Then they turned to us and said: "Do as you please with them, you can even choose to kill them." We did indeed beat them to death. It was our first revenge, even though we hadn't been liberated yet."* [413]

Did the "we" in this sentence mean that my uncle had participated in this summary act of murderous raw justice? I cannot answer this question, nor do I dare to make a moral judgement about it.

Inside Buchenwald, my father and his brothers encountered a surreal new order. Amongst other oddities was a street that the people in Buchenwald had labelled the Champs-Élysées, which was very close to the small camp. Why Champs-Élysées? On one side of the street was a small park, that was located next to the camp's infirmary. In its centre was a path which, due to its proximity to the park, became the place for "Sunday strolls" by the imprisoned. Opposite the infirmary was a cinema and a brothel in which enslaved women who had been forced into prostitution, were to sexually serve political and German (non-Jewish) prisoners who held higher positions. Their services led to rewards for various jobs and favours.[414]

Pamela Castillo Feuchtmann told me during my visit to the Buchenwald memorial site that the latrines were among the most important places in Buchenwald because the guards did not enter them out of fear of infection. As a result, bartering, exchanges of information and other social life took place in the safety of the stench of these latrines. My father had never mentioned such things, perhaps out of shame, but it

---

[413] Szwajcer, 1959, p. 258
[414] Pamela Castillo Feuchtmann, see before.

was said to be the only place of relative freedom.[415] My father's statement that he met in Skarżysko-Kamienna with his brothers and his father "in the bathroom" of Werk A comes close to describing such a place, only expressed in a more polite way.

There were daily roll calls in Buchenwald. My father had witnessed the camp band, which would sometimes ironically play the German folk tune "Alle Vögel sind schon da".[416]

Buchenwald remains a place of tensions between good and evil due to its proximity to the city of Weimar, a famous city of culture with its links to Bach and Goethe and the birthplace of modern German democracy and the Bauhaus Movement. In the camp, the Nazis tasked the enslaved workers with cultural tasks too, for example to manufacture replicas of Schiller's furniture. The central figure of the camp commandant was Karl-Otto Koch. He had the gate of the camp crafted with an ironic inscription. It read: "*Jedem das Seine*" ("To each his own") and it could and can still only be read correctly until this day from the inside. After he was found guilty of corruption, he was – "*Jedem das Seine*" – executed in the name of the German Third Reich by other Nazis in the very camp he had once led.[417]

Another anomaly of Buchenwald was the small zoo that Koch had established right in front of the camp. Visitors of the "master-race", mostly SS employees and their lovers on their days off, had full sight of not just animals behind fences, but humans behind fences (the camp's fences) too, supposedly those who were according to eugenic race theory members of the Jewish "subspecies" and not quite as human as Germans. Koch also ordered the manufacture of special "gift items", that were true souvenirs, illustrating the falling from grace and from all accepted human moral and religious conventions and norms by the

---

[415] ibid.
[416] ibid. "All the birds are already here." There were three string quartets in Buchenwald and even jazz was demanded by the SS leadership, according to the guidelines of the Third Reich, the latter was forbidden "degenerate music."
[417] ibid.

individual leaders of the Third Reich. There were paperweights made from the shrunken skulls of murdered victims in that special collection, much desired SS-trophies. Other items manufactured were bags and lampshades made out of human skin, that had been removed from the corpses of the victims of the camp. "These things may sound insane, but it is important to understand that the people behind these ideas lived outwardly "normal lives" as totally normal persons", the Buchenwald Memorial Site educator told me, and went on to show me photos from the family albums of SS-personnel, including Karl-Otto Koch.[418] They showed people posing with their family members with smiles for the camera.

The Communist German Republic that had ruled this area after the Second World War understood that horrible crimes had taken place in Buchenwald. However, they misled and falsified the remembrance, by wrongly emphasising Buchenwald as a place where the German Communist Party (KPD) leader Ernst Thälmann had been executed, which was true, but this was certainly not the only or main thing that happened there worthy of remembrance.

As my father only stayed in Buchenwald for a very short time, I won't say much more about this camp and would refer you to the book published by the Buchenwald Memorial Site Foundation: "*Buchenwald. Ausgrenzung und Gewalt*" (Buchenwald. Exclusion and Violence) for more information.[419]

---

[418] ibid.
[419] Knigge (2020)

22

Hasag Camp Schlieben

Schlieben, former railway station budling. From 1944 onwards, human transports were transported directly into the camp.

After twelve days of "paradise-like" circumstances, as my dad called it, he and his two brothers were ordered to mount an open-top train carriage on 14 August 1944. In some respects, that was already another lucky straw in a bad situation, because the worst period for occupants of the "small camp" in Buchenwald, where they were housed, was only just beginning. Thousands of people from other disbanded camps had arrived and were to be housed there in the coming months. It eventually would cause the premature death of countless people due to increased lack of hygiene and lack of food. Only a small minority survived, one of whom would later be well known as a man who tried to hunt down former Third Reich perpetrators and tormentors – Eli Wiesel.

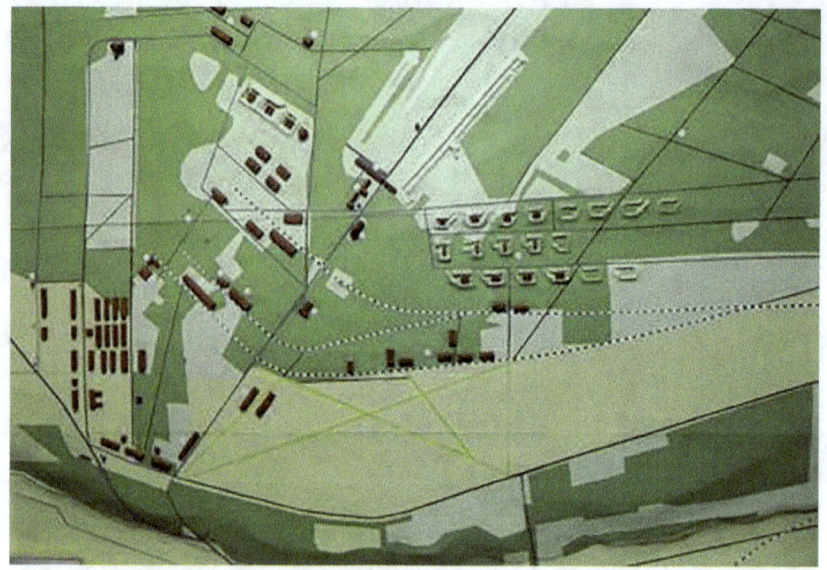

Model of the Schlieben Hasag plant in the memorial in Schlieben. Photo DZL.

From a distance, wherever that train passed by, its human cargo inside the open wagon would have been quite visible to anyone looking, including ordinary civilians in Germany along the track. The planned destination of the train was Schlieben in the state of Brandenburg. Schlieben was another strictly guarded Hasag camp, under the control of SS-Untersturmführer Hans Kempe and his subordinate Wehrmacht sergeant Richard Müller.[420]

---

[420] Martin Schnellenberg, „Die Schnellaktion Panzerfaust" in Dachauer Hefte (2005), p. 246

It was one of several new satellite camps of Hasag that included Taucha, Leipzig, Altenburg, Meuselwitz, Colditz and Flößberg.[421] In total, there were some 1,200 such Nazi concentration camps associated with various German companies.

Schlieben specialised in the production of carbine and gun ammunition, as well as in explosive rifle grenades, bazookas and parts for mines including anti-tank mines. According to information provided by today's memorial site, the enslaved workers who had joined from Skarżysko-Kamienna were mainly tasked with the production of anti-tank ammunitions.[422]

Schlieben was the result of a decision made in September 1944 by Albert Speer (Reich Minister for Armaments and War Production), granting Hasag special powers under the name "*Schnellaktion Panzerfaust*" – rapid action Panzerfaust. A revised tank design of the Soviet troops (T-34), which made existing German ammunition less effective, was the reason behind this decision. Production was to start by autumn and winter of 1944/45.[423] Paul Budin had already convinced SS Reichsführer Himmler to set up such new production sites in June 1944.

A total of 50,000 "Gretchen" handgun cartridges were to be produced. Hidden deep in a forest, the Schlieben factory was however not only a production site, but also a development and testing facility, putting 2515 people to work. Amongst these counted women and Indian prisoners of war.[424]

Having been housed in tents in Buchenwald, my father and his brothers were now assigned to live inside barracks. At the very least, these were fitted with wood-burning stoves, though in spite of being surrounded by trees, there was scarcely any firewood to feed them. Crate

---

[421] Ibid. 244
[422] My father spoke of" Kick and Lehmann." Jürgen Wolf noted that "Lehmann" at least meant the production department.
[423] Martin Schnellenberg: Die Schnellaktion Panzerfaust in Dachauer Hefte (2005), p. 237
[424] Martin Schnellenberg: Die Schnellaktion Panzerfaust in Dachauer Hefte (2005), S. 247

wood brought from work had to do. On the other hand, there was a complete lack of washing facilities.[425]

The work was similar to that they had known in Skarżysko-Kamienna, not the least because as the production of armoured ammunition at the Schlieben plant was carried out by former workers from the Skarżysko-Kamienna camp. My father and his brother worked in the transport detachment and delivered the not-so-heavy empty shell casings to the foundry.

My father remembered a few details of his days in Schlieben. Once, he said, he had dared to go into what he had called the "Italian Barack", where, as he went on to say, he had not been forced to work. Among these Italian prisoners of war, my father noticed one thing in particular: "*They sang all day long.*"[426]

A major challenge was something else. There was not enough to eat. My father told me about a morning "coffee", soup for lunch and one hundred grams of "heavy bread, like clay" for dinner.[427] Nothing occupied the minds of the imprisoned more than the question of whether the daily soup they would get, might contain a piece of potato. "*You would only talk about food!*" was how my father summarised his time in Schlieben.[428] Instead of potatoes, however, the soup contained mainly old noodles, alongside boiled insects and worms. Any reader, whose stomach turns with the thought of such a meal, should read on, as to what my father thought of it, given there was nothing else to eat: "*We ate it so wonderfully. It was very good, it wasn't bad at all!*"[429] As in Skarżysko-Kamienna, the Kapos kept the thicker bottom of the broth for themselves, my father remembered.

---

[425] Ibid.
[426] These were prisoners of war at the time of Pietro Badoglio, as I was told by the Memorial Site administration.
[427] Isaak Wargon, another slave labourer, confirmed these rations independently of my father, in Martin Schnellenberg: Die Schnellaktion Panzerfaust in Dachauer Hefte (2005), p. 247.
[428] Zylbersztajn, Wolf (2001), Cassette IV, 4:00
[429] Ibid. 5:00

As already hinted, the "prisoners" in Schlieben were not just Jewish enslaved SS-forced labourers. According to my father, some were also German criminals. One of them was a man who had been given a Kapo post and, according to my father, was called Erich. "He was a *Verbrecher!*" was all my father said and then immediately hurried on to talk about how many people had died in Schlieben. In my father's vocabulary, the word "*Verbrecher*", German and Yiddish for criminal, stood for nothing less than that person who was a brute abuser and murderer. Presumably there was a connection between the dead and people like Erich. And indeed, many people perished in Schlieben, but it wasn't only because of bad Kapos.[430] The aforementioned food restrictions and the extremely poor hygienic living conditions contributed too. Menasze Hollender, a Schlieben survivor, described how he had not been able to wash himself for some five months and that the entire camp-population was plagued by lice and other parasites. Similar to Werk C of Skarżysko-Kamienna, there existed also "*Prikiner*" in Schlieben, who would quickly fall ill and suffer agonising deaths due to the damage caused through their unprotected contact with tetryl and picric acid.[431]

"*A lot of people died there,*" was how my father summarised the conditions in Schlieben.[432] What didn't help was that Schlieben lacked unity amongst the enslaved Jewish population. They appear to have separated themselves according to their linguistic backgrounds. People from Hungary only regretted the deaths of people from their country, but not the losses of Jews from Poland and probably it was also the same way the other way around.[433]

---

[430] According to research by the Schlieben Concentration Camp Memorial, 222 prisoners (8 women and 214 men) died in Schlieben. 251 of the sick who were sent back to Buchenwald from Schlieben died there, 50 of the prisoners deported from Schlieben to Flößberg perished there and 30 in other camps. The number of prisoners who died on the evacuation transports from Schlieben has not yet been determined. Footnote with thanks to Jürgen Wolf.

[431] Martin Schnellenberg, the quick action Panzerfaust in Dachauer Hefte (2005), S. 248

[432] Zylbersztajn (2001) Cassette IV 6:00

[433] Ibid.

Ruins of the factories in Schlieben today. The buildings were built deep into the ground and fitted with a light roof to minimise damage in the event of an explosion. Photo DZL.

Starving, without any money and unlike in Skarżysko-Kamienna, without much access to the world outside (though see later on food) the camp that would facilitate smuggling operations, my father was desperate not to surrender to the fate of an eventual death. He kept looking for a way out. Incredibly, he found what he was looking for. With wit, and courage, he was able to locate a food-storage room.[434] During an unobserved and quiet moment he seized the opportunity and dug a hole from the outside right under the exterior wall and into the actual storage chamber. Putting his arm through, he struck gold – dried potatoes! In that manner, he was able to supplement his meagre diet with important and literally life-saving calories. It was again one of those moments that my father always referred to as "Mazel Sachen."[435]

---

[434] These dried-out potatoes were frequently supplied to concentration and labour camps during the Third Reich

[435] Mazel Sachen, yid. lucky things

Hasag Camp Schlieben

Kitchen / kitchen store in Schlieben. It was probably here (building on the left) that my father found dried potatoes by reaching through a hole he had dug himself. Photo DZL.

When I visited the Memorial Site constructed on what is left over from the original site in 2022, Dr Jürgen Wolf, a member of the board of the association that looks after the memorial site in Schlieben, walked with me to the very building which, as far as he knew, had been the camp's kitchen and food storage. Some 80 years later, the building was not only still standing but provided a home to some locals. It was incredible to stand there, and think about my father and if there had been nobody living in there, I would have liked to meditate on that and take my time to take it all in.

Martin Schnellenberg's research on the concentration camp in Schlieben suggested that there were also other ways to get a little bit more to eat than the Nazis had intended. Just as in Skarżysko-Kamienna, prisoners traded useful items they had crafted for food. And, whilst there may not have been a great market for other smuggled items, forced labourers who worked in the surrounding villages did indeed smuggle food into the camp, which they then exchanged for those aforementioned items in return.[436]

---

[436] Martin Schnellenberg, „Die Schnellaktion Panzerfaust" in Dachauer Hefte 21/2005, p. 247

My uncle Abraham described the conditions in Schlieben however as nothing but dire:

> *(In Schlieben) bitter days began again. Within but one month, we had to construct an entire factory where new anti-tank weapons were to be be manufactured. There was no food. The only consolation was that nobody was shot. But as there was nothing to eat, people were starving.*
>
> *In the meantime, the Red Army occupied the whole of Poland. They had already reached Kostrzyn, just 100 kilometres away from us. We were convinced that the Russians would come to liberate us. Unfortunately, the work became more difficult (at the same time). We worked by day and night. I and my brothers Wolf and Dawid worked night shifts.*

During one such night shift on 12 October 1944, one of the grenade factories exploded in the early hours of the morning. It was the so-called foundry in which the explosives for the bazookas were "cooked" and mixed. The initial explosion caused a chain of further blasts, the last of which occurred around 5.30 am. To this day, it is not entirely clear whether this was an act of sabotage, a tragic industrial accident or even an air raid, although Dr Jürgen Wolf, who runs the memorial site of KZ Schlieben, told me that it was in all probability down to an accident. The roof of the barrack my father had been working in had been blown off, though he and one of his brothers escaped without great injury. The third brother was however trapped under a beam. My father said that he was able to lift the beam and free his brother. At first it seemed, as if he did not sustain any major injuries either.[437]

Having survived this, the three fled with others into the nearby forest. It was not a minute too soon, because suddenly there was yet

---

[437] It is not clear which of the brothers was trapped. It is reasonable to assume that it was however, Dawid.

another explosion. This time it was so forceful, that, according to my father, the trees were shaking from it. Confused, they ran towards some houses where German civilians lived and where, according to my father, a German man helped them to examine Abraham's wounds and injuries, as he was bleeding. Other workers also reported running towards the villages. According to information provided by the memorial site of KZ Schlieben, workers fleeing the site ran not only into the neighbouring town town of Berga, but also into the neighbouring village of Striesa. Witness accounts confirmed that injured workers had been treated there.[438]

Soon enough young men in SS uniforms tried to gather some of the escaped back into the camp. There they were ordered to assist with the rescue and containment of the fire. The devastation they found there was immense, with debris scattered across the entire site. "*There was no-one at Lehmann's. Everyone was dead,*" said my father.[439] According to official figures, the explosions killed a total number of 96 of the enslaved workers.[440]

Here is the description of the event, as laid down by my uncle Abraham. In his account, he believed that the explosions were caused by US-bombing raids. The account also differs slightly from that of my father. In particular, my uncle believed he had walked to Schlieben on his own. He also described his state of mind as "having gone insane." It is conceivable that he simply found himself in a state of shock, and that could also have influenced the sequence of events in his recollections:

Suddenly, around one o'clock in the morning, we suddenly heard a loud explosion. The entire department of the factory where we worked was affected.

---

[438] During my visit with Dr Jürgen Wolf in August 2022.
[439] Zylbersztajn, Wolf (2001), Cassette IV 9:50. Jürgen Wolf stated that with "Lehmann" meant the "Production" department, the other department of the Hasag plant in Schlieben was the "Foundry".
[440] Martin Schnellenberg, The Rapid Action Panzerfaust, in Dachauer Hefte (2005), S. 250

It was only with great difficulty that I managed to get out of that place, after which I ran with whatever remained of my strength deep into the (neighbouring) forest without stopping. When I had run about a kilometre, a further sudden violent explosion overwhelmed me. I can still hear the sound of that explosion in my ears and shall never cease to forget it. The ammunition in the factory had blown up… The bomb dropped by American planes hit the target. Thousands of ready-made German bombs began to burn and to explode, fuelling such a (gigantic) fire that it seemed as if the entire world was on fire and now ablaze.

Plaque at the memorial site by amateur artist and journalist Hartmut Sommerschuh on the history of the Schlieben labour camp. Photo DZL.

I went crazy while at the same time I found myself bleeding from wounds. Nevertheless, I continued to flee from this terrible hell, where death lurked at every turn. Eventually I reached the town of Schlieben. There I was arrested and handed over to a doctor, who treated my wounds and asked me to return to the barracks.

The camp was three kilometres from the factory. On the way back, I met my two brothers, who had been already mourning me, convinced that I had succumbed under the rubble.[441]

---

[441] Szwajcer 1959, p. 258, translation by the author

23

Hammer's Marmalade

After the destruction of the factories, my father and his brothers went their separate ways. This was because my father was allocated to a new work task with a central heating company called Hammer Heating. His main function was to assist them with welding-jobs.[2] As my father recalled, German criminals sentenced to forced penal labour also worked alongside him there. I don't know what kind of people they were.

Apart from the address of the Hammer company, an invoice and a few advertising photos, no other documents could be found during the research. However the Schlieben-Berga Memorial Site was aware that Hasag also lent some of its enslaved labourers on to other companies. After I told the Schlieben-Berga memorial centre about my father's testimony, they initially knew nothing about the heating company he had cited. But they took the initiative and asked an elderly heating engineer in Schlieben whether he had ever come across this central heating company. To everyone's surprise, the man could not only remember the company, but also confirmed that it carried out different jobs in Schlieben during the war years. The memorial centre for forced labour in Leipzig (Gedenkstätte für Zwangsarbeit in Leipzig) further found out that the company in question, "Max Hammer", founded in 1884, which once had had its headquarters in Leibzig in Naumburgerstraße

31, was no longer in existence.. Their managing director in 1945 was a man who was listed as Herrmann Ulrich. Since the files of HASAG AG were destroyed, a direct connection could not be documented. But according to other local witnesses, the Hammer company would install radiators in private homes in Schlieben. During my visit to Schlieben I was shown a house where residents recalled precisely that.

My father appeared to have impressed his new German supervisors due to the speed and agility in which he completed the tasks assigned to him. It was a discipline he had acquired in the merciless hell of the factories of Skarżysko-Kamienna. Here it seemed to give him an advantage.

> *They were polishers, all master craftsmen, I helped them a lot and learnt a lot. They would say Wolf, go and get on that ladder. They thought a lot of me.*[442]

By "going up that ladder", my father meant that he did everything that was asked of him. My father therefore became the extra hand for anything there, including the cleaning of the rooms. And that turned out to be another straw of luck, for during one of these cleaning jobs, my father discovered several jars of preserved marmalade in one of the rooms. In his famished state, he didn't have to think twice about whether he should help himself. From now on, he did at every opportunity. Once again, he had found something that provided him with some additional caloric energy – Mazel Sachen! But what bothered him most of all was that his German work colleagues never thought of sharing their lunch provisions:

> *But when they ate – it was noon, one o'clock or half past twelve, they unpacked their sandwiches, zayre (Yid. – such big) slices. Sliced like that, the thin bread, with sausage, what do I know? We never had a piece of bread with butter at home – they cut it so nicely and*

---
[442] Zylbersztajn, Wolf (2001), Cassette IV 2:00

straight, thin slices. They ate – but that they would say: "You know what, take a piece too!" Here, (have some)![443]

He shook his head and continued:

Never! There was a woman, she was driving lorries. There were 14-year-olds there too – And she would eat and eat and the children had to watch. – Eat! But you ought to share a piece of bread! That, never happened![444]

My father often repeated this particular memory to his family, which is how I heard of it. He also recounted it in his testimony for the Shoah Foundation. From this particular emphasis, I take it that he understood it as a symbol of particular injustice and inhumanity shown towards him.

Bread and the little bit of jam he was able to eat covertly were of course still not enough to satisfy his starved body. What really appeared to have helped him were beetroots that grew in the surrounding neighbourhood, and which he appears to have picked up on his long walk to work. He braised them with a blowtorch and, although even that was never enough, he described the beets as something that was *wunderbar* – marvellous!*[445]

My father also remembered the names of his immediate superiors at Hammer. They were Master Walter and Master Schorsch, and he recalled that their swearing had made him laugh.

The Schorsch, if something didn't go, he said, Christ, Donnawetter, Kichl, nochamal![446]

---

[443] Ibid.
[444] Ibid.
[445] Ibid. 13.40
[446] Ibid. 14:10

24

Death Train to Terezín

Terezín in the year 2022. Photo DZL.

While my father had been working with the heating company, my uncle Abraham told me that he and his brother Dawid were initially forced to carry out salvage and clearing work after the explosions. They also had to salvage dead bodies out from the rubble, including people they had known from Szczekociny:

Our situation had become more tragic. German troops had arrived in the factory. We were told to clear the rubble. We were forced to pull out human body parts. After only two weeks, a new factory building was erected (by us).

The conditions continued to be inhumane, even though the Russians were coming ever closer. On 15 March (1944) I was transported away with others. One hundred Jews loaded into a train carriage were sent with me to the Czech Republic. For the entire journey, we had no more than two potatoes to feed ourselves. Only after a month travelling in these conditions, we finally arrived in Theresienstadt (Terezín). I will remember this journey for a long time, because over a thousand people died of hunger on the journey. The train stopped every other day, and the dead were dragged out. They were left in the fields to feed birds of prey...[447]

Jürgen Wolf from the memorial centre in Schlieben wrote to me that these memories were almost correct.[448] The second transport from Schlieben to Theresienstadt, which probably contained my uncle, departed from Schlieben on 14 April 1945. A week earlier, a similar transport train had also already left Schlieben. "On 21 April 1945, the prisoners from both transports arrived united in Theresienstadt."[449]

---

[447] Szwajcer 1959, p. 258f, translation by the author
[448] Personal e-mail 19.11.2022
[449] According to the Schlieben-Berga Memorial, around 1,500 people had been transported from Schlieben in two separate transports of around 700 people each. The transports were initially destined for the Flossenbürg concentration camp in Bavaria but ended up in Theresienstadt instead. Jürgen Wolf wrote to me that almost 200 prisoners from the second train were unloaded in Bautzen, where they were then forced to erect anti-tank barriers before being driven on foot towards Theresienstadt, which cost many of them their lives and before they were liberated by the Red Army 20 km behind the German-Czech border in Nixdorf on 8th of May. He wrote about the march and the deportations that it could be assumed that between a fifth to a quarter of the 1,400 prisoners, between 280 and 350 people, survived neither the railway transports nor the marches. Of the 1,400 people, only just under 1,100 arrived in Theresienstadt alive. E-mail 14.11.2022 and 19.11.2022

So it may "only" have been a week-long journey, but in the same way, without food and water, it may have felt to my uncle like an eternity and must have caused considerable suffering as well as fatalities.

Family members on my mother's side of the family, Karla and Max Elkeles and Arthur and Käte Lewandowski, had already been deported to Theresienstadt. Now members of my family on my father's side of the family also ended up in Theresienstadt – but only after the German-Jewish family members had already been deported to Auschwitz. Abraham describes his arrival in the former garrison town as confusing, because in Theresienstadt there was suddenly a greater freedom to move about.

> *When we arrived in Theresienstadt, the Jews were waiting for us with bread. They breathed new life into us. If the journey had taken a few more days, none of us would have been left alive.*
>
> *We were taken to a barrack and gradually regained our human appearance. We didn't leave the barrack for the entire first seven days and didn't know what our fate was going to be after that. There were thousands of foreigners from all over the world living in Theresienstadt. The whole town, which used to be an imperial fortress, was used. Every hour, hundreds of people were being brought here from various camps. We thought we could maybe survive here until liberation. In the meantime, however, rumours spread that the Germans had decided to blow up the entire town, but a miracle happened in the last moments before that.*
>
> *A white and red cross was placed on the roof of each house. In the last moments before liberation, so to speak, the city survived its possible total destruction. The lives of thousands of Jews were saved in this way.*[450]

Although he set the date of the liberation of Theresienstadt as 15 May, a week too late, my uncle wrote about the liberation by the Red Army, which actually took place on 8 May:

---

[450] Abrahams testimony in Szwajcer 1959.

However, this liberation cost the lives of thousands (in other ways). The starving people hurried to eat something edible. But the starving intestines could not tolerate this and brought about death rather than life. My 19-year-old brother Dawid, may God avenge his blood, was also one of these victims... The dead were burnt. The ashes of my brother I carried to Sosnowiec.[451]

Crematorium, Terezín incinerator, 2022. Photo DZL.

A document from Terezin / Theresienstadt confirms the death of my uncle Dawid Z "L on 30 June 1945 (20 Tamuz 5705).[452]

The reference to the starving brother Dawid is an indication of the great famine at the time of Terezín's liberation.

---

[451] Abraham's testimony in Szwajcer 1959. Šárka Neumanová, an employee of the Terezín Memorial, who guided me through Terezín during my visit in 2022, believed that my uncle Dawid's ashes could have been stored in a cardboard box due to a lack of urns.

[452] Terezinska Pametni Kniha (2000), directory number 482160,

There is neither a photo nor a description of Dawid Zylbersztajn from my uncles and my father. There is, however, one piece of information that describes him, at least in the eyes of his tormentors. On his Buchenwald registration card, he was listed at the moment of his arrival just under a year before his death on 5 August 1944 in these terms:

172 cm in height, middle-strong, with an oval face with brown eyes and straight nose. He had small ears and lacked two teeth. His hair was dark-brown, and he spoke Polish and German. In 1942 he had suffered from typhus. He was classified as a political Pole and Jew.

Neither my father nor Abraham ever spoke more than that about Dawid, or others. I lack any cconcept or description of his possible character, wider appearance, interests and ways. Not that it would have been impossible for my father and his two surviving brothers to describe such things. But for people like them it seemed better to bury agonising memories so that they did not overwhelm their conscious state of mind – in the silence of the night and in sleep the memories appeared anyway uninvited. Sadly, this meant, that they did not share enough on that account to the next generation, making the loss of people like Dawid even more considerable. Our ability to remember them is everything.

This is why I allow myself to play mind games. I imagine that Dawid would have been my favourite uncle and that Uncle Fiszl, who was the youngest, would have been even closer to me. I also imagine that my grandmother, and even my grandfather Herszik, would have reprimanded my father frequently about his duties as a father, and that our family on the Zylbersztajn side would have remained more intact after the war, if they all had been allowed to live.

A total of 155,000 people died in Terezín/Theresienstadt, 35,000 of them in Terezín itself and 83,000 after deportation from the camp, including members of my own family.[453]

---

[453] Details Terezin Museum

25

The Emaciated Persons of Flößberg

A long-time volunteer of the 'Flößberg Gedenkt' initiative shows an aerial photograph of the Flößberg camp from 1945. Photo DZL

"Dorten, that was a very hard camp! Very hard!"[454]

Wolf Zylbersztajn

---

[454] dorten, yid. there Zylbersztajn, Wolf (2001), Cassette IV 17:40

The Emaciated Persons of Flößberg

As Abraham and Dawid waited for the end of the war in Theresienstadt, my father's journey as an enslaved worker under German command continued. On 17 February 1945, he was ordered to board a train carriage and taken 100 km to the West to the German labour camp of Flößberg. Flößberg was a men only camp, which had only just been set up at the end of November 1944. Here, Hasag intended to continue the production of much needed anti-tank munitions. A total of 1400 enslaved forced labourers were to make that intention a reality. We know today that they ran out of time before production could start in earnest. Hans Zahn, who lived in a house in the woods right next to the camp, was able to observe the enslaved forced labourers from his home. He noted:

They were emaciated people! They came on foot from Bad Lausick and, although it was bitingly cold, were wearing only thin prisoners' clothes and clogs.[455]

Zahn was not the only local who knew about what was happening in the camp. The camp was located alongside the main linking road between the two villages of Flößberg and Beucha, where the parish priest also walked past every Sunday. It must have been easy to observe the misery from the road-side, believed Wolfgang Heidrich, a researcher of the '*Initiative Flößberg Gedenkt.*' He kindly walked me through dense forest and undergrowth to try to show me whatever was left of the camp. Apart from a memorial plaque and a cemetery, there exists no memorial site as such in Flößberg.

The camp and its Jewish enslaved workers would have been supervised by young SS soldiers, barely 18 or 19 years old, according to my father's testimony. He described them as people who acted arbitrarily and who spent most of their time chasing prisoners around the site. His

---

[455] Martin Schnellenberg, „Die Schnellaktion Panzerfaust", in Dachauer Hefte (2005), p. 260

initial task was the transport of very heavy metal pipes alongside others.[456] According to '*Initiative Flößberg gedenkt*', the work there included levelling and track work, clearing the forest, the construction of production halls, storage rooms and the building of a locomotive shed.[457] Manny Drukier, who also found himself as an enslaved worker, wrote in his memoirs that those who worked there, were in the most terrible condition: "(They were) *men whose life expectancy could be measured in days and weeks, who smelled badly and had thick beards, and who never took their lice-ridden blankets off their shoulders. We understood that we were sent here to replace those who had already died.*"[458]

The high death toll in Flößberg was once again related to a lack of sanitary facilities as well as insufficient food-rations, combined with extremely hard labour. The entire camp is said to have been infested with vermin and lice. Concerned about his hygiene, the enslaved worker Israel Polski was so desperate to clean himself, that he tried to wash himself with water from inside rain puddles.[459] The only food, Yaakov Gabr, another former enslaved worker recalled, consisted of a "soup of radishes and turnips, without bread."[460] The first commando leader (SS-Oberscharführer Strese) was said to have been so brutal in his treatment of those at his mercy that he was soon dismissed by the SS administration. It is hard to believe that anyone could be judged to be too brutal in the eyes of the SS – what kind of murderous monster must he have been? Officially he left his post due to illness.[461] However,

---

[456] Charles Kotkowky confirmed the presence of young SS soldiers from the Hitler Youth in his memoirs "Memoirs of a Survivor." He has many more memories of the Flössberg camp than my father. See also: Martin Schnellenberg, „Die Schnellaktion Panzerfaust", in Dachauer Hefte (2005), p. 259

[457] Katrin Henzel, The Flößberg Subcamp, in „Schriftreihe des Museums der Stadt Borna" (2007), p. 23

[458] Drukier (1996), p 165

[459] Martin Schnellenberg, „Die Schnellaktion Panzerfaust", in Dachauer Hefte (2005), p. 259, p. 261

[460] Ibid.

[461] Email from Wolfgang Heidrich to DZL on 20 November 2022

it is unclear whether this was due to a complaint from Hasag or whether the SS itself had raised concerns. He was certainly not dismissed out of pity, but rather to protect the SS, as Katrin Henzel of 'Initiative Flößberg gedenkt', assured.'[462] Wolfgang Heidrich, elaborated, that the problem the SS may have had with Strese was perhaps concerned with the public perception of the organisation, rather than the abuse itself. And yet we keep hearing that some of these people were completely "normal" Germans.[463]

Historian Martin Schellenberg wrote about Flößberg and Schlieben that, according to his research, the two camps were basically to be understood as death camps rather than labour camps, true to the maxim of "extermination through labour."[464] Katrin Henzel wrote about examples of these procedures:

> *Istvan Katona reports that dead prisoners are used as a deterrent and were left lying around for days. According to Charles Kotkowsky's memoirs, a prisoner named Rosen could no longer endure the beatings of an SS officer and committed suicide by throwing himself under a cattle wagon that was pulled by prisoners. The same man reported on the punishment of three Russian prisoners of war who had been caught by the SS team stealing potato peelings from the kitchen: they were beaten and forced to dig their own grave. As they lay motionless in the pit from weakness, the SS men threw stones at them and buried them "probably still alive".*[465]

---

[462] Ibid. S. 265

[463] This is how Pamela Castillo Feuchtmann of the Buchenwald Education Unit explained it to me. She rejects the belief that the Germans who had committed heinous and contemptuous acts against humanity in camps were particularly bad and out of the ordinary Germans.

[464] Ibid. S. 266

[465] Katrin Henzel, Das KZ-Außenlager Flößberg, publication series of the Museum of the City of Borna (2007), p. 25

FiThe "Flößberg gedenkt" (Flößberg remembers) initiative has been campaigning for decades for a fitting memorial for those who died in Flößberg. This cemetery, built with federal state subsidies, is now a first important step.

Others were "only" shot. In the jargon of the SS, such a death was then noted down as "acute cardiovascular failure".[466] Heidrich labelled the conditions in the camp as simply being" conditions for dying."[467]

It was therefore a hopeless situation that my father saw himself confronted with. Yet one morning amidst the despair he heard people calling his name. Shocked, he got himself ready. What awaited him? This could be nothing good! Had he done something wrong, was a "special treatment" awaiting him? For what? Expecting the worst, he suddenly caught sight of Master Walter, his former boss from Schlieben. He recited Walter's words 40 years later, probably true to the original: "*Come on! What have they done to you, those dogs? Fetch three other workers and come to work with me. Our company is here now.*"[468] My father quickly selected three people he knew and took them with him. By being transferred to the Hammer company yet again, my father largely escaped the catastrophic conditions in Flößberg. Many prisoners were sent back

---

[466] Wolfgang Heidrich, Death in the Flößberg Camp, publication series of the Museum der City of Borna (2007), p. 35
[467] Ibid.
[468] Dog" (as in the original)

The Emaciated Persons of Flößberg

to Buchenwald as invalids, others though did not make it. Only their dead bodies were returned. According to estimates, the total number of deaths in the muddy camp could have been 252 persons. All in all, the attempt to set up an armaments' factory in Flößberg cost 466 people their lives, including people deported to Flößberg from Schlieben.[469]

In March 1945, Allied warplanes began to attack the region. Two bombs fell very close to the Flößberg camp, though without causing too much damage. But on 5 March 1945, Flößberg's production facility was destroyed in another air raid. When after the attack some unexploded bombs had been discovered, it was of course the task of the enslaved forced labourers to defuse these weapons.[470]

---

[469] Wolfgang Heidrich, Tod im Lager Flößberg, publication series of the Museum of the City of Borna (2007), p. 34
[470] Ibid. p. 23

26

Train of the Dead and Half-Living

I assume that my father continued to live in the barracks in Flößberg while he was working for the Hammer company. But this chapter was soon coming to a close. The enslaved forced labourers understood from the increasing bombings and the US fighter planes visible in the sky that the end of the war was coming closer and closer. Perhaps liberation was near. Manny Drukier thought that the Germans would never allow people like him to fall into the hands of the Allies. He believed that they had witnessed too much, such as countless murders and abuses.[471] They could therefore be essential in later trials. Drukier was by no means wrong in his assumption.

Just a few days before the arrival of the US troops in Flößberg, on a "beautiful bright day", it was 13 April 1945, the camp fell into a state of confusion with SS soldiers who were rushing about. They ordered the forced labourers to leave their barracks immediately with the words "Alle raus!" – everybody out![472] The SS soldiers told them to get into already waiting cattle wagons as quickly as possible. My father had the

---

[471] Ibid. S. 168
[472] The date is given in Schellenberg, Martin (2005). "The Rapid Action Panzerfaust. Prisoners in the subcamps of Buchenwald concentration camp at the Leipzig armaments company HASAG. In: Dachauer Hefte 21/2005, p. 237 – 271.

foresight to take a hammer, a chisel and a knife with him, items which I assume he possessed because of his work at the central heating company.

Once the boarding was completed, he and the others found themselves in carriages that were so packed with people that they could only stand inside them. According to my father, those trapped inside with him were all sure that this could only be their final train transportation and that the Germans would soon gas them. He echoed Drukier by saying:

We were one hundred percent sure that they intended to kill us. We had seen too much, could testify to too much, they couldn't allow us to continue to live.[473]

And in fact, this was exactly the plan.

Here is my father's own description of this journey:

We were forever going (on the train), all day and it was bad! There was nothing to eat, nothing to drink, nothing at all… and I thought to myself, I'm not ready to give up yet.

It is possible to say more about what he tried to explain here. The train was to take its freight to Austrian Mauthausen extermination camp in order to kill off the labour force that was now no longer needed and indeed to eliminate their potential as witnesses. But after a day's journey, the train was far from reaching its destination. Without drinking water or food, some began to die, and by the end of the day some 15 to 20 people were dead. According to my father, these deaths were nothing but a "relief" within the crazy banality of the situation. The dead "gave" the still living a bit more space.

And still the train meandered slowly onwards. Eventually it reached Czechoslovakia. Many routes were no longer usable due to the ever approaching Allies and their direct targeting of railway lines. The search

---

[473] Zylbersztajn Wolf (2001), Cassette V 26:00

for possible re-routing options was on, which led to an endless back and forth and prolonged the journey and suffering of those trapped inside. Finally, at some point, the train stopped and the doors suddenly opened.

It was only a stop. The prisoners were ordered to throw any dead next to the railway track and proceed to bury them. My father said he also was ordered to help in that task. Local Czechs brought sandwiches, my father remembered. Afterwards, everyone was ordered to return into the train carriages and doors were shut again.[474] According to Manny Drukier's memoirs, there were now several more of these stops.[475] During one such stop, Drukier learnt that his father, who had also been onboard had lost his life inside another wagon, either for lack of water and food or because he had been murdered by the majority of Russian prisoners in that wagon in order to make room for the others. It was a merciless fight for sheer survival.

So far, they had lived through only the first half of what was later established to have been an almost two-week long odyssey. Jewish women whose transport carriages had been attached to the train after about a week (they came from the Venusberg concentration camp) also reported that there was little or no food or water, which drove many to insanity and death.[476] They reported that the SS guards would have taken a specific daily interest in the toll of new dead people inside the carriages.[477] Ibi L., one of the survivors amongst those women described her situation with the following words: "*The bodies stayed in the carriage, we travelled together with the bodies. My friend died beside me; I slept on her corpse. I don't think any of us were completely normal back then. We all suffered from high fevers. After a few days, the corpses were removed and those who were very ill were taken from the wagons to open platforms, where they all died.*"[478]

---

[474] Charles Kotkowky also reports on these loaves in his testimonies. In Memoirs of a Survivor
[475] Drukier (1996), p.196, in which Drukier says that in addition to eating bread and drinking water were also allowed to relieve themselves.
[476] Venusberg concentration camp was located near the Bohemian village of Trebusice
[477] Ciziborra (2015): KZ Venusberg, pp.88-98, according to files of the Federal Archives Berlin B162 /8375-77
[478] Ibid. p. 98f.

Helga Weiss, who was also on the transport and had already survived the hell of Auschwitz, managed to survive the journey and pass on her testimony after the Shoah. She remembered women from a number of countries, such as Greece and Poland, who looked "worse" than those, she was amongst. She then went on to describe her sight of the men, most likely those from Flößberg: "The men wear striped suits and look even worse than (all) the women."[479] Yalana L., another survivor, believed that 20 passengers died in the wagon each day.[480]

Due to these testimonies, including that of my father, I began to search for people wo could help me find more information about these train journeys. Through an extremely fortunate find, I came across Libor Schröpfer, the mayor of the Czech town of Holýšova.[481]

Schröpfer told me, when I visited the town later, that he came from a family that was part German and part Czech. His family members had both been in the Wehrmacht, but had also suffered as Czechs. In his neighbourhood, his family members were the only ones who had been able to remain in the Czech region after the war. All other Germans were forced to leave. Schröpfer grew up between these former fronts and under a third power, the later Soviet occupation. For a long time, he worked as the maths teacher at a local school, until a few years ago he decided to stand as mayor and was duly elected.

In this capacity as mayor, he saw it as his personal obligation to assist people like me and began some investigations in my name. He spoke to elderly witnesses and local historians.

According to what he found out, my father could have been on a train with a total of a length of 54 wagons, each single one with around

---

[479] Cziborra (2015): KZ Venusberg. P. 86 quotes Helga Weiss (2013): Und doch ein ganzes Leben, Cologne: Lübbe Verlag.
[480] Ibid. p. 104
[481] Holýšova has its own history in the Second World War. It is one of the few places where a prison camp was successfully attacked and liberated by Polish units instead of the Allies. Wolek (2020) Schröpfer was the only one who replied to my circular to all regional representatives in this region asking for information about these death trains.

50 people inside. Some were wagons from Oświecim (Auschwitz) as well as from the concentration camps of Gross Rosen, Buchenwald, from Freiberg and indeed from Flößberg. Most of the people locked in were Jewish-Polish nationals, but there were also Russians, Italians and a small number of Czechs among them. This long train travelled with its dead and half-dead freight of some 2,700 people via the Czech towns of Most (Brüx), Horní Bříza (Ober Birken), Nýřany (Nürschan), Stod (Staab), Domažlice (Taus), Klatovy (Klattau), Horažďovice (Horaschdowitz), České Budějovice (Budweis) and had Mauthausen as its final destination. The directions and routes changed constantly, depending on which tracks were still available and not destroyed.[482]

It is important to note that this is only an attempt of a reconstruction. Wolfgang Heidrich from the 'Flößberg Gedenkt' Group is also keen to reconstruct the routes. He questioned the route assumed by Schröpfer.

It led me to conclude that how and where the train my father was in passed will probably never be fully solved. But what is certain is that many people were forced to travel on trains like these for an extremely long time and were trapped inside them, and that all these trains ran through the Czech Republic.

If one follows Schröpfer's assumptions as an example, the train would have travelled from Domažlice (Taus) in the direction of Janovice (Janowitz an der Angel). Hence, it may have been near Horní Bříza where my father first got something to eat and thus regained the will to live. In fact, the survivor Hana Hnátová recalled how Czechs brought her and other people coffee and bread in Horní Bříza.[483]

Wherever it was, after his small renourishment, my father decided to take his faith in his own hands, not least because there was suddenly "a bit of additional space inside the carriage" due to more recently deceased persons.

---

[482] For example, the tracks were destroyed by an American air raid on 26 April 1945, Domažlická kronika 2010, pp. 144-149.
[483] Cziborra (2015) KZ Freiberg, I p. 100

The plan was to try to find a way to flee. If Libor Schröpfer's research is to be believed, the place where my father may have tried to escape could be not far from Blížejov. To escape, my father and 15 others, who also wanted to try their luck, first began to tear planks out of the wooden floor of the railway carriage.[484]

Referring to the tools he had brought along, my father described what happened next in the following words:

I had a chisel, I had a hammer, and I started breaking up the floor. The wagon was still standing, I was scared, because there were Werkschutz officers outside. – And we started breaking and breaking, it took (us) maybe two hours. It was a thick floor. We made a hole, lots of people helped. I wasn't alone, everyone helped. The bigger the hole was, the faster it went. They tore out whole chunks, you know?[485]

Then the train suddenly started moving again. It was time to attempt the escape. It was the biggest gamble they had taken so far into an uncertain ending. Did they hug each other and looked at each other's eyes for courage and reassurance?

The first person to disappear through the hole was a man my father knew well, named as "Mayer-Zernosovsky" in my father's testimony. My father himself was the third person to crawl through the hole, dressed in

---

[484] This also happened on another transport. However, SS-guards only realised this in Domažlice, where the train later stopped. As punishment, the passengers who stayed behind were beaten and whipped. According to witnesses on site, this happened on 11 May 1945. However, it may have been a few weeks earlier, as according to the Schlieben Memorial Site Group, the actual route became impassable from 26 April 1945, This would suggest the date 21 April 1945, one week after departure from Flößberg. Josef Beroušek and Václav Císler, both former employees at the Domažlice-Taus railway station, reported to have heard such terrible screams when these men were beaten up that they quickly fled the scene. But not before seeing a pile of stripped and beaten men in the last train carriage. They reported that blood was flowing from this carriage onto the tracks. Research by Libor Schröpfer and from Domažlická Kronika 2010 – the chronicle of the town of Domažlic 2010.

[485] Zylbersztajn, Wolf (2001), Cassette V

his striped Buchenwald uniform and taking his lice-ridden cover along with him.

**Transport cattle carriage from below.
Exhibition object, Auschwitz, 2002, Photo DZL.**

The escape hole was situated directly above the carriage's axle, onto which my father now stepped. There he saw what he referred to as a "wire" to the other axle. My father held on between this and the wire, as he described it, until his body was hanging just above the surface and then allowed himself to fall onto the centre of the railway track. He survived the fall unharmed, and just a few moments later he saw the train moving away behind him. He noticed a patch of forest next to the track and quickly ran into it and found the other two escapees there.

Left behind in the railway carriage, others now also tried their luck and one after the other dropped out off the train. It would only be a matter of time before one of the guards would notice one of them and raise the alarm, and indeed they soon had the train stopped and the search for the runaways began.

According to Libor Schröpfer, all this probably took place near Blížejov (Blisowa) on 25 April 1945. There had already been several successful escapes from trains in the area during that time. When I visited Schröpfer in the Czech Republic in April 2022, a man told me how his grandparents had hidden four escapees and delivered potatoes to others in the forest.

When I asked the man what might have motivated his grandparents to do this, he replied that local Czech people had only two options: either to do nothing or to actively try to help. In any case, handing the escapees over to the German authorities was totally out of question. Nobody would have done such a thing, the man was certain. Czech women had repeatedly tried to care for people locked in the wagons by bringing them some provisions. Hitler Youth officers guarding the trains were said to help themselves first before they allowed the provisions to reach the people inside the carriages.

Manny Drukier described how he and a boy called Leon had also tried to make a hole in the floor of his carriage. To their frustration their hole was discovered by the guards, for which Leon was beaten up. Subsequently, the hole was sealed again. In spite of the set-back Drukier was determined to try to flee, and he later managed his escape by jumping out of one of the train windows.[486] A woman called Hana Hnátová jumped out of a roof hatch together with several others and survived to tell her story too.[487] Others, such as Rikica-Radmilla Slozberg, who had previously been interned in the Freiberg concentration camp, failed in her escape attempt. After jumping out of a window, she was immediately spotted and pursued by SS guards who shot at her. She survived with injuries and was returned to the railway carriage.[488] Drukier confirmed that there were armed train guards on the trains ready to shoot without hesitation.

---

[486] Drukier (1996), p. 172
[487] Cziborra (2015), KZ Freiberg, p. 100
[488] ibid. p. 101

But back to my father's attempt to escape, where he was still hiding in the small, forested area. He and the others soon realised that there was a village located on one side of the railway track and that they had to move. Together he and the others approached the village and quickly entered one of the houses. The man living there didn't take long to comprehend the situation and handed the group bread and, when that didn't satisfy their hunger some potatoes as well.

As they wanted to return into the forest, probably on the man's advice, they were however unexpectedly spotted by two ethnic German policemen on bicycles. With an imperious "Halt! Halt," they ordered the fugitives to stop. My father was close enough to be able to make out an eagle on their caps. In his own words:

I thought all the effort was worth nothing, that now I'm dead! What was I supposed to do? I just headed for the village. I run and run until I spotted some water, a small water and a small bridge over the water. And I entered the water. And there was a tree in the water. I hid, with my head between the trees. And I saw little children, eight to ten-year-olds, running back and forth across the bridge. Later I learnt that they were children of a boarding school for ethnic Germans. They'd already finished school, it was dusk, about five or six o'clock.

And I see them, and they don't see me, and they don't find me. And then it got all quiet. It got dark, and it was snowing, I could remember that too. I get out of the water and lie down right in the square and I ask myself: What should I do now?[489]

After I had passed on these specific accounts of my father's escape to Libor Schröpfer, he believed that my father's descriptions corresponded well with a local village called Blížejov (Blisowa). The village is situated about ten kilometres from Domažlice, and at its end there is a small

---

[489] Zylbersztajn, Wolf (2001), Cassette V 4:30, translation into English by author

river, the Zubřina, with a small bridge running over it. The description of a nearby forest also fitted with the area and what's more, there were Czechs and Germans living in the village alongside a large boys' school that was used to accommodate German refugees from the East, which could apply to the "boarding school" mentioned by my father.

Zubřina River, near the village of Blížejov (Blisowa) Czech Republic. You can make out a bridge in the background. Was my father hiding here? Photo DZ

Whether this was in fact the correct location will never be totally verifiable; The "water" as my father called it, could likewise refer to the artificial pond in the centre of the same village, but there is no bridge there and there are no trees, at least not today. Schröpfer considers the possibility that my father was hiding in the centre of the village as unlikely. However, there are still houses and barns around the village's pond today, which suggests that people could have spotted somebody like my father, for that was exactly what happened. Emerging from the water, my father remembered hearing someone shouting to him in Czech: "Poor man, run into the forest." But my father said that he was unable to follow this advice. The cold water had most probably caused hypothermia. My father first lost control of his limbs and then his will to live!

"Let them get me now and shoot me and all this shit is over. It's enough!", were the words he used to recall that very moment during his testimony to the Shoah Foundation decades later.[490]

Amid this deep and desperate gloom in the stillness of the increasing darkness surrounding him, a glimmer of hope arose when he suddenly spotted a nearby shed, locked with two beams. The thought of a shelter, even if only for a short time, suddenly spurred him on again, although apparently with the last of what remained of his strength. He got himself up, approached the shed, examined the door and managed to open it.

"And I look in and see, it's marvellous!"[491]

Entering the shed my father discovered two goats and above them, accessible only with a ladder, a hay loft. But even better than that, he felt the sudden warmth induced through the presence of the two live animals! He rid himself of his soaked clothes, climbed up the ladder, stretched himself out, covered himself with the straw and fell into a deep sleep on the spot. He was only woken in the morning by shouting in German. What did that mean? Were they looking for him? Surely no-one knew where he was? Or perhaps the man who had shouted something to him had called the alarm? It was only when no one came that he discarded his doubts. Instead, he discovered something life-giving: beetroot! Left as feed for the goats, but cut with the knife he still possessed, it became an instant meal to him. Not only that, but there was drinking water too.

---

[490] Zylbersztajn, Wolf (2001), Cassette V
[491] Ibid

Train of the Dead and Half-Living

"I had water, I ate – I was king!" [492]

After about three days, someone finally entered the shed. It was an elderly man about 60 years of age who climbed up the ladder to fetch some hay. As he reached for the hay, however, he got hold of my father's feet.

Saying nothing, the man left and returned after a while but this time together with his wife. In Czech and German she tried to explained to my father that he didn't need to be afraid. On the contrary, they soon began to bring him food, goat's milk, turnips and other things. My father thought he had been there for a week, but it was probably *two* weeks in total.

In his testimony he gave a vivid account of how he experienced liberation. It had started when US troops were crossing through the village and were being welcomed loudly by the excited locals. That day has a date. Most of the Czech Republic was liberated on 4 May 1945.

---

[492] Ibid. 9.45

When I visited the area in April 2022, Libor Schröpfer told television and radio stations about my imminent visit. There was a lot of interest. I told the media that the hiding of my father and other escapees from the trains and camps by people who didn't have much themselves was a symbol of selflessness. Despite all the adversity in their own lives, they acted humanely. Especially in this age of self-centredness, such selflessness can never be taken for granted. Exhausted people like my father were neither beautiful to look at, nor were they clean or wore respectable clothes, nor did they carry anything of value. They came as strangers and yet Czechs helped them out of human kindness and perhaps to some degree also in a spirit of resistance against the Germans. In spite of the end of war appearing to be imminent and but a question of time, hiding people could still be a risky undertaking. Through their strong commitment to freedom, which lasts until this day, they helped people who evidently possessed even less freedom than themselves. Libor Schröpfer, who was still the mayor of Holýšov at the time of my visit when the Russian invasion of the Ukraine had just begun, told me that his municipality had just agreed to welcome 300 Ukrainian refugees. He admitted that there were differing opinions on the merits of this effort. The understanding and awareness of how the previous generations helped and rescued people who were foreign and completely at their mercy was something these communities could be proud of. I thanked Schröpfer and Jiří Červenka, the mayor of Blížejov, whom I visited briefly with Schröpfer again in the name of my family.

27

Survival after Liberation

The woman (wife) came and announced that I was free and could come down. And when I came down, I saw how many Czechs – the whole village – had gathered around me. Everyone brought something to me. Everyone wanted to do something good.[493]

Wolf Zylbersztajn

Do chronicles or written down memories concerning the end of the war exist, which perhaps recorded that moment of liberation from the Czech perspective and mentioned a man that could have been my father. Unfortunately, none could be found, but there are some traces. Schröpfer wrote to me this in an E-Mail:

> *...the Czech descriptions of the Second World War highlighted the global political events but contained but a minimum of data about the end of war events in the village. In the chronicles of other villages and towns in the Domažlice area we found however a few accounts concerning those death transports. There exists repeated information about how the*

---

[493] Ibid.

Czech population was trying to bring food to the prisoners, and how some prisoners had escaped from the transports, or that the transports stopped at various railway stations and in which direction they then travelled, etc.[494]

In the euphoric moment of liberation, celebrating the survival of that "poor man" who escaped the fangs of the Germans, was an expression of the Czechs' own personal and collective emotions concerning the liberation, given that they had been hostages to the German Third Reich themselves. Many knew what had gone on inside those carriages of the train transports and what kind of people were inside and what their condition was; it had been in this area where trains had stopped frequently and where the Czechs had provided them with something to eat.

The advance of liberation was also overwhelming for my father. My father's body seemed to have been in sheer survival mode for years. Now with it all being over, its tiredness and frail state became apparent, and my father simply collapsed. Suddenly feeling quite ill, my father had to be taken by the villagers to nearest hospital in Dormazlice, where he had been treated for a few days and speedily recovered. After a thorough final examination, he was soon discharged.[495]

My dad travelled initially to Pilsen and then to Carlov, a town with a DP camp.[496] How he did so, I don't know, because he must have had no money, unless he was given some by locals, the US-authorities or was carried free of charge. Inside the DP camp in Carlov he spotted his fellow escapee and survivor from the death train, Mayer-Zernosovsky. He also had survived his escape, but he had a relatively fresh scar in his face caused by chains that were hanging at the end of the train, which had hit him right in the face as he was lying on the track. My father seems to have escaped these.

---

[494] Libor Schröpfer Email to me, 1 October 2020, own translation
[495] Manny Drukier also experienced this after the liberation and had to be taken to a hospital in Chelmna by the Czechs. Drukier (1996)
[496] DP- Displaced Persons, camp for refugees and displaced persons, often of the Red Army.

And what can be said of the others who had escaped from the railway carriage together with my father?

Yakub Kupperberg, who had also been on the train and, like my father, was a Jewish survivor from my father's town Szczekociny, told my father a few years later that he had seen how many of the other escapees were soon tracked down and shot on the spot as punishment and were then buried in a ditch by the track. Kupperberg, on the other hand, was transported onwards until the train reached the Mauthausen death camp in Austria. There he was soon standing naked, so he reported, awaiting his gassing, when US troops surrounded and finally liberated the camp. He survived! If my father had not run away, one or the other fate would have awaited him too.

In Carlov, my father was able to get a job in a canteen that served US-military personnel. For him, there could not have been a better job. It meant that he had enough to drink and eat, whilst he also had some work. As a result, it didn't take too long for my father to reach his normal weight again.

"I literally expanded," he joked as he was looking back in 1996.[497]

Eventually he decided to travel on to Poland, first to the town of Częstochowa, where he had once known a cousin. He hoped that this cousin might have survived the war. In fact, he not only found him, but, to his great delight, also found his brother Abraham there, who he learned had survived in Theresienstadt. Perhaps it was part of a plan they had made, that if they were to survive, they would first meet in Częstochowa. From now on, every time the brothers met, a bizarre discussion as to who of the two of them had suffered more since they left Schlieben, would emerge and last their entire lives.

From his brother Abraham my father also learned that their little brother Dawid had not made it and that he had died just after his liberation. Abraham showed my father the urn that contained Dawid's

---

[497] Zylbersztajn (1995)

ashes.[498]

They then decided to return to Szczekociny for the first time since the end of the war. There they intended to visit a farmer with whom their father had left some tools and bits and bobs before they had to leave Szczekociny. That perhaps was also part of a plan for the day the war had ended. It may have been only three years that had passed since, but unfortunately, this old farmer had died during that period. His son, described as a strong, muscular and tall Catholic Pole, is said to have approached my uncle and my father and told them to get lost. He claimed that their belongings had been taken by the partisans. One has to ask why he resorted to such threatening degrees of malice when supposedly others had taken possession of it? My father disciplined his outraged brother, who was ready to argue with the man. "He could even murder you for that now, and it's not worth it", my father told him.

I wrote an entire article in English about this scene after my father's death in 2011, entitled "On the Possibilities and Impossibilities of Being a Neighbour." It was about the audacity of former neighbours and the coexistence of different communities, also with reference to my current home, London.[499]

I asked myself, how it could be that former neighbours could become so nasty. I tried to explain what the reason behind such behaviour might be and what could be done about it.

The only thing my father and his brother found in Szczekociny was money that they had buried somewhere together with their father. But the joy of finding the tin with the money inside was short-lived, because after opening it it turned out that the notes had become completely unusable, as water had penetrated the tin and destroyed the paper notes.

Being unwelcome in their hometown and birthplace, the two

---

[498] Szwajcer (2010)
[499] Zylbersztajn (2011)

Survival after Liberation

brothers moved to the nearby town of Sosnowiec. I don't know why they chose this town, but they probably knew people there. An identity card dated 2 February 1946 gives 36 Modrzejowaka Street as their place of residence, a street not far from the town centre.[500]

The first thing they took care of in Sosnowiec was the burial of the ashes of their brother Dawid. On 15 August 1945, they lowered the ashes into the earth of the Jewish cemetery in Sosnowiec.[501] It was to be the only real grave of the members for the Zylbersztajn family who had perished in the Shoah.

Kaddish for Dawid Zylbersztajn in August 2022 (In liberal Judaism, the Kaddish may also be recited alone). Photo DZL.

When I visited the Jewish cemetery in Sosnowiec decades later in August 2022 to recited the Jewish funeral prayer, the Kaddish, for Dawid, we (my friend Imran Manzoor helped me in the endeavour) were unable to locate the grave itself. So, I prayed in front of a memorial commemorating the victims of the Shoah instead.[502] After I was finished

---

[500] Karta Rzemieslnicza 34076408 Card number GVI-lw/8/46
[501] Szwajcer (2010), p. 260
[502] In liberal and reformed Judaism, which I was a member of then, Kaddish can be recited alone. These days I am a member of a more traditional "Masorti" community.

a butterfly rose above the cemetery in the strong sun. I imagined it was the spirit of Dawid.

Dawid Zylbersztajn ze Szczekocin, zmarły 30 czerwca 1945 roku w getcie Theresienstadt, już po jego wyzwoleniu. Była to ostatnia osoba pochowana na cmentarzu w Milowicach.

Whatsapp message to me at the end of October 2022.

Perhaps it symbolised my uncle's spirit, dancing around the graves in delight that a relative had honoured and not forgotten him.

Three months following my visit and totally out of the blue, I received a Whatsapp message from Poland with a photo attached. I was asked if the grave depicted on it could be that of my uncle. I looked at the stone. It seemed as if it had been hidden under the soil. No one had looked for a Dawid Zylbersztajn in the cemetery for almost 80 years, until I praised G.d in Dawid's name with my reciting of the prayer for the dead, the Kaddish. Now three months later, the message of the photo was clear. I mean in the form of the Hebrew words repeated so often in the Holy Scriptures: "Hineni!" – here I am! So that's where my uncle's mortal remains had been placed. I plan to travel to Sosnowiec again sometime and pray once more at the actual grave so that his soul can find its rest, perhaps that time with a minyan, if at all possible.[503]

Moisze, my father's eldest brother, had also survived the war and escaped the atrocities committed by the Third Reich in Yangiyul in Uzbekistan. The worst he had to deal with was poverty. After the end of the war, he too went in search of his family. He expected the worst. A friend in Breslau gave him the tip to check in the town of Sosnowiec, and so he did. The joy of seeing two of his brothers again after all those years must have been as immeasurable, as it must have been painful to learn about what happened to the rest of the family.

Reunited, the three brothers had to find a way to survive in Sosnowiec. To this end, they opened a shoemaker's workshop, and soon afterwards a shoe shop. They made a good living from it. My father soon owned a motorbike, a Triumph 500. As life slowly returned to normal, my uncle Abraham and my aunt Ruszke (Rosza, née Sliberberg) met and fell in love. They were soon married and expecting a child, my cousin Zwika. Did my father also have a girlfriend in Sosnowiec? I didn't hear anything about such developments from him.

But my father did seem to be flirting a bit, as appears to be evident on some old photos from that time in which my father can be seen in the company of ladies. I also think I overheard my mother talk about someone he was supposed to have married.

Most of the survivors who ended up in Sosnowiec and Poland after the war probably saw their old home country as but a temporary home. One of the main reasons for this was a renewed rise in antisemitic attacks, pogroms and acts of violence against Jews.[504] These had begun shortly after the end of the war.

In April 1945, there were antisemitic rumours spreading in the Polish town of Chelm that three Jews had committed a child abduction. The same claims were made in towns such as Lublin, Rzeszow, Tarnow and

---

[503] minyan – required minimum number of persons for higher prayers like the Kaddish.
[504] Engel (1998)

Sosnowiec, until these nasty rumours reached their murderous climax in the town of Kielce on 4 July 1946. There, between 38 and 42 people had been murdered in a pogrom-like night driven by an angry mob that had stormed a house where Jewish survivors had been lodging.[505] According to historian David Engel, these riots were rooted in age-old antisemitic prejudices that had led to the persecution of Jewish people in the Middle Ages, for example in England in the 12th and 13th centuries. Engel thinks it should also be understood in the context of the Russian occupation of Poland and the underground movements against it.[506] Jewish people were seen as objects between the two fronts. Prejudice led to the scapegoating of Jews for anything. This sealed the future of Polish Jews in their country of birth after the Shoah. Whether they were hated by the Polish underground or by communists or ordinary Poles did not matter in the end. The result and the consequences were the same. In 1946, 244,000 Jewish people were said to still be living in Poland, a final high point after which numbers only continued to decrease rapidly.

In an interview with the online newspaper "*Times of Israel*", the Polish historian Lukasz Krzyzanowski stated that antisemitism permeated all areas of society after the war. Antisemitic crimes were often not investigated.[507] Even if survivors, like my father and his brothers, had tried to build a new life for themselves, they were unable to do so, as Krzyzanowski's own research in his book "*Ghost Citizens*", about survivors in the town of Radom, 216 kilometres from Sosnowiec, proved.[508] Hardly any of those who returned there after the war decided to stay on. However, when I visited Sosnowiec in 2022, I discovered about a dozen more recent graves in the old Jewish cemetery, people who had died in recent decades, that indicated that at least a few Jewish people had remained there. The majority,

---

[505] ibid
[506] Ibid. On antisemitism in the English Middle Ages, see also Zylbersztajn-Lewandowski (2022)
[507] O'Malley (2020), quoting the Polish historian Lukasz Krzyzanowski. Translated by the author
[508] Ibid. and Krzyzanowski (2020)

however, had emigrated, often to the United States, others to Palestine, later Israel, less often, including my father, to Western Europe.[509]

In January 1951, the time had come for the brothers to leave Poland for good. My father got rid of all his tools and sold them. They were probably too heavy and lumpy to take with him on any journey. His brother Moisze and his wife Chava "Chavtje" (born Zandweiss, 1925) would not leave Poland until six years later.[510] When they finally decided to make their move they went straight to Israel. Their only daughter, my cousin Hannah, was born in 1955 just before they left Poland.

My father's own departure from Poland was not a simple border crossing. He had said, that he paid some human traffickers ten US dollars to cross from the Czech Republic into Austria. Converted into today's value, that would have been around 1800 Euros.[511] He could then travel on to Germany via Austria with less trouble.

Germany? Why did a Polish Jewish survivor of the Shoah or any survivor of the Shoah want to go to Germany, the country of the perpetrators, I asked my father in an interview in 1995. Apparently, it had less to do with Germany.

> *I didn't like the Communism that was coming. Communism was bad. I could no longer work under Communism. You couldn't have your own property; the state took everything. I was a professional leather worker – I made boots. That was what my father taught me before the war. But with Communism, I couldn't continue doing that, so the situation was bad. The government wanted everyone to work in co-operatives, called Spczelnas. I didn't like that. I wanted*

---

[509] Ibid.
[510] Many of Chavtje's siblings and parents were murdered in the Shoah.
[511] The same amount is about 1500 Pounds (2025). 1,786.18 Euro https://usd.mconvert.net/eur/1950, retrieved on 18/11/2023 Calculated after inflation, the amount in November 2022 was around 115 Euros, see https://fxtop.com/de/inflationsrechner.php?A=10&C1=USD&INDICE=USCPI31011913&DD1=31&MM1=01&YYYY1=1951&DD2=26&MM2=11&YYYY2=2022&btnOK=%C3%84equivalent+calculate, retrieved on 27/11/2022

to be independent, but people like me were labelled as capitalists. We knew that, unlike Poland, Germany was (now) a free country – that's what Polish Jews who were already in Germany (told us). They were the ones who knew how to cross the border... Only Polish Jews went, non-Jewish Poles didn't go to Germany.[512]

It's interesting that my father described himself as marginalised, hated and not welcomed back home, not as a "true Pole".

After crossing the border, my father first found himself in a DP camp near Linz. From there, his journey continued towards the Bavarian capital Munich. Many other survivors had the same plan. In addition survivors from one of the largest Bavarian DP-Camps, the one in Föhrenwald near Wolfratshausen, would move to Munich, just 30 kilometres away. Reason enough for my father to check out the city: "*I wanted to go there and see what was going on.*"[513]

Was my father aware that some survivors from Szczekociny had already held a small memorial service for the murdered souls of their town in Munich back in 1947?[514] However, most of this first group of survivors were already in or on their way to Israel, by the time my father arrived. Zionist representatives had also tried to persuade my father to immigrate to Israel. But my father had received letters from his brother Abraham and others who were already there, in which they described the situation in Israel as difficult and that they had to live in camps.

"I'm an old jumper", he told the interviewer from the Shoah Foundation, justifying the fact that he jumped out of the moving train destined for Italy as it looped itself over a hill near the Austrian town of Villach. The journey had been organised by the Zionist organisations to bring Jews, including my father, to Israel.

---

[512] Zylberstajn (1995), p. 2
[513] ibid
[514] Szwajzer (2010), S. 96

I wanted to leave for Israel. But those were difficult years, 1951, 1952. Israel was in such a mess, politically and economically. So, I thought I'd wait a bit. America was out of the question, by the way – I never knew anyone there.[515]

There were also other survivors of the labour camp Skarżysko-Kamienna who had settled in Munich. In 1947, the former German Hasag foreman Karl Herold was recognised by one of these survivors. Herold had been one of the few Germans in Skarżysko-Kamiennas who did not use their privilege and power to torture or murder Jews, but on the contrary, had been ridiculed at the time for his defence of one of the enslaved forced workers.

Now, after the collapse of the Third Reich Herold and a group of Jewish survivors decided to try and report Herold's former colleagues to the authorities. Some had continued to work in Leipzig after the war, as if nothing had happened. Following investigations, a far-reaching criminal trial against these opened on 15 November 1948 in Leipzig's Congress Hall. It was the largest trial to date in the Soviet occupied zone, which, according to reports, was initially attended by some 5,000 people with up to 1,500 persons in the audience each day.[516]

---

[515] Zylbersztajn (1995), S. 5
[516] Frey (1949), p. 21-24

28

My German Friends Grandfathers

Grandfathers innocent! German Grandfathers!
Heroic Grandfathers –
objected NSDAP since the beginning.
Sacrificing Grandfathers – hid Jews in their Homes
Rebelling Grandfathers –
not voting for Adolf Hitler
Unknowing Grandfathers –
who didn't know the extent
of horrors done to the People of Israel.
Pacifist Grandfathers –
who never saw the battlefields.
Moral Grandfathers –
who were not part of the SS
Duty observing Grandfathers – being great German soldiers

I wished I had a Grandfather, just like yours,
were it not for the regrettable fact, that his life was taken away
by other Germans' Grandfathers.

My German Friends Grandfathers

In spite of these great Grandfathers, there is one Grandfather,
who doesn't fit the rest. Somebody I knew once admitted:
Daniel, my Grandfather still is today supporter of the Reich.
I am certain that he killed Jews.

Ashamed and shattered I must reveal this fact to you,
which I can't change. Instead of hiding the truth
and to pretend that I am the grandson to a
Yad Vashem hero without a tree.

Poem, written in 1996. Published in an issue of "Second Generation Voices" of that time, in which descendants of Shoah survivors wrote. Slightly adapted by author for this English Edition of Zol Zayn Shulem.

29

Judgements

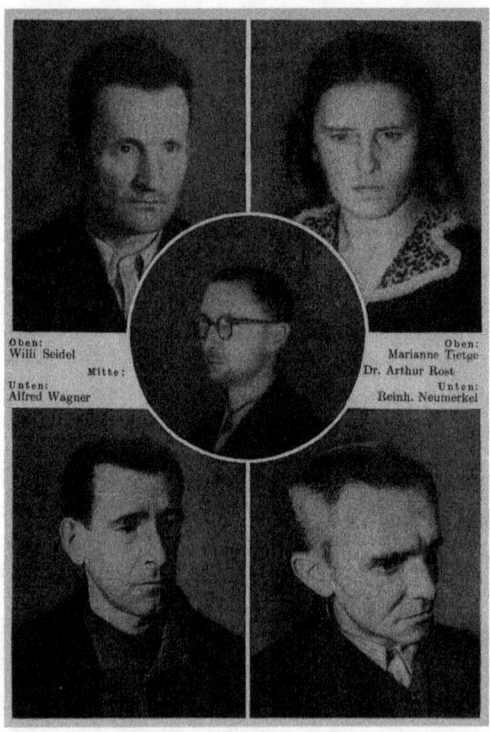

The human faces of racists, murderers and sadists. The core-accused of the Third Reich operations in Skarżysko-Kamienna of the German company Hasag during the trials in Leipzig. Illustration Frey (1949).

Of the just over 3,000 Jewish inhabitants of Szczekociny, only around 200 survived. One family in Szczekociny, according to the memorial book *Pinkes Szczekocin*, was particularly marked by the Shoah. Around one hundred members of the Koplowicz family died between 1939 and 1945, most seemingly murdered. The only survivor was Bejlusz Fajgenblat (née Koplowicz). After the war, she decided to make her home in Israel.[517]

In my father's immediate family, only my father and two brothers remained still alive in late 1945, although some cousins and his father's sister (his aunt) and her husband (his uncle) also survived the Shoah. The latter did so due to their flight to Communist Russia immediately before the German invasion.

I have written this book around much of what my father could remember and had passed on. But some of his memories could not be placed in a particular location. They happened in some of the places where he had been both a victim and witness. These accounts ought not to be lost, even though I am unable to attribute them to a particular place:

In one of the camps my father said that a Jewish prisoner had been locked in an outdoor building without either food nor drink. The guards passed their time with bets on how long it would take for this person to perish. My father told me that he and others in the camp heard the man begging for some water. The man hoped for a turn of his misfortune until the very end, by knocking against the door to draw attention to himself, until finally, probably after a couple of days, nothing more could be heard.

Another story he told was about dogs in one of the camps. The animals were misused and encouraged to attack people. I only remember fragments of the stories but have developed a lifelong aversion towards German shepherd dogs since I was a child because of that, perhaps having learned that Hitler owned this type of dog, or even less consciouly because my father was dismissive of this breed. This testimony from the

---

[517] Szwajzer (2010)

trials against those who were responsible for the crimes committed in Skarżysko-Kamienna leaves no uncertainty regarding how dogs were misused, and most likely my father's memories were from there:

> Rost (Dr Arthur Rost, director of the Skarżysko-Kamienna factory) always appeared with his dog – earlier there was a case when two people were killed by this dog... I saw how (some) people (who were only hungry and wanted) to eat. I happened to be just outside to relieve myself. That's when I saw how Dr Rost set the dog on those people who wanted to rest... Yes, I personally saw that the people were dead (later). They were covered in blood. They were two men. One aged 17, the other aged 20.[518]

That Dr Rost set his dog on prisoners purely for his sadistic entertainment had also been observed by others. Put under cross-examination, Rost even confessed himself, that he had set his German shepherd dog on prisoners, and that they were seriously injured by its bites.[519]

My father also told me that he had seen small children being smashed against walls as if they were rags, killing them in this barbaric and despicable way.

Another comment my father made was that German women in the camps treated the enslaved Jews worse than the men. Perhaps he was thinking of one specific woman in Skarzisko-Kamienna: Marianne Tietge (née Haubold). Tietge is listed in the court documents as a mother of children, but in the camp she was known for kicking into mens' private parts. She also was said to take pleasure from whipping people she had control over with a special hose that was modified with exposed wires to cause more damage.[520] She also had her victims pay her for the favour of not sending them to their deaths. Women too could be her

---

[518] Statement by Max Diamant, in Frey (1949), p. 34. (freely translated by author)
[519] Frey (1949), p. 14
[520] Frey. (1949) S.74

victims. Some witnesses reported that she enjoyed throwing heavy boxes onto the heads of some of those under her control.[521]

While Tietge and many others were brought to justice as a consequence of the trial, the main person responsible for the camp, Paul Budin, was not. Budin had taken his own life inside the Hasag main administration building on the night of 14th of April 1945, shortly before the US army entered Leipzig.[522] His suicide strongly suggests that he was quite possibly aware that Hasag's use of totally exposed and enslaved workers would be met with little sympathy from the Allies. It also means that he may have guessed that his penalty could be a severe punishment, maybe a death sentence. He was too much of a coward to face up to this, to be questioned by others and to admit these crimes, as the main person responsible for the factories.

Indeed, in December 1948, Arthur Rost, Willi Seidel, Alfred Wagner and Reinhard Neumerkel were sentenced to death by the Leipzig district court, for their parts in the crimes inside the Hasag factories in Skarzisko-Kamienna. No doubt, had Budin lived, he most probably would have faced the same sentence. In the case of those sentenced to death, the judges observed that they had shown no indication of a possible shift of conscience. They concluded that for that lack of hope for repentance of their crimes, "German's should be freed from these people once and for all."[523] Felix Krebs and Marianne Tietge were given life sentences. Fifteen other German employees of Hasag were sentenced to imprisonment lasting between six and 15 years and three employees received a prison sentence of up to three years. All assets of the ten main accused that could be traced were ordered to be confiscated.

Only a few of the supervisors and foremen from Schlieben and Flößberg, many of whom had tortured and tormented their workers, were brought to justice. One of them was a Schlieben foreman who

---

[521] Frey (1949), p.17, p.66 and p. 74
[522] Klein (2009), p. 14
[523] Ibid, pp. 90-93

personally administered 49 lashes with a dog leash to Eli-Yahu Winkler, on the antisemitic grounds that "the Jews are beating us." Winkler survived the Shoah and testified.[524] Jürgen Wolf from the memorial centre of KZ-Schlieben knew of the following persons that were sentenced after the war: Viktor Leo Thomas Lamkewitz who was a foreman in the foundry and was nicknamed "The Boxer" in the camp because he conducted himself with particular brutality towards prisoners, received a life sentence. Works manager Erich Gustav Graichen was given a prison sentence of up to eight years for his own mistreatment of the enslaved forced labourers. Karl Richard Müller, the head of the SS guard team and transport leader of the first evacuation transport to Theresienstadt, was sentenced to one year in prison. He was said to be exceptional for not having harassed or mistreated any prisoners and was even acquitted in the end.

Heinrich Lütscher, Flößberg's commanding officer, was sentenced to three years in prison by a US military court in 1947 for the cruelty he showed towards the enslaved forced workers.[525]

The sentences concerning some of the other larger camps mentioned within Zol Zayn Shulem, will only be mentioned briefly. Compared to the smaller camps, where my father was, there is more information published about these. Due to the fact that there is less known about Skarzisko-Kamienna, Schlieben and Flößberg it is given more of a mention here. But for very brief reference, many but not all of the persons who run Auschwitz and Auschwitz Birkenau, Buchenwald as well as Dachau, were caught, and considerable number received death sentences, others got away with imprisonment. Some like Josef Mengele, who conducted medical experiments on Jewish victims in Auschwitz escaped justice. Concerning the people who run Treblinka, only prison sentences were handed out.

During my research, I also tried to find out who Master Walter, from the heating installation company Hammer, really was, because he had

---

[524] Martin Schnellenberg, „Die Schnellaktion Panzerfaust", in Dachauer Hefte (2005), p. 259, p. 270
[525] Personal e-mail Jürgen Wolf, 19.12.2022 with reference to Stichting voor wetenschappelijk onderzoek van nationaal-socialistische misdrijven, 2021

not only treated my father relatively well, but had pulled him out of the hell of work with heavy pipes in Flößberg. Although that was in part out of self-interest, it was one of the many contributing factors in my father's survival. I would have been interested to know if he had revealed anything to his relatives over the rest of his living years. All I found is that the Hammer company had indeed signed up to the exploitation of enslaved forced labourers from Buchenwald.

Further details about the employees of the company and their identities were also lost.

A cemetery in Flößberg, which was quickly created after the war to draw an end to this disturbing chapter, was in 1951, in the early days of the GDR, transformed into a memorial-site to remember the plight of political victims of National Socialism. This was despite the fact, that most of the enslaved labourers in Flößberg had not been political prisoners of the Third Reich. Most victims had simply been Jewish. Nearly six decades later, with the fall of the Iron Curtain, this selective and arranged memorialisation was rectified.[526] In the years that followed interested and engaged local Germans tried to dig into the real history of the camp. They even contacted my father, though he refused to collaborate. It was left for me, years after my father's death, to pick up the scraps of his life story and write them down as a whole story as best I could.

This also raised difficult questions about my father's experiences, not just regarding the later camps. Could it be that my grandfather's selection as a member of the *Judenrat* of Szczekociny gave him and in extension my father and his brothers privileges over others?

Strigler writes in the "*Factories of Death*":

Only later, when things became tight in the shtetl and everyone without exception was sent to certain death, did some of the Judenrat come (to Skarzisko Kamienna) in exchange for money. It was no

---

[526] Stefan Walter, „Eine unangenehme Sache – Der Häftlingsfriedhof von Borna", in Schriftreihe des Museums der Stadt Borna (2007), p. 52

> wonder why they were so full of hatred. Natek (name) had a mania for seeing only enemies in every newly arriving transport. If you arrived that late to the camp, it was a sign that you had money beforehand, with which you could protect yourself at the expense of others (or) that you were part of a Judenrat. He could have skinned the new arrivals, take the cruellest revenge for the six months that were lost to him, compared to the others.[527]

However, the position of the *Judenrats* was varied. In ghettos like Warsaw or in death camps, they were jointly responsible for deciding who had to be sent for deportations and who not, truly a question of certain death or being permitted to hang on. As far as I know, my grandfather was never responsible for carrying out any such selections. Until September 1942, the time of the total evacuation of Szczeociny, there were no large deportations and removals from the town. The task of the *Judenrat* in Szczekociny was rather to organise and provide for labourers or to satisfy the hunger for loot of their German and Volksdeutsche tormentors. Nevertheless, the "privilege" of the position may have had something to do with the fact, that my father and grandfather were able to escape the great deportation to Treblinka, although my father clearly stated that it was the fact that his father had made boots for an SS man without pay. So at best it was the privilege of access to this German. Did it help? My father and his father were allocated to the group of "skilled labourers" allowed to survive, but on the other hand, they were in fact skilled and experienced leather workers. If they had an apparent "privilege" it was not even good enough to save other relatives. The brothers Dawid and Abraham came to Skarżysko-Kammienna on their own account. At best, my grandfather possibly saved his son Abraham's life when he sent shoes with money hidden inside. But did you have to be a *Judenrat* for that? It was Abraham himself who had sent for help from the camp. As my father and his father were moved on to the

---

[527] Strigler (2017), p. 153

Radom ghetto, the status of a former *Judenrat* in Szczekociny no longer played any role in the selection process there. All that mattered were a few banknotes to the right person in the right moment.

It may be, however, that in Skarżysko-Kamienna, the Jewish commander of the camp, Fela Markowiczowa could have been impressed by the fact that my grandfather was a *Judenrat* member. She therefore may have given him a better position. She may very well have been looking for people who resembled her role, even though my grandfather is said never to have played roulette with human lives. The "*Kommandata*", as she was called, is also said to have had a preference for people who came from her own neighbourhood. A *Judenrat* who came from Szczekociny, just 100 kilometres from Skarżysko-Kamienna, may not have held the worst of cards.

But the money that my father had brazenly stuffed into his "cushion from heaven" upon his arrival in Skarżysko-Kamienna, fully aware of the threat of an immediate death sentence, which he was able to smuggle through security unnoticed, may have been much more crucial to his survival and that of his father and brothers than any previous positions. On the other hand, in Buchenwald, Schlieben and Flößberg and on the death train to Mauthausen, deprived of his money, it was luck and proactive thinking alone that kept my father alive. My uncles Abraham and Dawid were also just "fortunate", until Dawid's luck ran out in Theresienstadt just moments after the liberation.

It was the same chutzpah and presence of mind that later brought about an escape route from the death transport to Mauthausen. What would have happened if my father hadn't escaped from the train? I have already mentioned that the train made it to KZ-Mauthausen. That train arrived at Mauthausen or Gusen station four days after my father's escape on 29 April 1945. After disembarking, the weakest people were immediately shot by SS guards.[528] Stefan Walter, head of the "*Initiative Flößberg gedenkt*", wrote:

---

[528] Email from the director of the Floessberg Memorial by Stefan Walter, 18 July 2020

From the accounts of survivors, it is clear that the prisoners of Flößberg found themselves in a physically and hygienically desolate state when they arrived in Mauthausen. Their clothes were heavily soiled, and they were covered with lice. Ferenc Kornfeld, a survivor, reported that the disinfection and decontamination measures that followed their arrival were sometimes associated with considerable ordeals. After an initial shower, the prisoners presumably had to walk barefoot and naked to the so-called "Russian camp" of Mauthausen, where they were then to be housed. Here they had to climb into cold vats of water again. Survivor Stephen Casey reported that he was given his old prisoner clothing back after disinfection, while Ferenc Kornfeld reported that he and others were only given a blanket as (new) clothing. The survivors did not report any more abuse or killings after the disinfection and accommodation in the camp. However, it was checked for people who had died on the plank beds, and their bodies were removed. The liberation of the Mauthausen camp took place on 5 April 1945, after which prisoners who had previously been in Flößberg died in Mauthausen from the hardships they had suffered. Stephen Casey reports the death of a friend after liberation.

What can be said about the final deportation train, then? Stefan Walter said that on 13 April, 1144 prisoners were deported from Flößberg. It is not known precisely how many of these arrived alive in Mauthausen. No named records of the transport exist. Estimates range between 200 (Ferenc Kornfeld) and at best 600 people (Bernard Steif) who made it. This means that a third or even half of all those trapped inside the trains perished during the journey. They died miserably of thirst, starvation, suffocation or during their escape attempts.

What my father wanted to pass on to posterity was that he never understood how Germans could invade a foreign land. He said he could neither forget, nor forgive. Forgiving was an act of the murdered, and forgetting was not possible for him. In 2001, at the time of his interview at the Shoah Foundation, self-confident right-wing nationalist politics was already stirring up in Germany, as well as in other European countries, not the least in France, where antisemitism was on the rise. My father found it hard to swallow the German politeness of the post-war pseudo-state. For him, it hid the true face of Germans. The evidence for that, he said, was the rise of the right-wing nationalists and the apparent inability to sufficiently marginalise them or adequately prosecute the murderers of the Third Reich era. What would have made of the rise of the AFD in 2025 as Germany's main opposition party?

My father spent the rest of his life trying to comprehend what had happened between 1933 and 1945. To him it was the worst murder conducted in the history of mankind. It was the worst, he argued, because it wasn't about land or resources, "we had nothing of much worth. It was nothing but theft and plunder!". The only reason for the attacks, as he understood it, was a racially motivated genocide that murdered and persecuted people for no other reason than that they were Jewish. "*They only wanted to murder and take lives and spare no-one, not even small children*", he repeated again and again.[529] Humanity had never seen such "*Verbrecher*", or "criminals", he would say. He added that he never expected that they would allow people like himself survive.

After the falling apart of Yugoslavia, my father agreed that what happened in Bosnia and other parts of the former republics constituted genocide. At the same time, however, he opposed attempts by Germans to understand the Shoah as only an example of the potential for human cruelty, because of the brutality and the extent and speed of the slaughter he had witnessed. That was in his view unprecedented. When I confronted him with Hans Dollinger's "*Black Book of World History*", a book in which the German historian attempted to record all the massacres and mass murders of the last 5,000 years in global human history, my father remarked that man was his own worst enemy.[530]

---

[529] Zylbersztajn (2011), Cassette V
[530] Dollinger (2002)

"*Homo homini lupus*" was one of his favourite quotes – "Man is a wolf to man." That quote was ironic, when you think of the fact that my father's own first name was Wolf. Nevertheless, as far as he was concerned, there would be a unique place for Germans in human history, as a condemned people: "Oh, may they be cursed!"[531]

And yet it was he who had been living in Germany since 1951. His justification for this was that Hitler's dream of a "*judenfreies Deutschland*" – a Germany free of Jews – would be refuted every day he lived on.

But his life in Germany was without peace and restless. As I will report later, there were constant discussions about the role of Germany and Germans and later parallels were being made between Nazi crimes and Israeli actions. Like many of my Israeli relatives, my father always responded with words similar to these: "*Let the Nazis try to fight us in our own country with our army.*"

It was pride in the strength of the Israeli armed forces that stood behind such words. Such strength symbolised for him the best guarantee that what had happened to him would never happen again.

He was not opposed to the independence of Palestine alongside Israel. He was in favour of two states and the end of the Israeli military occupation of most regions in the West Bank and Gaza. It was the subject of frequent discussions between him and other survivors. The talk was usually not about whether Palestinians had a right to their own state, but whether and how Jews could live safely in Israel. He did not live to see 7th October 2023, but he saw something similar in the years of Israel's many clashes with its neighbours and the terror. Those who had done such things before deserved a "*shwarzn sof*" – a black end – or the force of Israel. Nevertheless, peace was something to strive for. He attentively followed the peace process with Egypt's Sadat, with King Hussein, even the rapprochement between Rabin and Arafat, while political figures such as Gadaffi, Amin, Khomeini, Assad and Saddam Hussein belonged to the category of "*Verbrecher.*"

---

[531] Ibid.

Judgements

Another topic in connection with the Shoah was the question of G-d. "*Where was G-d, where was he?*" my father often mocked. My aunt Ruszke, on the other hand, was certain that G-d had saved her. My father replied: "Why (save) me and not the others, why little children?" He no longer prayed. He honoured those he had lost in the Munich synagogue in Reichenbachstraße during Yizkor on Yom Kippur. And that was that.

Less than ten per cent of the Jews in Szczekociny survived the Shoah. My father said that not one of his original school friends survived the war. His family was exceptional, with three surviving brothers.

Before this book moves on to the time after 1945, I would like to leave the last words to my father.

I have seen what happened in the former Yugoslavia. One slaughtering the other. That is very bad. But the murders committed by the Germans in the Second World War, the world has never seen the like of such crimes.

All under the age of five – I saw how they threw them onto a lorry and drove them out of the city, where they murdered them. Little children! And then they buried them in a vast ditch. I don't think that what the Germans did can be found anywhere else. Despite all the terrible events in the world today. There is no nation that I have seen in my life that could be worse than the Germans. They were true racists. History has known no worse, they stamped over the dying and the dead.[532]

---

[532] Zylbersztajn (1995), p. 21

30

Amsterdam and Munich after the War

1947 in the Netherlands. From left to right: My grandmother Maria, my mother Corrie, my aunt Gerda, my uncle Edi and my great-grandmother Cor.

Amsterdam and Munich after the War

At the end of the Second World War on 5 May 1945, the Lewandowski Family was sitting in their apartment at Haarlemer Straat 29 in Amsterdam, gathered around the radio-set. "Dad suddenly announced that the war was over and was just happy", my mum told me. My mother was merely six years old. She said that initially it was still dangerous to go out on the streets, because there were still executions being carried out by prowling, vengeful Germans and their henchmen.

After the war, the Lewandowski family lived finally without fear in Haarlemer Straat.

The family was blessed with more children My mother's brother Eduard was born in 1947, Louise in 1950. For their father, these were late children, as he was now 60 years old.

My aunt Gerda told me that my grandfather often visited Amsterdam's theatres with my mother, as she was the eldest, thus picking up on his old passion, about which he wrote already during the First World War. My mum remembered many of these visits, especially those to the opera.

"My father loved music", she often emphasised. One story she frequently repeated was how the family sat around her father when he played and sang old German favourites, amongst them "Mein Vater war ein Wandersmann." Between my grandmother and my grandfather, my mother remembered, it was my much older grandfather, who appeared to be the more caring parent. "Dad always went out with us children. He took us with the little ones in their pram for strolls on Sundays. My mother didn't do that. She always preferred to work in the shop instead."[533]

The postwar years were a time of reconstruction for many, the Lewandowskis in Amsterdam included. My grandfather had been concentrating on developing his own new lingerie brand he called GELE, after the two letters of his first and second name. Now with the war over, he finally had the opportunity to showcase his work again and with seeming success, as he was given an award at the Amsterdam fashion exhibition of 1951.

---

[533] · personal conversation

My mother with a friend, c.a. 1949/50, Amsterdam. Own photo.

At the same time my mother was finally able to enjoy some school education. In a photo taken around 1950, we can see my mother, aged ten or eleven, sitting next to a school-friend. According to her own perception, she identified completely as a Dutch girl at the time.

But her father could not seem to shake off the memories of the previous home he had been forced to flee from. Despite having a relatively happy family in Amsterdam, he kept considering a return to Munich. This was not because he was minded to try suing for compensation and to see if any of his old possessions could still be traced. He had German return papers issued as early as 1949 and in 1951, presumably shortly after the successful exhibition, he decided to leave everything in Amsterdam behind and to relocated to Munich, taking his wife and all the children, including my mother, with him.

At around the same time, the first tribunal regarding the flat that the Germans had taken possession of took place before the judges of a

British-administered restitution court. Initially it appeared promising. According to my cousin Claudia and the stories her mother Gerda told her, my grandfather also sold a property that was not disputed (probably near near Schliersee) during this time in order to come to some money for himself and his family. However, it wasn't enough, because according to my mother, the property wasn't worth much.[534]

GELE employee at the exhibition in Amsterdam, 1951, my grandmother Maria on the far right.

---

[534] I remember that the property may have been at the lake Schliersee or near the lake Tegernsee, or in between the two. This was mentioned to me by my mother. She also reported once that she was with my grandfather in Tegernsee Brewery. In any case, both lakes are close to each other, so it was somewhere in this region.

The attempt to get compensated for his apartment at Beichstraße 9 in Schwabing, which was auctioned in his absence in 1935, or to receive some compensation, failed.

It was not a straightforward case. My grandfather had fallen behind with his mortgage payments in 1932 but had a repayment agreement in place. He owned money on two mortgages, one worth 22,000 Reichsmark and another one to the value of 3000 Reichsmark. The repayments depended on my father receiving rental income on his property, among other things. But after Hitler had risen to power, his antisemitic tenant, Herr Braml, refused to pay his rent. In addition, my grandfather had a tax and duty remission that he had been granted by the Munich tax office cancelled. This happened after the tax office learnt that my grandfather was of Jewish descent, as documents in his files still reveal to this present day.[535] So the city of Munich, together with the Bavarian mortgage bank, collaborated directly or indirectly to force the situation that led to sale of the house in 1936. This is why my grandfather had the postwar restitution court examine the case. Unfortunately, he lost both before the judges 1951 and on appeal in 1953. The main argument of the defence, with which the judges appear to have agreed, was, that my grandfather had difficulties with the repayment before the onset of the Third Reich. Another argument was that it was only from 1939 onwards that decisions were explicitly made *against* Jewish property owners.

The obvious fact that my grandfather had already been sent to Dachau concentration camp for six months in 1933 was totally ignored by the judges, as if it had been of no consequence. The debt, the persecution and the antisemitic tenant were simply considered as matters apart. The defence also emphasised the fact that my grandfather had "only" been a "half-Jew" who was of a "Christian denomination" during the Third Reich and that he possessed a Nazi contact due to his service in the First World War. This contact was the Nazi finance minister Ebb,

---

[535] File B 126/61234 and 563 Federal Compensation Office Düsseldorf in the Federal Archives, Koblenz, "Supreme Restitution Court", pp. 2-3

who had served in the same unit as my grandfather and to whom he had threatened to write in his despair. But the fact that my grandfather had been deprived of his freedom in 1933 and had been beaten up severely several times, and that he had been told before his decision to flee to Holland in 1935 that "next time, he wouldn't get out (of Dachau – the adjective "alive" can certainly be inserted here), none of this seemed to bother the judges, as long as the bureaucratic proceedings of the taking possession of and auctioning of the flat did not reveal itself traces of overt antisemitism. The fact that the system had already victimised my grandfather severely left them unimpressed.

In 1936, when the forced sale was taking place, my grandfather had already been living in the safety of the Dutch capital, Amsterdam. Both of his two Munich-based lawyers failed to summon up the courage to represent and defend him in the case, because of his background and incarceration – in other words, dealing with my grandfather's case could get you in trouble with the authorities of Reich. The inventory of the flat was also confiscated, according to the legal documents filed later. A list from 1951 of the possessions confiscated in 1936 mentions paintings by Friedrich Kaulbach, Jan Weissenbruch, Keller, Franz v. Lenbach, Gritzner, "Siebermann" (probably Max Liebermann), Ludwig Eibl and three other oil paintings.

One of the two aforementioned lawyers, Otto Meyer, stated after the war in his testimony that every time my grandfather, his client, approached the authorities about his property, the situation got worse, and that even he himself, Meyer, had witnessed remarks about my grandfather's identity.

Here is Otto Meyer's letter, which I discovered in the archived trial papers of 1952:[536]

> Lawyer Dr Otto Meyer Munich Maximilianstraße 29
> Munich, 16 November 1950 Mr Gerhard Lewandowski
> Munich
> Nymphenburgerstr. 217

b. Röhrl

As your legal representative in the period before and after your arrest by the Gestapo, I know that you repeatedly discussed with me the issues that arose from your persecution as a half-Jew. In particular, these related to the struggle for your property at Beichstrasse 9, made more difficult for you to sustain, because your tenants no longer wanted to pay you rent as a "Jew" and no longer paid it, so that you got into ever greater financial difficulties, especially with authorities such as the central tax office and the city's treasury. As often as you addressed the authorities concerning the pay of the rents and taxes due for the property, you were treated dismissively (lit. shown the cold shoulder) everywhere, referring in particular to your status as a Jew and calling it an impertinence that you had even dared to attempt any appeals. I was also spoken to very stupidly, whenever I intervened on your behalf. Similarly, the behaviour of your bank (Bayer. Vereinsbank) was doomed to failure for the same reasons, and it was therefore not possible for me to intervene successfully, in order to prevent the forced sale of your property.

I would ask you to name me as a witness at the Reparations Office, where I can confirm the accuracy of the above information under oath at any time.

Yours sincerely,
Dr Otto Meyer

---

[536] translated by author

The other lawyer, Paul Lermann, even admitted after the war that he was no longer able to represent my grandfather in 1936, because he, Lermann, had himself become a member of the NSDAP at the time.[537] He wrote:

On reflection, it was an unreasonable and impossible task for me to intervene in these circumstances, if I didn't want to expose myself to danger... It had happened to me shortly before at the Political Police Station, when I petitioned for a Pole, that I was told very clearly, what interest I had, in acting as a German lawyer for a Pole.

Although my grandfather was eventually granted a short extension of ten days in January to explain his affairs, his flat was auctioned off and soon sold on. In his submission to court after the war, my grandfather pointed to the fact that his inability to pay fees in time was due to the arrests, the racism displayed to him by the authorities and the refusal of the tenant to pay his rent on grounds of his antisemitism. All this owning to policies of the Nazi regime, which ultimately led to his hastily arranged flight to Amsterdam in order to save his life, the last link in the chain of humiliation and deprivation,

In spite of the full support of the well-known Munich lawyer Siegfried Neuland (1889-1969) in assisting my grandfather (Neuland had been the Vice President of the Jewish Community in Munich and later its president), my grandfather lost both the initial, as well as the appeal case, and that in spite of the fact, that the three judges of the US Court of Restitution Appeals were Americans.[538] Neither court wanted to agree to any explicit discrimination in this case and did not consider the situation in which my grandfather had found himself to be significant enough in order for them to rule in favour of my grandfather.

---

[537] File of the 1952 case. NSADP, Abbreviation for Nationalsozialistische Partei Deutschland, the National Socialist Party of Germany, Hitler's Party

[538] Ibid

My grandfather's former lawyer Paul Lermann wrote in a letter in 1950, before the trials began, the following lines:

In my opinion, if political persecution had not played a role and if he had not been half-Jewish, Mr Lewandowski would have been able to organise his circumstances in such a way, that no seizure-proceedings would have been initiated at all. However, difficulties arose precisely because Mr Lewandowski, as a politically persecuted person, was forced out of his normal business activities.[539]

According to my uncle Marcello's recollections, my grandmother was offered an increased pension of 1,000 Deutschmark (after my grandfather's death), but under an implicit demand. In return for the pension, she was not allowed to initiate any further claims or legal proceedings concerning my grandfather's case, a condition that had also been imposed on my grandfather earlier (see next chapter).

As a widow without sufficient resources, a stranger to Munich and a mother of four, she had little other choice but to accept the offer before her. My grandfather's property had been destroyed during the war and the house in which the apartment stood had been rebuilt at some stage with six floors. The per square metre rate in the area was recently valued to exceed 10,000 Euros.[540]

Other residents of Munich, Germans without Jewish ancestry and who were not political opponents of the Nazi system and thus were not tortured by the Political Police or in Dachau, did not encounter any problems during or after the war.

---

[539] Paul Lermann, Adalbert Str 25 Munich, 20 September 1951
[540] In the year 2022

Case No. 484

as it would be an additional requisite that the carrying-through of the execution sale represent itself as an instance of abuse of a governmental act. They assigned it as irrelevant to the issue that the Jew contracted debts as a cause of the persecution, that Lewandowski had been in political confinement, that he had to flee to Holland, and that the tenants of the house, in several instances, had refused to pay the rent to the Jew.

The two lawyers Otto Meyer and Lermann had been named as important witnesses in the briefs. They were supposed to testify on the treatment which Lewandowski received by the authorities.

Mr. Stoeckel had been named as witness on the attitude held by the tenants as regards the payment of their rents. The courts found it proper to do without a hearing of these witnesses. However, that view of the courts is incorrect and presents a violation of law for the testimony of the witnesses would have convinced the court that Lewandoswki had been even individually persecuted and that the execution sale was the result of those measures of persecution.

III.

It appears necessary to point out in this case that the foregoing considerations as to whether this or that trend of thought should be followed were, as a matter of fact, superfluous for the claim asserted by Lewandowski is well-founded even if one wanted to follow the fundamental conception of the Munich courts and of the Hamm Oberlandesgericht. For it cannot be denied that the discriminating circumstances are given which serve also to support the charge of an abuse of a governmental act.

Kopie aus dem Bundesarchiv

Original page of the defence lawyer of my grandfather, Siegfried Neiland.

Zol Zayn Shulem I: Zores

Case No. 484

IV.

Consequently, I petition the Court to grant the following motions:

I. The decision of the Munich Oberlandesgericht of 24 July 1951 and the decision of the Munich I Landgericht of 27 November 1950 shall be set aside.

II. The order of adjudication of 23 June 1936 shall be null and void.

III. The restitutor Horst Hammer shall return to the claimant Gerhard Lewandowski the real property Beichstrasse 9,

or as an alternative,

after setting aside the decisions of the Munich Oberlandesgericht and of the Munich I Landgericht, to remand the matter to the Munich I Landgericht for a new trial and decision.

/s/ Siegfried Neuland
Attorney-at-Law

for the Copy:
/s/ Siegfried Neuland
Attorney-at-Law.

Kopie aus dem Bundesarchiv

Original page of the defence lawyer of my grandfather, Siegfried Neiland.

31

The Lewandowskis in Munich

In 1951, the Lewandowskis initially resided in the flat of a friend of my grandfather in Grillparzerstraße 51. But even this somewhat more upmarket address could not hide the fact that for my mother and her siblings, but also for my grandmother, the rushed move to Munich tore them out of their familiar and social network in Amsterdam and the Netherlands. This small partially Dutch family had now moved to the land of the "*Rodmoffen*" – as Germans were dismissively called in the Netherlands. And it was not just people like them who had suddenly moved to Germany, but, in particular, former Dutch collaborators of the Nazi state too.

I couldn't find out much about those years, but I did discover that my grandmother, who my mother described as distant and reserved (Quote: "she had the children and then didn't want to take much care of them"), employed a nanny called Johanna. My aunt Gerda remembered being punished by her teacher at school with beatings on her fingers, because she had made mistakes when attempting to speak German. My mother said, she didn't experience anything like that, and as far as she was concerned, thought it wasn't so bad. But my aunt Gerda was younger than my mother. It was a story aunt Gerda would recall often, perhaps an indication how traumatic and unjust she felt it was.

The old Lewandowski flagship store in Theatinerstrasse and the shops in Neuhauserstrasse, Sendlinger Strasse and Färbergraben had all been destroyed in the allied bombing raids. The brothers Gerhard (my grandfather), Bruno and Wilhelm Lewandowski tried to rebuild five of the remaining corset and underwear shops and reopened them "with great difficulty", Alfred Lewandowski wrote later.[541]

From a fashion point of view, the post-war years were in fact not a bad time for corsetry. Film stars such as Sophia Loren, Gina Lollobrigida and Marilyn Monroe had made bras that emphasised the female form acceptable. The age of the petticoat also dawned on Europe. In addition, bodice panties, so-called corselets, came into fashion.[542]

However, the hopes and ambitions of rebuilding the former fashion empire were soon dashed through unsuspected departures.

The first setback came when in 1953 Bruno passed away. Erna, his surviving wife, now had to run the shop on her own. Willi Lewandowski allegedly still owned three shops, one on Marienplatz (where there is currently a bakery and shop), a shop in his wife's name (Stingelwagner) in Unterföhring and another in Fürstenriederstraße in Munich. About these we read in an advert from the early 1960s:

> In 1947, Wilhelm Lewandowski worked tirelessly with his wife, Mrs Hella, née Stinglwagner, to open the Werk Building at Landshuter Allee 162 and a shop on the corner of Neuhausestraße at Pschorrblock… A branch was opened at Augustinerstraße 36 in 1953 and another in 1956.[543]

Although my grandfather, as many witnesses confirmed, was an experienced businessman who wanted to rejoin his brothers in the effort of rebuilding their lives in Munich, he was plagued by great financial worries, due to the unsuccessful restitution claim. His daughters also remembered this

---

[541] Lewandowski (1981)
[542] Bauer (2014), p.12
[543] Advertisement from the early 1960s, private archive, Philipp Lewandowski

The Lewandowskis in Munich

in conversations with me. To be able to support his family, he finally accepted a compensation pension of just 227 Deutschmark per month, around 600 Euros in today's currency.[544] However, in order to "benefit" from this pension "as compensation for his (poor) health", he was told by the restitution authorities to waive his rights to any further complaints and claims.[545]

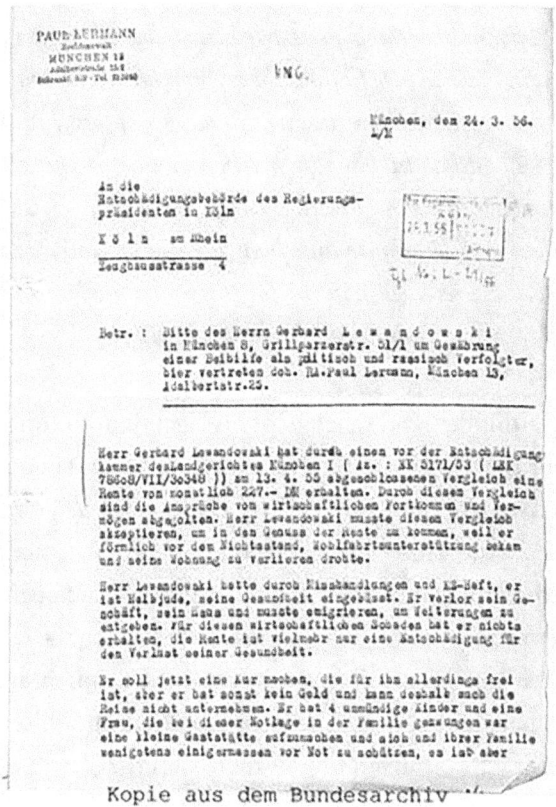

Letter from the files on my grandfather Gerhard Lewandowski.

---

[544] This pension was paid to him from 13 April 1955. File from the German Federal Archives of the compensation authority of the district president in Cologne, relating to Gerhard Lewandowski 1563, previously IW-HNG-4-21/56. Converted value of approx.. 600 Euros (2022).

[545] Federal archive file on Gerhard Lewandowski B126/61243, letter from his Lawyer Paul Lermann on 24 March 1956

His former lawyer, Paul Lermann, wrote on 24 March 1956 that my grandfather had been forced to agree to this involuntarily:

> Mr Gerhard Lewandowski received a pension of 227 DM per month as a result of a settlement concluded before the Compensation Chamber of the Munich I Regional Court (case no. EK 517½3 (LEK 78608/VIII/30348)) on 13 April 1955. The settlement settled claims for economic advancement and assets. Mr Lewandowski had to accept this settlement in order to benefit from the pension because he was formally dependent on social welfare and was in danger of losing his home.
>
> Mr Lewandowski has lost his health due to the abuse and imprisonment in a concentration camp, he is half-Jewish. He lost his business and his house and had to emigrate to escape further persecution. He received nothing for this economic loss; the pension is merely compensation for the loss of his health.

I consider this demand to let go of his legal right to continue his case as a victim of the Third Reich to be downright scandalous on the part of the West German authorities. Why did the *Wiedergutmachungsamt* (the restitution office) interfere in a search for natural justice and forbade my grandfather, on the basis of a small pension, to continue to try to question them and have the circumstances concerning the forced auction of 1936 and his persecution further examined through available legal channels? What right did Germans in particular and after all have to demand such exclusion from one of their victims?

Just one year later my grandfather found himself seriously ill and on top of that deeply in debt. His lawyer reported that my grandmother had opened a small restaurant for a short time in order to get by, given she had her four children to support and that my sick grandfather was supposed to go to a health spa but didn't even have any clothes. On top of that, rent and heating costs totalling 400 DM plagued my grandfather. The compensation authority in Cologne finally appeared to recognise hardship and granted my grandfather a one-off emergency payment of DM 1,000.

The Lewandowskis in Munich

A further application from his lawyer in September 1955, requesting a "business start-up capital" of DM 5000, was, however, rejected.[546]

On 5 October 1956, my grandfather's doctor, Dr. G. Vorberg, reported that his patient suffered from a severe heart condition and coronary disease caused by his mistreatment "as a Jew", and that the financial hardship had put him in a state of constant mental agitation. His state of health had worsened.[547]

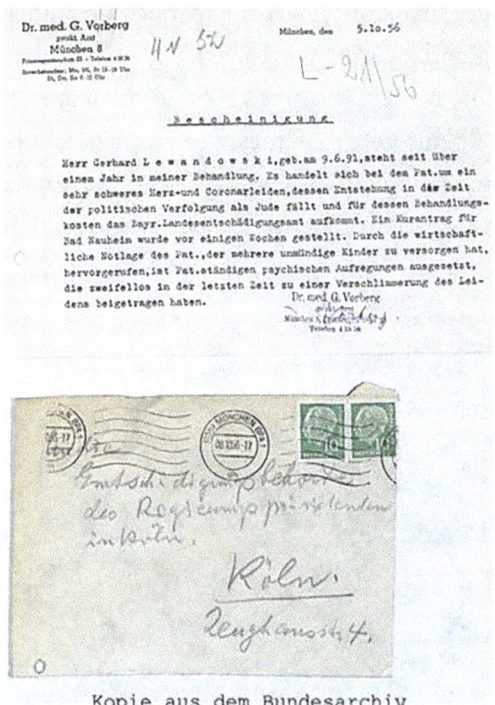

Kopie aus dem Bundesarchiv

Letter from Gerhard Lewandowski's doctor to the compensation authority in Cologne.

---

[546] Federal archive file Gerhard Lewandowski. 1563, letter from Paul Lermann, Mümchen. Interestingly, my grandfather's lawyer Paul Lermann emphasises in this letter that Gerhard Lewandowski was brought up as a Protestant and never belonged to the Jewish faith. However, the reason for this can be explained by the request for help in a state of emergency emanating from non-Jewish victims of Nazi persecution. Six months earlier, Lermann had described Gerhard Lewandowski as a "half-Jew."

[547] Federal archive file Gerhard Lewandowski, 1563.

Zol Zayn Shulem I: Zores

I discovered a photo of my grandfather, showing him during this period. He is standing proudly in a neat suit with his daughters Gerda and Corrie, my aunt and my mother, in front of newly opened tiny shop in his name. He holds a cigar in one hand, and his expression leaves no doubt, as to what this picture aims to express: At last! In line with the requirements of the rebuilding of the Lewandowski corsetry and ladies' fashion chain, the photo says something else: My grandfather's daughters now represented his hopes for the future. According to my mother, the shop was but very small, but it was the spark of a relaunch, nevertheless.

But all hope and joy were short-lived. My grandfather succumbed to acute heart failure on 10 December 1956 at the relatively young age of 64, just short of being able to witness the marriage of his first daughter, my mother, even though my father had met my grandfather before he died and, according to my parents, the two men had liked one another.

My grandfather's death also occurred before the widening of compensation and restitution for victims of the Third Reich through the German Federal Compensation Act of 1956, the Federal Restitution Act of 1957, and the Federal Compensation Act of 1965.

On reflection, the sum of 5,000 DM my grandfather had requested to start his business, was far less than the total amount my grandfather had lost through the forced sale of his house. Without the National Socialists coming to power, his lingerie and corsetry business might also have recovered from the global depression. In view of everything that had once belonged to the Lewandowski Family in Munich and Berlin, not to mention the "value" of the murdered Lewandowskis, had they remained alive and been able to continue their businesses and jobs, it is shameful that victims were given so little help in rebuilding their lives. Grief and agitation caused by representatives of the German state, the physical and mental injuries inflicted and his torture through beatings and incarceration certainly advanced the premature death of my grandfather.

My father would also spend the rest of his life arguing with the restitution authorities. The reasons are obvious, and they also apply to my grandfather Gerhard. German authorities either did not understand the extent of what reparation payments, so-called "*Wiedergutmachung*", were supposed to be paid out for, or they did and kept a low profile, i.e. they didn't pay or only paid the bare minimum.

Edi (Eduard), the only boy among the Munich Lewandowski siblings, is said to have later tried to continue the small business that my grandfather had rebuilt and left behind At some point he gave up. A few years later, Gerda and my grandmother were to try their luck with a small lingerie shop in the village of Zorneding (between Ebersberg and Munich), where my aunt lived from the 1970s onwards. They sold made-to-measure lingerie, which my aunt Gerda had to sew and sometimes, according to my uncle, had to work through the night for. She had learnt how to make such undergarments through a former Jewish employee of my grandfather after the war.

As already mentioned, my grandfather's small pension had been transferred to my grandmother following his death, with the condition that there would be no further claims.

Not everyone in the family faced the same difficulties as my grandfather, or his brother Bruno, who was simply unable to find a renewed purpose for his life after the tragic loss of his only daughter.

The exception was Alfred, my grandfather's youngest brother. The only brother, as far as I could establish, possibly the only one out of the entire Lewandowski Family in Munich as well as Berlin, who had joined the Wehrmacht, was also the only person who managed to expand and succeed, in terms of business, after the war.

This had its start with him continuing to manufacture bandages in whatever was left of the Lewandowski family business after the war. Before her death, my aunt Gerda claimed, that, as far as she knew, Alfred had had the remains of the factory transferred into his name without his brothers' knowledge or consent. To what extent this was correct is unclear. However, what can be said with certainty is that Alfred was not lacking in business acumen and talent. And so, between 1948 and 1960, he built and reigned over 5,500 square metres of factory floor and office space, as well as a combined electricity producing power-station and sawmill powered by a water stream.

I can only remember that at some point in 1981, I caught sight of the anniversary publication for the 125th anniversary of the "Lewandowski Company" which Alfred had produced. I was quite taken aback by it. In the pamphlet Alfred introduced himself as representing the inheritance and next generation of the entire Lewandowski Business History. The second page of the anniversary publication states: "Formerly part of the company association: Jacob Lewandowski, Kladau, Lewandowski Brothers. Berlin, David Lewandowski, Munich. Today's group: ALV Alfred Lewandowski Vebandstoff-Fabiken, Elektrizitätswerk Bettmansäge K.G, Lewandowskische Liegenschaftsverwaltung, Bau- und Grundwertungsabteilung Pöcking, Upper Bavaria."[548]

---

[548] Lewandowski (1981)

Alfred remained curiously silent about the Jewish identity of his great-grandfather and his father in the pamphlet, and did not shy away from showing himself with a picture during his service under Feldmarshall Rommel in North Africa. He also said nothing about the persecution of his brother Gerhard or the murder of many of his cousins, uncles and aunts in Berlin nor the process of Aryanisation of the Lewandowski company in Berlin. Decades later, while conducting research for this book, I met Alfred's grandson Philipp, who, had just as many questions about the Lewandowskis as I did, and especially about his grandfather.

32

Jewish Refugees in Munich

After my father had escaped the train arranged for him by the Zionist organisation by jumping once again off a train, the one that was supposed to take him to Italy, he hurried across the Alps on his way to Munich. Munich had become a temporary home to thousands of Jewish survivors within the US-occupied zone of postwar Germany. The number of Jews of Eastern European descent living in the greater Munich area in 1947 was impressive, allegedly no fewer than 75,000 people.[549]

Here in "Mjelowa", as Polish Jews had called Munich's Möhlstraße in Bogenhausen, with the experience he had gained and the money he had earned in Sosnowiec, my father was able to open a small shoemaker's workshop, in which he even employed some shoemakers, who were Jewish survivors like himself.[550]

In the tradition of his father's trade, he would measure and cut the uppers for the shoes, whilst the shoemakers would sew, nail and glue the shoes together. Some people, he said, would order more than one

---

[549] Anna Holian, Möhlstraße and the reconstruction Jewish economic life in post-war Germany, in Maier (2018). S. 2

[550] Maier (2018), p.76 Remember that my father insisted, that he was a leatherworker, cutting the leather, rather than a shoemaker. The distinction appears to have been important to him. It appear to have been traditionally separate.

pair at once, for example if they intended to travel on to places like the United States, England or Israel. An envelope that I found amongst my father's papers has survived over all those years, and shows a pre-printed return address, which stated:

Poln. Riding and Officer Boots
WOLF SILBERSTEIN MUNICH 27 – Möhlstraße-30

Möhlstraße, a street situated in an area of Munich with large, elegant homes, and which a certain Heinrich Himmler had once called his home (Möhlstr. 19) during the Third Reich (then, with direct proximity to Hitler's private apartment at Prinzregentenplatz 16), literally became after the war the very centre of Jewish postwar life.[551]

"Möhlstraße was home to small shops selling cigarettes, coffee, nylon stockings, fabrics, watches and silverware, as well as fresh fruit, vegetables and kosher meat, and often at low prices."[552] Some of these goods came from Eastern Europe, others from US stocks.[553] Lilly Maier, who researched Möhlstraße academically, wrote that in the first years after the war, this market in Munich helped to alleviate some of the deficits in the general food supply, and thus had an implicit vital function for many of the non-Jewish German citizens of Munich."[554] Even after the German currency reform, this "Jewish Market" remained a cheaper option than most other markets. This postwar Jewish quarter consisted of some 100 to 130 temporary and improvised shops. There was a Jewish kindergarten, a school, a pharmacy, a clinic for the sick, a place for prayers, as well as cafés and restaurants, grocery shops, textile shops, jewellers, furriers, bookshops and shops that sold Jewish ritual objects.[555] Similar centres,

---

[551] Willibald Karl, Möhlstraße in Munich-Bogenhausen, in Maier (2018), p. 21
[552] Anna Holian, Möhlstraße and the reconstruction Jewish economic life in post-war Germany in Maier (2018). S. 26
[553] Zylbersztajn (1995), p. 3
[554] Maier (2018), p. 36
[555] Ibid. and p. 29

built by immigrants, often refugees, can be found anywhere around the world even today.

But there is a very important question if indeed the Jewish Möhlstraße of Munich resembled something that could be described as a "*Schwarzmarkt*", a shady "black," illegal, taxes and standards undermining black market? Certainly, the Munich Police of the time was in no doubt that it was. But historian Juliane Wetzel rejects this label in her study on Jewish DPs. As to what concerned lower prices she notes that the American military authorities, but also German authorities, furnished the DPs with rather generous licences to sell non-priced goods as a reparative gesture.[556] Even more goods were purchased through contacts the Jewish survivors had with US soldiers, who procured goods in so-called PX-base shops, grocery stores and supermarkets for US military personnel.[557]

Raid by the Munich police in Möhlstraße on 4 July 1949.
Photo: Rudi Dix. Courtesy of the Munich City Archive.

---

[556] Juliane Wetzel: „Mir szinen doh." Munich and the surrounding area as a refuge for Holocaust survivors 1945-1948. In: Martin Broszat et al.(eds.): Von Stalingrad zur Währungsreform. On the social history of upheaval in Germany. Munich 1988, pp. 327-364, as cited in Maier (2018) p. 39

[557] Maier (2018), p. 80

It should be noted at this point that the accusation of running a Schwarzmarkt against Munich's post-1945 Jewish population was almost synonymous with the vocabulary the German Nazi regime had used until 1945. At the Wannsee Conference in 1942, the State Secretary of the newly annexed territories in Poland, Dr Josef Bühler, justified in his words, the need to eliminate the Jews, because, they posed supposedly a great danger as carriers of epidemics and creators of disorder inside the economic structures of Germany because of, and here you have it in black and white, the Jews' apparent "constant black market trading."[558]

The contacts and friendships that were forged between the survivors in Möhlstraße could often last a lifetime. They certainly were the basis of my father's Jewish life and friendships until his death. Another fundamental characteristic of the Jewish Möhlstraße was that it was closed on Shabbat but open on Sunday, unlike the rest of the other shops and stores in Munich, the capital of the still very Catholic Bavaria.[559] Möhlstraße played a role in the lives of many. Even Munich's long-time representative of its Jewish Community Charlotte Knobloch, a Jewish survivor herself, gave Möhlstraße a mentioning in her biography. Others however called the same street an eyesore.[560]

But why on earth did the Jewish survivors build up all of this in Munich's Möhlstrasse out of all places? Is there a reason for it? Firstly, the American occupying forces had some of their administrative buildings in the area, including those for aid and partner organisations that supported the Jewish refugees and survivors. Amongst them were the *United Nations Relief and Rehabilitation Administration* (UNRRA) and the *American Joint Distribution Committee* (AJC). Nearby were also the most important local aid organisations, the *Munich Jewish Committee* and the *Central Committee of Liberated Jews*, as well as the *Jewish Agency for Immigration to Palestine*, the Jewish educational and training

---

[558] Arad (1999), p. 13
[559] Maier (2018), p. 37 and p. 42
[560] Knobloch (2012) p. 113 Michael Brenner (1995), p. 74.

organisation *ORT*, and the *American Hebrew Immigrant Aid Society*.[561] [4] The reason for this was the fact that this area had remained relatively unscathed by the war damage seen in other parts of Munich.

The survivors were able to obtain houses and flats from the occupying forces, whose proximity had a "calming" effect in the event of any problems with the Germans. This was not without good reason. In 1946 an Auschwitz survivor had been shot at by the German police during a search in a DP camp near Stuttgart, after which the Americans had prohibited the police all access to DP camps.[562]

When direct US control ended, raids by the Munich police increased. They were soon accused of displaying classic antisemitic behaviour. Historian Lilly Mayer analysed internal correspondences from within the police directorate and found many similarities to reports from the Third Reich era. For example, the Jewish survivors in Munich were described as "Do-Nothings", parasites, a plague, a disgrace, as a rabble with criminal physiognomy and as loitering anti-social elements in their hundreds. The police chief at the time, a certain Mr Pitzer, even referred to his apparent fight against the black market as a "purge." The non-Jewish Germans were seen as victims of the former.[563] Mayer wrote that the general impression Germans had of a "displaced person" was of a person with apparent high level of criminality. Alas the survivors were accused of using dishonest methods to enrich themselves, quite in the antisemitic tradition of the "usurious Jew", associating anything seemingly foreign as an evil danger to Germans.[564]

Before my father had arrived in Munich, a police raid in Möhlstraße in 1949 had reached the headlines of newspapers around the world and led to fierce criticism.[565] Then, after the Munich-based *Süddeutsche*

---

[561] Anna Holian, Möhlstraße and the reconstruction of Jewish economic life in post-war Germany in Maier (2018). S. 25
[562] ibid.
[563] Maier (2018), p.49
[564] Ibid.
[565] ibid.

Zeitung published an antisemitic letter addressed to their editor, the Jewish community had enough, and organised a huge protest in Munich.[566] Nevertheless the police continued to harass the Jewish survivor community. There were further police actions in 1950 involving as many as 1,000 police and customs officers especially ordered into Munich from all over Germany. Similar police actions against Jewish survivors continued at least until 1954.

There is a serious question to be asked here, perhaps it even constitutes a shameful accusation: could it be that the deplorable treatment and the exaggerated surveillance of the new Jewish citizens of Munich fuelled their exodus from the Bavarian capital? Could the number of Jewish citizen, not only here but in the rest of Germany, have remained much higher without this harassment? It may have been a stroke of luck that my father only arrived in Munich after the largest confrontations by the Munich Police, because I am almost certain that he would not have been able to tolerate such treatment and that he would have packed his bags yet again. In the same way the Munich police had treated many people like my grandfather Gerhard during the Nazi era, the "new" post-war police possessed an interest in the new Jewish neighbourhood that can only be described as obsessive, characterised by an unrepentant urge to harass Jews.

But let me focus at least for a moment on these new Jewish residents of Munich. Who were they, how did they live? To start with, they were mostly single, without family support of any kind, and almost all were eager to make a living somehow. One of the many people my father remembered was a certain Hertz Rieger, who later set up a soon world-famous and Munich-based fashion house for furs and who made a name for himself due to his rather extravagant lifestyle. He became very wealthy in the 1960s and 1970s, before the business went into an unstoppable and rapid decline, as fur increasingly lost its appeal. But my father had

---

[566] In Ronen Steinke, Die Adolf Bleibtreu Affäre. Wie ein antisemitischer Leserbrief in der Süddeutschen Zeitung 1949 eine Straßenschlacht auslösen, in Maier (2018), pp. 52-63

met Rieger before his success. He remembered him with these words: "You ought to have seen how he still had a car-load full of *shmattes*."[567] Perhaps there was a touch of jealously in that; after all, one sold quality made shoes, carefully crafted, whilst the other started off with *shmattes*.[568]

And even those who sold *shmattes*, would have surprised anyone. Had survivors endured years in poor and unkempt conditions, after years of suffering, this group of people desired to be as far removed from the nightmares they had just lived through as possible. For men, this meant searching for the very best suits, in particular Polish and Italian tailored garments, which, according to my father's memories, were of superior quality and more fashionable than what was available on the German market at the time. Numerous photos of my father and his acquaintances prove this and show him and the others in sharp, smart suits. Supposedly, they checked out the latest cuts from Italian fashion magazines and then tasked Jewish tailors in town – "all master tailors", according to my father – to copy the patterns and cuts.[569]

As my father reported, not only Jewish survivors from Poland lived and worked in Munich at the time, but also those from Hungary, Romania and Greece. According to him, however, most came from Poland.[570] Hence it is not surprising that the lingua franca around Möhlstraße was Yiddish.

During that time my father lived in Eduard-Schmidt-Straße, on the east bank of the Isar, the river that cuts itself through Munich, and where he rented a room from a German family. He got the room through a Jewish acquaintance who had left Germany and who passed on his room to my father. Despite the room being situated inside a family home, my father claimed that he had almost no contact with this family other than paying his 30 Deutschmark rent. Nor were there any other contacts with non-Jewish Germans, not even for business.

---

[567] *shmattes,* yid. Stuff, junk
[568] Rust (2010)
[569] Zylbersztajn (1995), p. 7
[570] See also Maier (2018), Ben-Zion Witler (1907-1961) who confirmed the same.

This only changed once most of the Jewish survivors had left Germany, having travelled on to America, Israel and other destinations. Many Jews had no real desire to live in Germany after what they had endured. According to my father's estimate, some ninety per cent of the Jewish DPs left Munich soon.[571] "When there were less Jews that remained, I had no choice but to have contact with Germans in order make a living", he explained. In fact, most of the Jewish businesses had disappeared after 1954. By 1957 there were but 25 businesses and shops left. Nevertheless, "Mjelowa" remained a centre of Jewish life into the late 1970s. I remember, for example, visiting the Jewish primary school, it was called Sinai Schule, together with my parents, in that neighbourhood. But mum and dad decided that it was "too far" away from home for me to go there.[572]

The historian Tobias Winsel confirms that the departure of survivors was very much the aim of the Munich city administration and the Free State of Bavaria. The few Jewish people who stayed behind, like my father, were in fact the exception, people, who resisted the pressure.

> *Bavaria was only intended to be a stopover for emigration; complete integration into economic life was not welcomed. One of the reasons for this was that the strong presence of DPs led to their rejection amongst the Bavarian population. There was a strong aversion to Jewish, mostly Eastern European, DPs, which reinforced by the fact that they were seen to be associated with black market transactions and other offences. The alleged high criminality of the DPs in Bavaria – which usually never corresponded to reality – was therefore increasingly perceived negatively and as an argument for their expulsion.*[573]

---

[571] Ibid. p. 3
[572] Anna Holian: Möhlstraße and the reconstruction. Jewish economic life in post-war Germany, in Maier (2018). p. 31 Regarding the Sinai Primary School: "far," because there remains the question of whether it was far in distance to the place where we lived, or far, measured by the distance my father had chosen to take to religious Judaism, as the school taught Judaism in the familiar religious way to children, including all customs, prayers and festivals, beside Hebrew reading and writing.
[573] Tobias Winsel: Mandated "Duty of Honour" – Reparation for Jewish Nazi Victims

The deportation of these "foreign undesirables" thus remained quite in line with Bavarian tradition. In particular, the spirit of Gustav von Kahr and everything that followed him, was still alive and well in spite of the Holocaust.[574]

Winstel goes on to say that the German state even rushed to make reparation payments to Jewish survivors after 1945 precisely so that the unwanted Jewish population – in their words – "the DP problem" – would vanish as quickly as possible. Too bad that some people, like my father, invested these funds into their businesses and shops; moreover, that in the years that followed people like him even demanded more compensation than those quickly paid-out sums. In his case exactly the opposite to that indended happened: Jewish survivors of the Shoah from Eastern Europe remained in post-war Germany!

As already hinted, due to the disappearance of most of the survivors by emigration, my father began to accept (non-Jewish) German customers out of necessity. Some were trouble. A certain Baron von Lanke became one of my father's non-Jewish German customers. Having heard that there were Jewish-Polish shoemakers in Möhlstraße, he hurried into the quarter to see my father and ordered the type of riding boots that the Polish cavalry once wore.[575] My father remembered:

> *He may have been able to admire them during service in Warsaw during the war. I don't know what he did there. I can guess, you know. He must have been a high-ranking officer – I didn't ask.*[576]

So, my father cut the leather pattern and asked a trusted shoemaker that he knew to put the patterns together. However, it then all got a bit complicated and the 80 DM he had been given as the purchase price was not enough to cover the expenses for the necessary leather, the

---

in Baumann and Heusler (2004), p. 217 (own translation)
[574] Gustav von Kahr, see in the chapter: The Lewandowskis
[575] The spelling of the name is uncertain. It could be also Lancken or a different version.
[576] Zylbersztajn (2015) p. 5

shoemaker's labour and the additional soles. When my father informed his customer that the finished boots would have a higher price, he received an angry reply, stating that my father was contractually bound to the agreed price. In addition, the baron sued my father for breach of contract. The case went to court. According to my father, the presiding judge heard all the arguments, and my father said, he explained the costs in detail which justified the final sale price of 120 Deutschmark. In the end the judge felt that the increased price was totally justified. And so, my father continued: "When the baron finally received his boots, he even gave me 140 Deutschmark – 'because of their good quality'." And not just that, he advised my father to place an advert in a riding magazine. It didn't yield the desired demand, although my father started making boots for a riding school in Munich as a result.

At this time, my father met an acquaintance who wanted to open a pizzeria in Munich's Kirchenstraße and who was looking for a business partner. The opportunity was the beginning of my father's career as a restaurant owner and the end of his shoe and boots manufacture, although he would always quality check any shoes I bought. As I was into solid mountaineering boots for a long time, he was usually satisfied.

My father described the restaurant, whose customers were mainly US soldiers with money to spend, as a "*Bombengeschäft*", in other words the success was explosive. Experiencing the exponential possibilities with a restaurant compared to shoe manufacture, he began to dream of opening his own restaurant, together with a Greek acquaintance (the man had worked in Munich during the war years and had stayed on after the war) on one of Munich's key shopping streets, Leopoldstraße. The business started well again, but because there were problems with disappearing takings and my father believing that the acquaintance was not fully trustworthy, he opened up another restaurant a few streets further away.

Working hard, my father's German was initially weak. He recalled his poor knowledge of German. One of his often-repeated anecdotes was how he asked for a "*Braut*", a bride, instead of some "*Brot*," bread, wrongly translating the Yiddish word *broyd* in a restaurant, to the entertainment of the waiter. To improve his language skills, he began to read German newspapers, but at the same time subscribed to Israel's Yiddish weekly newspaper, "*Letzte Najes*" from Tel Aviv, arranged through his brothers. As long as I knew my father, he had also continued a subscription of the Southern German daily liberal broadsheet *Süddeutsche Zeitung* as well.

Living alone without a family, many Jewish survivors in Munich soon longed for company. As there were only a few Jewish women amongst them, my father, like all the others, even began to spend evenings where he and his friends escorted German non-Jewish young ladies.

"We didn't talk about the war," he reflected, adding that there continued to be no contact with non-Jewish German men.[577] Accompanied by Jewish friends, he and the ladies visited dance events. Some of the Jewish survivors fell in love with the non-Jewish German women and, as my father put it, "unfortunately" soon some of his Jewish acquaintances decided to marry these women.[578]

The geography between where he lived in Munich's Eduard-Schmid-Straße and where he initially worked in Möhlstraße explains how my father and my mother eventually came to meet. My mum lived at the time with her family in Grillparzerstraße, which is roughly between Möhlstraße and Eduard-Schmid-Straße. It was while shopping that my father spotted my mother for the first time. The two of them must have had a brief conversation and the rest is history, as you say. My father confessed that he initially assumed my mother was indeed a young non-Jewish German woman like everyone else. After my mother told him about her family, my father thought he had struck gold. A non-Jewish German woman, he felt, would have been difficult for him to get along with or for his family in Israel to meet. But he believed that this young woman, part Dutch, part Jewish-German, not minding her Dutch-Lutheran upbringing – even that was better than a German – would not cause such complications. That said, there was a big age difference between the two of them. My

---

[577] Ibid. p.8
[578] Ibid.

mother was just 18 years old in 1956, my father being 37, twice as old. As they had met before my grandfather's death in December 1956, my father told me that he even had met my grandfather Gerhard, and that it had gone well. Certainly, my grandfather could hardly comment on age differences, given the age difference between my grandmother and himself. For my mother, my father was a connection to her Jewish grandfather and a degree of security in a family with financial difficulties. Perhaps too, she had little appetite for relationships with German men, who could very well have been Nazis and part of the lot that caused so much pain for her father. I think both conveniently ignored, that my mother's paternal grandmother was German and non-Jewish.

Wedding picture of my parents 1962. Private photo of author.

And thus, in the end, my father and my mother got married initially in a civil ceremony in 1962. As far as I know, in terms of Jewish weddings, it was rather complicated for both of them to get married according to Jewish rites, as my mother had neither been raised Jewish nor had a Jewish mother. I was told the rabbinate raised concerns, although my mother's Jewish background warranted exceptional procedures. In the end, three rabbis were said to have witnessed the act and to have approved the marriage. I am unable to verify when this happened. But what I can be sure about and will report in the second part of this two-book series, my mother did in the end make a full orthodox conversion to Judaism.

For a Leben, a Nayen

(yid. "To a new life")

This is where Zores, the first part of this two-book series Zol zayn Shulem ends. It reports the events that took place before my birth in 1969 and the result of research over many years. I am almost certain that new insights and details will emerge over time. I may also have missed certain facts or not been aware of them, or I may have misunderstood details, perhaps made mistakes.

Prior to writing this book there existed but torn-apart leftovers, which somehow, I had to gather and try to tie them together, as well as I could, so that a picture emerged.

I was totally unaware how many members of the Berlin Lewandowski family had been murdered. Quite a few details remained hidden or lost, because the generation of my parents, my mum and dad included, kept too much for themselves, either because they did not want to explain it, or could not explain it, unwilling to go to painful places, or because they simply did not know, or had forgotten.

In the second part of the series, which I called Faroys, the Yiddish word for forward, I will offer to readers a mostly autobiographical insight and reflection regarding my childhood and youth amongst Jewish survivors of the Shoah in Germany and Israel. These reveal in part a well-hidden world full of contradictions, in particular for my generation. We had family members who had seen and experienced the worst imaginable and whose families and worlds were destroyed and lost and who, I think it is correct to say, lived in Germany with mixed feelings.

On the other side was the young post-war generation, born and educated in Germany, who day by day were in contact with non-Jewish Germans, many of whom became friends. The modern post-war German non-authoritarian pedagogy of the late 1960s and 1970s had a healing potency not just for non-Jewish Germans who questioned their parents and grandparents, but also for people like myself. At the same time traditional German non-reformed education methods continued to cause pain and marginalisation for many young people, including myself.

Growing up in the Olympic Village of Munich meant that my home was an amazing futuristic car-free playground, but also the location in which the terrible drama of the terrorist attack of the Israeli Olympic Team in 1972 had its beginning.

Munich was as much a beautiful, enchanting and green city as much as it had been the former centre of the pre-war Nazi era, "die Stadt der Bewegung." Any buildings such as the *Nordbad* Swimming Pool or the *Haus der Kunst* (House of Art), the Königsplatz or the Odeonsplatz serve as reminders to that period, alongside the houses and apartments, which are no longer owned nor occupied by Jewish families due to Germany's grim history.

My father remained very much shaped by the experiences he endured before 1945. He tried his very best to build a new life. He gave a brave face to the public, granting little insight into his emotional uprooting, nor did he consciously allow himself to go back to those places he very much remembered, as I would learn. But as he aged, his world was increasingly marked by bitterness, not the least due to the lack of professional psychological care and services offered to survivors – not that many felt that they needed it. My father was as much a difficult, as well as a warm and friendly person and he was a massive fan of the football club FC Bayern München. I have some stories for you to read, about the rows of Bayern Munich supporting Jewish holocaust survivors inside the Munich Olympic Stadium, the home of the club between the 1970 and 2000s.

Mum had made her own experiences during the war years as a little girl. The traumatic experiences of her father appeared to have had an impact on her too. On top of this she was torn out of her former home of Amsterdam and the Netherlands and taken by her father into the country of the Germans, the very people that most in the Netherlands had referred to as bad and as occupiers, unless they were also Nazis. It mattered little that Germany was the former home of her father, whose attempts to get back what was lost remained wanting.

As I turned 16, I decided to continue my education in Israel, rather than in Germany, in order to connect more with Judaism and perhaps subconsciously to escape the claustrophobic – not without reason – world of my parents. When I returned to Germany after obtaining the equivalent of A-Levels, bureaucratic narrowness by a Bavarian state official led to the fact that I did not take advantage of my right to build a life in Germany. I not only studied in the United Kingdom, but met my wife to be there, which meant that London became my home instead.

In spite of the distance from Germany with a relative independent life, the past, even that before I was born, kept revisiting me, both consciously and subconsciously. Years later I learned that I was marked by some of the typical signifiers of what is known as the "Second Generation." Those who are children and grandchildren of Shoah survivors are a mixed and very diverse lot. Trauma experts and psychologists have been able to identify at least some patterns that many of us appear to have in common, some to lesser degrees, others more, some may deny they have these at all.

I wanted to understand more about this, principally to be able to leave the shadows of the past behind me. These shadowa had a bearing on some of the decisions I made in my life. In that sense it is important to understand that the Shoah did not just end in 1945, or with this first part of the two-book series I labelled Zores.

Our parents no longer trusted the world and its people and experienced fear for us. They tried to protect us, and yet their worries deprived us of some freedoms. Behaviour patterns had to be reviewed, decades after the traumatic experiences that gave cause to them and brought about challenges for a generation of people who clearly had not personally lived through the horrors of the Shoah.

And whilst all of this took place, the world continued. New and ancient variants of racism and of Jew-hatred showed themselves, whilst at the same time Israel, the country founded to provide a solution to the hate, found no rest. In England I was also a migrant. But the experience of the Shoah meant less, and was often misunderstood behind assumptions about me as a migrant from Germany with a noticeable German accent.

Through the shared life with my wife and later my daughter I soon learned about racism and hate directed against people with darker colours of skin. The town in which my wife had grown up was built on the back of what is referred to as Mafaa, or the transatlantic slave trade in African people. The longing for Africa and the return of her ancestors from the Americas and England to Freetown, can be seen as not dissimilar to the return of Jewish people to Israel. In fact, Freetown was sometimes described as the "Zion of Africa."

All this said, it would not have come to this book, had I not made the decision to share some of my experiences, above all, in order to try to give hope. The life stories of people of the „Second Generation", after the Shoah – I am but one single example with an array of individual and particular experiences – are part of a triumph over deserts composed of ash. Any one of these triumphs came with its own unique challenges and details. Only a small part of my generation, children of survivors who were born and raised in Germany, remained in Germany. There will be much more about all of this in the second part of the book.

Literature, Sources and Archives

Videos, Films and DVDs

Ruth Boronow Danson and Leslie Brent Talk at St. Paul's Steiner School (2016) *https://www.youtube.com/watch?v=7eC5hYSTTg8* und *https://www.youtube.com/watch?v=vHPanFrtI4o*
(Accessed 27.3.2021)

Lemer, Shulem & Shira Choir (2015). Avinu Malkenu, Sirreel Productions.,LLC, *https://www.youtube.com/watch?v=anPJFBzVC2c* (accessed on 26.3.2021)

Loipedinger, Martin: Julius Pinschewer. Klassiker des Werbefilms, Absolut Medien GMBH, Berlin, 2012

Robinson, Ken (2006). Do Schools kill creativity? Tedtalk Februar 2006, *https://www.ted.com/talks/sir_ken_robinson_do_schools_kill_creativity?language=en* (accessed on 26.3.2021)

Samura, Sorious (2000). Cry Freetown, Insight News TV. First shown on CNN, 3.2.2000 Unorthodox (2020). Netflix Serie, Anna Winger & Alexa Karolinski

USC Schoah Foundation:
Rozah Zylberstayn, Interview 33278, 8th Sept.1997
Wolf Zylbersztajn, Interview 51541, 21.2.2001

Yale University Library (1983). Holocaust Testimonies, Leon S., Edited Testimony (HVT-8025) *https://www.youtube.com/watch?v=ErtPjsisYLg* (accessed am 18.8.2020)

In Germany

Archiv der Gedenkstätte KZ Sachsenhausen
Arolsen Archives
Bayerisches Staatsarchiv
Berliner Stadtarchiv
Frohburger Kommunalarchiv
Gedenkstätte für Zwangsarbeit Leipzig
Staatsarchiv Landshut
Staatsarchiv Sachsen
Stadtarchiv große Kreisstadt Borna
Stadtarchiv der Landeshauptstadt München

In Israel

Yad Vashem

In the Netherlands

Delfer Nationaal Archief (NA),
Nederland Stadsarchief Amsterdam

In Poland

City Archive Szczekociny, Polen

In USA

New York State Archives
United States Holocaust Museum

Other Sources

Hedges, Chris (1993). New York Times 30. Juli 1993, Acquittal in Jerusalem; Israel Court Sets Demjanjuk Free, But He Is Now Without a Country, *https://www.nytimes.com/1993/07/30/world/acquittal-jerusalem-israel-court-sets-demjanjuk-free-but-he-now-without-country.html* (accessed am 8.7.2020)

Lewandowski, Alfred (1981). 125 Jahre 1856-1981. Das Haus Lewandowski, Jubiläumsschrift

Mythos Erwin Rommel. Der Wüstenfuchs als Wegbereiter des Holocaust, Der Spiegel, 27.08.2007, *https://www.spiegel.de/geschichte/mythos-erwin-rommel-a-946888.html*, (accessed on 05.07.2020)

My Heritage, Website

The Record from Hackensack (2011). New Jersey (Hackensack), 18.11.2011, S. L4

Zylbersztajn, Daniel

(1995). Wolf Zylbersztajn interviewed by his Son Daniel Zylbersztajn (privat, unveröffentlicht)

(1997). London Back Radio & The Community, MA Dissertation, Goldsmiths College, University of London

(2004). The Effectiveness of Imagery Facilitated Instructions / Idiokinesis for Improved Performance Outcomes from (in) Pilates Novices, MA Dissertation, Brunel University, West-London

Internet Pages /Online

ADL (2019). ADL Global Survey of 18 Countries Finds Hardcore Anti-Semitic Attitudes Remain Pervasive. 15.11.2019 *https://www.adl.org/news/press-releases/adl-global-survey-of-18-countries-finds-hardcore-anti-semitic-attitudes-remain* (accessed on 2.9.2022)

Avraham, Alexander (2010). Sephardim. YIVO Encyclopedia of Jews in Eastern Europe. *https://yivoencyclopedia.org/article.aspx/Sephardim* (accessed on 4.4.2021).

Barakat, Amiran (2004). Poland to Remove Public Toilets Built on Jewish Cemetery, in Haaretz, 22. November 2004 online *https://www.haaretz.com/1.4763449* (accessed on 26.2.2021).

Barne, Donna, Pirlea, Florina. (2019). Money sent home by workers now largest source of external financing in low- and middle-income countries (excluding China), World Bank, 2.7.2019, *https://blogs.worldbank.org/opendata/money-sent-home-workers-now-largest-source-external-financing-low-and-middle-income* (accessed on 22.11.2020).

Bonikowsky, Laura N. (2013). Editorial: The Arrival of Black Loyalist in Nova Scotia, The Canadian Enyklopedia, updated 2020, *https://www.thecanadianencyclopedia.ca/en/article/black-loyalists-feature* (accessed on 14.5.2022).

Bryc, Katarzyna, Durand, Eric, Macpherson, Michael, Reich, David,and Mountain Joanna (2015). The Genetic Ancestry of African Americans, Latinos, and European Americans across the United States. In *American Journal of human Genetics*, 2015 Jan 8; 96(1). 37–53. (accessed on 3.2.2021).

Campbell, Lucy (2021). David Lammy praised for Response to radio caller who Said he was ‚not Englisch', The Guardian, 29.2.2021 *https://www.theguardian.com/world/2021/mar/29/david-lammy-praised-for-response-to-lbc-caller-who-said-he-was-not-english* (accessed on 30.3.2021).

Caroll, Rory (2000). Pope says sorry for sins of Church. Guardian 13.3.2000 *https://www.theguardian.com/world/2000/mar/13/catholicism.religion* (accessed on 2.9.2022).

Central Bureau of Statistics (2023). Israel in Figures – Rosh Hashana Selected Annual Data 2023, 13.9.2023 *https://www.cbs.gov.il/en/mediarelease/Pages/2023/Israel-in-Figures-Rosh-Hashana-Selected-Annual-Data-2023.aspx* (accessed on 15.3.2024).

Cole, Michael (2020). Holy war in the city of knives: antisemitism and football on the streets of Krakow. In Open Democracy, 17.9.2020 *https://www.opendemocracy.net/en/countering-radical-right/holy-war-city-knives-anti-semitism-and-football-streets-krakow/* (accessed on 2.9.2020).

CST (2024). Antisemitic Incidents 2023, 15.2.2024, *https://cst.org.uk/public/data/file/9/f/Antisemitic_Incidents_Report_2023.pdf* /accessed on 10.3.2024).

Curry, Andrew (2019). Parents' emotional trauma may change their children's biology. Studies in mice show how. In American Association for the Avancement of Science (AAAS), doi:10.1126/science.aay7690, 18.8.2019, *https://www.sciencemag.org/news/2019/07/parents-emotional-trauma-may-change-their-children-s-biology-studies-mice-show-how* (accessed on 11.4.2021).

Daniel Counter Blog (2008). Leon Zelman „Shoa survivor „extraordinaire" *https://danielscounter.blogspot.com/2008/01/leon-zelman-sa-shoa-survivor.html* (accessed on 28.2.21).

Daniel Counter Blog (2009). „Untermenschen" and „Asylum Seekers": 8.1.2009, *https://danielscounter.blogspot.com/2009/12/london-refugee-conference-in-january.html* (accessed on 28.2.2021).

Daramy, Ade (2016). Remittances are three times greater than aid – how can they go even further? The Guardian, 11.5.2016, *https://www.theguardian.com/global-development-professionals-network/2016/may/11/remittances-three-times-greater-aid-sdgs* (accessed on 22.11.2020).

Dayan, Linda (2023). Thousands Attend Funeral of Slain Canadian-Israeli Peace Activist Vivian Silver, Haarez, 16.11.2023, *https://www.haaretz.com/israel-news/2023-11-16/ty-article/.premium/thousands-attend-funeral-of-slain-canadian-israeli-peace-activist-vivian-silver/0000018b-d9cd-d423-afb-fbef6e360000* (accessed on 15.3.2024, paywall).

DeCelles, Katherine (2016). Minorities Who ‚Whiten' Job Resumes Get More Interviews, Havard Business Schoo , *https://hbswk.hbs.edu/item/minorities-who-whiten-job-resumes-get-more-interviews* (accessed on 30.10.2020).

Departament Badań Demograficznych (2012). Raport z wyników Narodowy Spis Powszechny Ludności i Mieszkań 2011 (accessed on 2.9.2022). *https://stat.gov.pl/cps/rde/xbcr/gus/lud_raport_z_wynikow_NSP2011.pdf*

Devlin, Hannah (2015). Genetic study reveals 30% of White British DNA has German ancestry. The Guardian, 18.3.2015, *https://www.theguardian.com/science/2015/mar/18/genetic-study-30-percent-white-british-dna-german-ancestry* (accessed on 30.3.2021).

Devlin, Hanna (2018). First modern Britons had ‚Dark to black' skin, Cheddar Man DNA Analysis reveals. The Guardian 7.2.2018, *https://www.theguardian.com/science/2018/feb/07/first-modern-britons-dark-black-skin-cheddar-man-dna-analysis-reveals* (accessed on 30.3.2021).

Doktor, Lara (2008). Liebestöter ziehen noch, in Süddeutsche Zeitung, 16.09 2008, *https://www.sueddeutsche.de/muenchen/adelinde-dilz-liebestoeter-ziehen-noch-1.690968*, (accessed on 3.7.2020).

Dollinger, Hans (2004). Schwarzbuch der Weltgeschichte. 5000 Jahre der Mensch des Menschen Feind, Erfstadt: Area Verlag.

Duffel, Nick (2014). Why Boarding schools produce bad Leaders, in The Guardian, 9.6.2014, *https://www.theguardian.com/education/2014/jun/09/boarding-schools-bad-leaders-politicians-bullies-bumblers* (accessed on 27.3.2014).

Ebbighausen, Rodion (2016). Erfolgreich an deutschen Schulen: vietnamesische Kinder, 05.05.2016 *https://www.dw.com/de/erfolgreich-an-deutschen-schulen-vietnamesische-kinder/a-19237644* (accessed on 30.3.2021).

EdgeHist (Youtube Kanal der Fakultät für Geschichte an der Edgehill University), Daniel Zylbersztajn: On the Difficulties of Memorialising Jewish Victims in Europe: Munch, 1972. *https://www.youtube.com/watch?v=iAEnz9yJUfI&t=1s* (accessed on 19.9.2023).

Engel, David (1998). Patterns Of Anti-Jewish Violence in Poland, 1944-1946, Yad Vashem Studies Vol. XXVI, Jerusalem 1998, S. 43-85, Online *https://www.yadvashem.org/articles/academic/patterns-of-anti-jewish-violence.html* (accessed on 12.4.2021).

Enthoven, Victor (2016). Slavery in Dutch America and the West Indies, Oxford Bibliographies, DOI: 10.1093/OBO/9780199730414-0230 *https://www.oxfordbibliographies.com/display/document/obo-9780199730414/obo-9780199730414-0230.xml* (accessed on 24.2.2023).

Filkins, Dexter (2015). Shot in the Heart, in The New Yorker, 19.10.2015, *https://www.newyorker.com/magazine/2015/10/26/yitzhak-rabin-assassination-israel-oslo-peace-accords* (accessed on 15.3.2024).

Frankel, Leora (1992). Out There: Israel; Pilgrimages With Reggae. New York Times 11.10. *1992/ https://www.nytimes.com/1992/10/11/style/out-there-israel-pilgrimages-with-reggae-beat.html* (accessed on 17.2.2022).

Francis-Tan, Andrew and Mialon, Hugh. M (2014). 'A Diamond is Forever' and Other Fairy Tales: The Relationship between Wedding Expenses and Marriage Duration (September 15, 2014). Zugang: SSRN: *https://ssrn.com/abstract=2501480* or *http://dx.doi.org/10.2139/ssrn.2501480* (accessed on 23.1.2022).

Grant, John N (2015). Jamaican Maroons in Nova Scotia, Canadian Enyklopedia, updated 2019, *https://www.thecanadianencyclopedia.ca/en/article/maroons-of-nova-scotia* (accessed on 14.5.2022).

Gilad, Elon (2014). What does your Jewish Name mean? in Haaretz, *https://www.haaretz.com/jewish/.premium-what-does-your-name-mean-1.5244607* (accessed in 2021).

Gritz, Linda & Michael Katz (2020). Boston Workers Circle, Arbeter Ring Yiddish Sing, 22.6.2020 *https://circleboston.org/sites/www.circleboston.org/files/event_files/Yiddish%20Sing%20booklet%2006_22_20-comp_Part1.pdf* (accessed on 2.4.2021).

gov.uk (2018). Ethnicity Facts and Figures: Population of England and Wales. Updated 2020. *https://www.ethnicity-facts-figures.service.gov.uk/uk-population-by-ethnicity/national-and-regional-populations/population-of-england-and-wales/latest* (accessed on 20.2.2022).

gov.uk (2020). Ethnicity Facts and Figures. Renting Social Housing. Erneuerte Version 4.4.2021 *https://www.ethnicity-facts-figures.service.gov.uk/housing/social-housing/renting-from-a-local-authority-or-housing-association-social-housing/latest* (accessed on 20.2.2022).

Heath, Deana (2018). British Empire is still being whitewashed by the school curriculum – historian on why this must change, in The Conversation, 2.11.2018, *https://theconversation.com/british-empire-is-still-being-whitewashed-by-the-school-curriculum-historian-on-why-this-must-change-105250* (accessed on 27.2.2021).

Higgins, Charlotte (2011). Historians say Michael Gove risks turning history lessons into propaganda classes, in Guardian, 17.8.2011 *https://www.theguardian.com/politics/2011/aug/17/academics-reject-gove-history-lessons* (accessed on 27.03.2021).

Hilgert, Romain (2018). Aberglaube mit Pressehilfe, in d'Lëtzebuerger Land, 29.06.2018 *https://www.land.lu/page/article/408/334408/DEU/index.html* (accessd on 28.3.2021)

Hope not Hate (2016). Cable Street, *http://www.cablestreet.uk/* (accessed on 14.8.2020).

House of Commons Library (2020). Research Briefing, 2.12.2020, *https://commonslibrary.parliament.uk/research-briefings/sn06077/#:~:text=in%20the%20year%20ending%20December,other%20EU%20countries%20excluding%20Ireland* (accessed on 18.3.2021).

House of Commons Library (2023). Constituency data: Ethnic groups, 2021 census, 29.3.2023, *https://commonslibrary.parliament.uk/constituency-statistics-ethnicity/#:~:text=Across%20England%20and%20Wales%2C%2082,20%20constituencies%20by%20ethnic%20group* (accessed on 15.2.2024).

Houston, Peter (2022). The Week Junior, keeping children reading with magazines they want to read. In Whats New in Publishing? *https://whatsnewinpublishing.com/the-week-junior-keeping-children-reading-with-magazines-they-want-to-read/* (accessed on 14.11.2022).

Janes, Jerome (2013). Pope John Paul II's Divided Loyalties to Jews. Forward 17.7.2013 (accessed on 2.9.2022).

Janzen, Cornelius (2023): Antisemitismus-Vorwürfe: Offener Brief an Roger Waters: „Unmoralisch," in ZDF Heute, 21.11.23, *https://www.zdf.de/nachrichten/politik/pink-floyd-roger-waters-antisemitismus-vorwuerfe-israel-100.html*, (accessed on 10.3.2024).

Jerusalem Post (2020) Arson feared after second fire in a week at Neve Shalom, Jerusalem Post, 7.9.2020 *https://www.jpost.com/israel-news/arson-feared-after-second-fire-in-a-week-at-neve-shalom-641346* (accessed on 15.3.2024).

Jewish Agency (2023). Jewish Population Rises to 15.7 Million Worldwide in 2023, 15.9.2023, *https://www.jewishagency.org/jewish-population-rises-to-15-7-million-worldwide-in-2023/* (accessed on 15.3.2024).

Jewish Chronicle (2022). Man arrested on suspicion of religiously aggravated assault on father of batmitzvah girl, 8.11.2022 *https://www.thejc.com/news/news/man-arrested-on-suspicion-of-religiously-aggravated-assault-on-father-of-batmitzvah-girl-2P44Ztf4vk2I3Kl7NGXI41* (accessed on 17.12.2022).

Jewish Policy Institute (JPR) (2011). Key trends in the British Jewish community: A review of data on poverty, the elderly and children. *https://www.jpr.org.uk/documents/Key%20trends%20in%20the%20British%20Jewish%20community.pdf* (accessed on 20.2.2022).

Jewish Policy Institute (JPR) (2024). Jews in the UK today: Key findings from the JPR National Jewish Identity Survey, 8.2.24. *https://www.jpr.org.uk/reports/jews-uk-today-key-findings-jpr-national-jewish-identity-survey* (accessed on 10.3.24).

Jiao-Yang Tian, wie Wang, Yu-Chun Li, Wen Zhang, Yong-Gang Yao, Jits van Straten, Martin B. Richards & Qing-Peng Kong (2015). A genetic contribution from the Far East into Ashkenazi Jews via the ancient Silk Road.. In nature Briefing, Scientific Reports, Scientific Reports Vol 5, Article Nr. 8377, 11.2.2015 *https://www.nature.com/articles/srep08377* (accessed on 8.3.2021).

Kaldor Mary and Vincent, James (2006). United Nations Development Programme Evaluation Office: Case Study Sierra Leone. Evaluation of UNDP Assistance to Conflict Affected Countries. New York, United Nations. *http://web.undp.org/evaluation/evaluations/documents/thematic/conflict/SierraLeone.pdf* (accessed on 22.1.2023).

King, Susan (2015). HBO's 'Night Will Fall' chronicles making of WWII Holocaust film, in Los Angeles Times,25 Jan 2015, Online *https://www.latimes.com/entertainment/tv/la-et-st-hbo-night-will-fall-alfred-hitchcock-20150126-story.html* (accessed on 17.3.2021).

Klären, Jutta (Red.) Bundeszentrale für Politische Bildung (Herausg.). (2010). Jüdisches Leben in Deutschland *https://www.bpb.de/izpb/7643/juedisches-leben-in-deutschland* (accessed on 10.8.2020).

Kotkowsky, Charles (ohne Datum) Memoirs of A Survivor, in Mervin Butovsky und Kurt Jonassohn (red). Memoirs of Holocaust Survivors in Canada, Concordia University Chair in Canadian Jewish Studies *http://migs.concordia.ca/memoirs/kotkowsky/kot_mem.html* (accessed on 10.8.202).

Lewis, Paul (1991). U.N. Repeals ist ,75 Resolution Equating Zionism With Racism in New York Times, 17.12.1991. *https://www.nytimes.com/1991/12/17/world/un-repeals-ist-75-resolution-equating-zionism-with-racism.html* (accessed on 15.3.2024).

Lori, Aviva (2007). Is there a doctor in the House? in Haaretz, 11.10.2007 *https://www.haaretz.com/1.4984036* (accessed on 17.2.2022).

Luh, Jürgen (2022). Schlagwort: Novembertage. T-RECS #51: Ein öffentlicher Mann. Der deutsche Kronprinz Wilhelm 1930 bis 1934. Recs, Research Center Sanssouci. Für Wissen und Gesellschaft. 15.8.2022 *https://recs.hypotheses.org/tag/novembertage#_ftn61* (accessed on 4.9.2022).

Marks, Joshua Robbin (2019). Sephardic and Mizrahi Jews in Ashkenazic Lands, The Times of Israel, *https://blogs.timesofisrael.com/sephardic-and-mizrahi-jews-in-ashkenazic-lands/* (accessed on 4.4.2021).

Matiluko, Seun (2021). Census 2021: Why we need to acknowledge the differences between black people in Britain, The Voice online, 22.3.2021, *https://www.voice-online.co.uk/opinion/2021/03/22/census-2021-why-we-need-to-acknowledge-the-differences-between-black-people-in-britain/* (accessed on 30.3.2021).

Mcpherson, William (1999). The Stephen Lawrence Inquiry. *https://assets.publishing.service.gov.uk/government/uploads/system/uploads/attachment_data/file/277111/4262.pdf* (accessed on 7.4.2023).

Neuer, Hillel C (2023). Antisemitism and Discrimination Against Israel at the United Nations. UN Watch, 22.6.2023, *https://docs.house.gov/meetings/FA/FA06/20230622/116138/HHRG-118-FA06-Wstate-NeuerH-20230622.pdf* (accessed on 15.3.2024).

Ohio, Margaret Amaka (2017). Racism in Public Discourse in Poland. A Preliminary Analysis. In Edutainment, 01 (2016). *https://www.asc.uw.edu.pl/wp-content/uploads/2020/06/RACISM-IN-PUBLIC-DISCOURSE-IN-POLAND.-A-PRELIMINARY-ANALYSIS.pdf* (accessed on 2.9.2022).

Okolosie, Lola (2020). White guilt on its own won't fix racism': decolonising Britain's Schools, in The Guardian, 10.7.2020 *https://www.theguardian.com/education/2020/jun/10/white-guilt-on-its-own-wont-fix-racism-decolonising-britains-schools* (accessed on 27.3.2020).

O'Malley, JP (2020). Historian: Polis society shunned Jewish survivors returning from Nazi camps, in The Times of Israel, 19.12.2020, https://www.timesofisrael.com/historian-polish-society-shunned-jewish-survivors-returning-from-death-camps/ (accessed on 12.4.2021).

Parker, Fiona & Murphy, Michael (2023). Jewish families leaving synagogue 'targeted' by pro-Palestinian Demonstrators, Daily Telegraph, 11.11.2023, *https://www.telegraph.co.uk/news/2023/11/11/protesters-extreme-anti-semitic-signs-pro-palestinian-march/* (accessed on 15.3.2023, Paywall).

Peters, Freia (2011). Die besten deutschen Schüler stammen aus Vietnam. Die Welt, 6.2.2011 *https://www.welt.de/politik/deutschland/article12458240/Die-besten-deutschen-Schueler-stammen-aus-Vietnam.html* (accessed on 30.3.2021).

Pew Research Centre (2016). Israel's Identity, 8.3.2016, *https://www.pewresearch.org/religion/2016/03/08/identity/#:~:text=Israeli%20Jews%20are%20nearly%20evenly,associated%20with%20their%20ancestral%20roots* (accessed on 15.3.2024).

Priddy, Sarah & Torrance, David (2919). Contribution of the Jewish community to the UK. House of Commons Library Debate Pack. *https://researchbriefings.files.parliament.uk/documents/CDP-2019-0149/CDP-2019-0149.pdf* (accessed on 20.2.2022).

Pullan-Sheffield, Amy (2018). DNA suggests Yiddish began on the Silk Road, in Futurity, 20.4.2016 *https://www.futurity.org/yiddish-ashkenazic-jews-1143632-2/* (accessed on 8.4.2021).

Pybus, Cassandra, Candlin Kit & Petterd Robin (2009). BlackLoyalists.info (Australian Research Council, Univ. of Sydney), Internetseite ist archiviert unter *https://web.archive.org/web/20150905172923/http://www.blackloyalist.info/about/* (accessed on 15.5.2022).

Reuters & Times of Israel (2024). UNRWA report claims some agency employees admitted Hamas ties under Israeli coercion, Times of Israel, 9.3.2024, *https://www.timesofisrael.com/unrwa-report-claims-some-agency-employees-admitted-hamas-ties-under-israel-coercion/* (accessed on 17.3.2024).

Roumani, Mourice M (2020). First, Libya's Jews Were Deported. Then the S.S. Stepped in, Haaretz, 8.08.2020. *https://www.haaretz.com/world-news/2020-02-08/ty-article-magazine/.premium/first-libyas-jews-were-deported-then-the-s-s-stepped-in/0000017f-f7ed-d2d5-a9ff-f7ede3b30000*, (accessed on 15.9.2023).

Samuels, Ben (2023). Too Little, Too Late | Eight Weeks After Oct 7 Massacre, UN Women Condemns Hamas' Use of sexual Violence Against Israeli Women, Haaretz, 2.12.2023, *https://www.haaretz.com/israel-news/2023-12-02/ty-article/.premium/after-eight-weeks-un-women-condemns-hamas-use-of-sexual-violence-on-oct-7/0000018c-2b09-dc03-a9ec-3f7ba0190000* (accessed on 15.3.2024).

Sidiqque, Haroon (2019). Minorit ethnic Britons face ‚shocking' job discrimination, The Guardian, 17.01.2017. *https://www.theguardian.com/world/2019/jan/17/minority-ethnic-britons-face-shocking-job-discrimination* (accessed on 28.2.2021).

Stichting voor Wetenschappelijk Onderzoek van Nationaal-Socialistische Misdrijven (2021). Justiz und NS-Verbrechen, Deutsch/deutsche Verfahren (JuNSV – Deutsch/deutsche Verfahren *https://junsv.nl/junsv-01/junsv/inhvzbrdddr.htm* (accessed on 28.12.2022).

Taylor, Diane (2018). It was like a family: Remembering the Mangrove, Notting Hill's Caribbean Haven. The Guardian 15.9.2018. *https://www.theguardian.com/uk-news/2018/sep/15/remembering-the-mangrove-notting-hill-caribbean-haven* (accessed on 18.2.2022).

The Baroness Casey Review. (2023). *https://www.met.police.uk/police-forces/metropolitan-police/areas/about-us/about-the-met/bcr/baroness-casey-review/* (accessed on 7.4.2023).

The Guardian Editorial (2019). The Guardian View on creativity in Schools: a missling ingredient, 18.10.2019, *https://www.theguardian.com/commentisfree/2019/oct/18/the-guardian-view-on-creativity-in-schools-a-missing-ingredient* (accessed on 26.3.2020).

The Sutton Trust and The Social Mobility Commission (2019). Elitist Britain, *https://assets.publishing.service.gov.uk/government/uploads/system/uploads/attachment_data/file/811045/Elitist_Britain_2019.pdf* (accessed on 26.3.2021).

Times Educational Supplement (2020). ‚Little or no evidence' that phonics improves reading, in Times Educational Supplement (TES), 22.01.2020, *https://www.tes.com/news/little-or-no-evidence-phonics-improves-reading* (accessed on 27.3.2021).

Travis, Alan (2017). Number of Romanians and Bulgarians in UK rises to 413,000: The Guardian, 11.10.2017 (accessed on 18.3.2020).

Trepka, Tomasz (2016). Potworne tajemnice skarżyskiej fabryki,Echodnia, 18.09.2016 *https://echodnia.eu/swietokrzyskie/potworne-tajemnice-skarzyskiej-fabryki/ar/c3-10528324* (accessed on 28.05.2020).

Van Dam, Andrew, (2022). People from elite backgrounds increasingly dominate academia, data Shows first-generation academics were always rare. Now they're vanishing. In Washington Post, 8.7.2022 *https://www.washingtonpost.com/business/2022/07/08/dept-of-data-academia-elite/* (accessed on 25.1.2023).

Vyas, Shekha (2014). East End producer Rockboi turns his hand to being a rapper, Hackney Gazette, 9.1..2014, *https://www.hackneygazette.co.uk/news/east-end-producer-rockboi-turns-his-hand-to-being-a-rapper-1-3838532*, (accessed on 10.11.2020).

Wikipedia: Blooms Restaurant *https://en.wikipedia.org/wiki/Bloom%27s_restaurant* (accessed on 16.8.2020).

Williams, Len (2020). Inside Brick Lane's Mosque That Was A Synagogue That Was A Church, in Londonist, 17.2.2020, *https://londonist.com/london/history/brick-lane-mosque-east-london-church-synagogue-hugenots* (accessed on 16.8.2020).

Wolke, Karol (2020). The liberation of the german concentration camp in Holýšov, Czech Republic, by the Polish Armed Forces in The Warsaw Institute Review, *https://warsawinstitute.review/issue-2-2020/the-liberation-of-the-german-concentration-camp-in-holysov-czech-republic-by-the-polish-armed-forces/* (accessed on 26.4.2022).

Yad Vashem: Anti-Jewish Violence in Poland After Liberation, *https://www.yadvashem.org/articles/general/anti-jewish-violence-in-poland-after-liberation.html* (accessed on 1.3.2021).

Yad Vashem: Names of Righteous by Country *https://www.yadvashem.org/righteous/statistics.html* (accessed on 28.2.21).

Youth Against Racism in Europe: Stopping the BNP in Tower Hamlets, *http://www.yre.org.uk/towerhamlets.html* (accessed on 16.8.2020)

Zeleznice v Prorektoratu (Eisenbahnen im Vizerektorat) *https://www.fronta.cz/utoky-na-zeleznice-v-protektoratu* (accessed on 24.6.2020)

Yoman: Szczekociny – Jewish Cemetery & Gravestones, in Hebrew, Israelische Nachrichtensendung, Channel One, *https://www.youtube.com/watch?v=huiYtzrAwmg* hochgeladen auf Youtube oYossi Bornstein 21 März 2007 (accessed on 28. Februar 2021).

Wade, Lizzie (2018). Genetic study reveals surprising ancestry of many Americans, Science Mag18.12.2018 *https://www.sciencemag.org/news/2014/12/genetic-study-reveals-surprising-ancestry-many-americans* (accessed on 30.3.2021).

Zeewusarchief, Niederlande: Slave Voyage aboard the Unity. *h*ttps://www.zeeuwsarchief.nl/en/themepage/slave-voyage-aboard-the-unity/the-voyage-history/ (accessed on 11.11. 2022).

Zylbersztajn-Lewandowski, Daniel (2008). School of Peace in Oasis of Peace, by Daniel Zylbersztajn for Oasis of Peace UK, Internet Archive *https://archive.org/details/Mp3SchoolInOasisFinal1* (accessed on 19.11.2020).

(2011), The possibilities and impossibilities of being a neighbour, Open Democracy, 4.11.2011, *https://www.opendemocracy.net/en/possibilities-and-impossibilities-of-being-neighbour/* (accessed on 25.6.2020).

(2012a). That's The Way to do it. Punch and Judy Turns 350, DW Online, *https://www.dw.com/en/thats-the-way-to-do-it-punch-and-judy-turns-350/a-15707807* (accessed on 24.2.2021).

(2012b). Großkonzerne bei Olympia: „Gesund, nachhaltig, zertifiziert", taz, die Tageszeitung, 29.7.2012 *https://taz.de/Grosskonzerne-bei-Olympia/!5087971/* (accessed on 24.2.2021).

(2012c). A Better Way? What can food co-operatives offer in the Age of the Supermarket? London Resoance FM 103.4 *https://archive.org/details/ABetterWayWhatCanFoodCo-operativesOfferInTheAgeOfTheSupermarket* (accessed on 24.2.2021).

(2012d) Nappy Change, The Challanges of contemporary fatherhood (as broadcasted on London Resonance FM 104.4, March 2012 (accessed on 24.2.2021). *https://archive.org/details/NappyChangeTheChallangesOfContemporaryFatherhoodasBroadcastedOn(2012e)*. Lieber rot als britisch, taz, die Tageszeitung: 2.9.2012, *https://taz.de/!571166/* (Tazarchiv, accessed on 18.3.2021).

(2012f). Ernüchternd und erleichternd: taz, die Tageszeitung, 13.8.2012, *https://taz.de/Kolumne-London-Eye/!5086649/* (accessed on 18.3.2021).

(2012g). Genetischer Reduktionismus ist falsch, in taz, die Tageszeitung, 9.8.2012 *https://taz.de/US-Forscher-ueber-Rassismus-im-Sport/!5086963/* (accessed on 30.3.2021).

(2013). Die Macht der Pedale, Zeit Online, 7.8.2013 *https://www.zeit.de/reisen/2013-08/london-fahrradrennen* (accessed on 24.2.2021).

(2013a). Wahlerfolge britischer Rechtspopulisten. Ukip on the Block, taz, die Tageszeitung, 14.5.2013 *https://taz.de/!5067407/* (accessed on 18.3.2021).

(2013b). Nach dem Mord in London:„England, England, EDL! EDL!", taz, die Tageszeitung, 23.5.2013 *https://taz.de/Nach-dem-Mord-in-London/!5066858/* (accessed on 18.3.2021).

(2015). Die Überlebende *https://taz.de/!215237/*, taz die Tagezeitung, (accessed on 24.2.2021).

(2015a). Haltestelle Olympiapark, Jüdische Allgemeine. Haltestelle Olympiapark, 15.1.2015 *https://www.juedische-allgemeine.de/kultur/haltestelle-olympiapark/* (accessed on 19.9.2023).

(2016). Zwischen den Welten, taz die Tageszeitung *https://taz.de/Nach-dem-Grossbrand-im-Grenfell-Tower/!5436291/* (accessed on 24.2.2021).

(2016a). Wahlkampf um Parlamentssitz von Jo Cox: Eine Schauspielerin soll's richten: taz, die Tageszeitung, 18.10.2016, *https://taz.de/!5345863/* (accessed on 18.3.2021).

(2016b). Eine Schwäbin in Kent, Jüdische Allgemeine, 10.05.2016, *https://www.juedische-allgemeine.de/?p=25477* (accessed on 23.3.2021).

(2016c). Arm aber erfolgreich, taz, die Tageszeitung, 25.6.2016 *https://taz.de/Migrantenkinder-in-Tower-Hamlets/!5303675/* (accessed on 26.3.2021).

(2017). Im Schatten der Strahlen, taz die Tageszeitung, 21.2.2017, *https://taz.de/Atomkraft-im-Nordwesten-Englands/!5382462/* (accessed on 24.2.2021).

(2017a). Nach Anschlag auf Londoner Moschee :„Jetzt könnt ihr mich umbringen", taz die Tageszeitung, 19.6.2017, *https://taz.de/!5418939/* (accessed on 18.3.2021).

(2017b). Die Auswirkungen des Terrors: Manchester United?, taz die Tageszeitung, 28.5.2017, *https://taz.de/!5409852/* (accessed on 18.3.2021).

(2017c). Nach dem Anschlag von London nicht nachgeben, taz die Tageszeitung, 4.6.2017 *https://taz.de/!5417678/* (accessed on 18.3.2021).

(2017d). Couscous & Co: Jüdische Allgemeine, 15.6.2017, *https://www.juedische-allgemeine.de/juedische-welt/couscous-co/* (accessed on 29.3.2021).

(2018). Als Austauschjude in Belsen, Jüdische Allgemeine, 29.11.2018 *https://www.juedische-allgemeine.de/?p=2009487*, (accessed on 9.1.2022).

(2019a). Mayday, Mayday, taz die Tageszeitung, 24.3.2019 *https://taz.de/Brexit-Demos-in-Grossbritannien/!5582690/* (accessed on 23.3.2021) .

(2019b). 15.5.2019: Brexit Reloaded *https://taz.de/!5592134/* (accessed on 23.3.2021).

(2019c). Im Armenhaus der Brexiteers: taz, die Tageszeitung, 17.10.2019 *https://taz.de/Grossbritannien-und-die-EU/!5629650/* (accessed on 23.3.2021).

(2020). I was there, A rare photo from the hell of the Schoa, Medium, 21. April 2020 *https://link.medium.com/p2TiT9xmU6* (accessed on 30.5.2020).

(2020a). Labour suspendiert Corbyn, taz die Tageszeitung, 29.19.2020 *https://taz.de/!5724684/*

(2020b). Die Türsteher vom Ärmelkanal, taz, die Tageszeitung, 20.9.2020, *https://taz.de/!5711448/* (accessed on 23.3.2021).

(2020c). Labour suspendiert Corbyn, taz, die Tageszeitung, 29.10.2020 *https://taz.de/!5724684/* (accessed on 23.3.2021).

(2021). Große Herzen, harte Fäuste, taz, die Tageszeitung, 23.11.2021 *https://taz.de/Juedischer-Antifaschismus-in-England/!5814040/* (accessed on 23.11.2023).

(2022). Antisemitismus in Großbritannien. Bundeszentrale für politische Bildung. *https://www.bpb.de/themen/antisemitismus/dossier-antisemitismus/* (abgerufen 10 April 2022).

(2023). Mahnwache für alle Toten in Nahost: Gegen den Hass, in taz, die Tageszeitung, 4.12.2023, *https://taz.de/Mahnwache-fuer-alle-Toten-in-Nahost/!5978206/* (accessed on 10.2.23).

Literature

Adorno, Theodor (1994). The Stars down to Earth, Abingdon, Oxon: Routledge Classics

Ahmed, Imitaz (2022). Recognising the 1991 Bangladesh Genocide. An Appeal for Rendering Justice. Public Diplomacy Wing, Ministry of Foreign Affairs, Government of the Peoples Republic of Bangladesh, Dhaka: Nymphea Publication.

Ali, Shahrazad (1992). The Blackwoman's Guide to Understanding the Blackman, Philadelphia: Civilized Publications

Arad, Yitzhak (1999). Belzec, Sobibor, Treblinka. The Operatioon Reinhard Death Camps, Boomington: Indiana University Press

Bajohr, Frank (2002). Aryanisation in Hamburg, New York Oxford: Berghan Books

Bookbinder, Susan (2013). Izyk cheated Death many Times, but died before his Son restored Jewish History to Szczekociny, in Jewish Telegraph (Großbritannien), 16.8.2013

Baddiel, David (2021). Jews Don't Count, London: TLS Books

Bakó,Tihamér & Zana, Katalin (2020). Transgenerational Trauma and Therapy, London & New York: Routledge

Bauer, Hannah (2014). Vom Korsett zum Büstenhalter. Einfluss gesellschaftlicher Extremsituationen am Beispiel der zwei Weltkriege auf den Unterwäschemarkt Nordersted: Grin Verlag

Baumann, Angelika (Red.) (1995). Jüdisches Leben in München, München: Buchenberger Verlag

Baumann, Angelika & Heuslert, Andreas (2004). München arisiert. Entrechtung und Einteignung der Juden in der NS-Zeit München: C. H. Beck

Baumann, Zygmund (1991). Modernity and Holocaust, Cambridge: Polity Press

Barbier, Muriel & Boucher, Shazia (2005). Die Dessous, Berlin – New York: Parkstone

Beimler, Hans (2019). Im Mörderlager Dachau, Köln: PappyRossa Verlag

Boas, Franz (1904). Some Traits of primitive Culture: *Journal of American Folclore,17:* 243-254

Bornstein, Izyk Mendel (2009). B-94, The Spirit of the Survivor, Rosh ha-ayi, Reborn Roots

Bornstein Yossi, Piskiewicz, Angnieszka, Skrzypzyk, Miroslav & Wieczorek, Anna (2017). Szckeocinski Festiwal Kultur Zydowskiej YAHAD-RAZEM. 10 lat, Wloszczowa: Drukania Kontur

Brenner, Michael (1995). Nach dem Holocaust. Juden in Deutschland 1945–1950. München: C. H. Beck

Brenner, Michael, Jersch-Wenzel, Stefanie & Meyer Michael A. (1996). Deutsch-Jüdische Geschichte in der Neuzeit, 4 Bde., Bd.2, Emanzipation und Akkulturation 1780-1871, München: C. H. Beck

Brenner, Michael (2019). Der lange Schatten der Revolution. Juden und Antisemiten in Hitlers München 1918-1923, Berlin: Jüdischer Verlag im Suhrkamp Verlag

Brooke, Kevin (2003). Russian History, Spring-Summerr 2003 / Printemps-Ete 2003, Vol. 30, S. 1-22

Campbell, Mavis C. (1990). The Maroons of Jamaica, 1655–1796. Trenton, NJ: Africa World Press

Cleaver, Eldridge (1968). Soul on Ice. New York: Dell Publishing

Clouder, Christopher & Rawson, Martyn (2004). Waldorf Education, Edinburgh: Floris Books

Cohen, Mark (2014). Prologue. The "Golden Age" of Jewish-Muslim Relations: Myth and Reality, in Meddeb, Abdelwahab and Stora, Benjamin. A History of Jewish-Muslim Relations: From the Origins to the Present Day, Princeton: Princeton University Press

Cziborra, Pascal (1996). KZ Venusberg. Der verschleppte Tod, Bielefeld: Lorbeer Verlag

Cziborra, Pascal (2015). KZ Freiberg, Geheime Schwangerschaft, Bielefeld: Lorbeer Verlag

Dachauer Hefte 21 (2005). Häftlingsgesellschaft, Dachau: Verlag Dachauer Hefte

Darke, Diana (2020). Stealing from the Saracens: How Islamic Architecture Shaped Europe, London: Hurst

Dollinger, Hans (2002). Schwarzbuch der Geschichte, Köln: Area Verlag

Drukier, Manny (1996). Carved in Stone, Holocaust Years – A Boys Tale, Toronto: University of Toronto Press

Epstein Helen (1995). Die Kinder des Holocaust. Gespräche mit Söhnen und Töchtern von Überlebenden. München: H. C. Beck.

Fanizadeh, Andreas (2021). Die Deutschen vor El Alamein, in taz, am Wochenende, 27/28 März, S.12

Feldman, Deborah (2012). Unorthodox, New York: in the original bei Simon & Schuster, als Übersetzung bei Secession Verlag, Zürich, 2016

Frey, Hans, (1949). Die Hölle Kamienna, unter Benutzung des amtlichen Prozessmaterials zusammengestellt, Berlin, Potsdam: VVN

Garwood, Aldred (2021). Holocaust Trauma and Psychic Deformation, London &New York: Routledge

Gibaszewski, Krzysztof (2015). Hasag. Historia obozu pracy przymusowej w Skarżysku-Kamiennej, Skarżysko-Kamienna, Krzysztof Gibaszewski & PjS Agencja Wydawniczo-Poligraficzna

Gilman, Sander (1991). The Jew's Body, London: Routledge

Gilroy, Paul (1987). The Cultural Politics of Race and Nation, London: Hutchinson

Gilroy, Paul (1993). The Black Atlantic – Modernity and Double Consciousness. London: Verso Books

Gilroy Paul (2000). Between Camps: Nations, Cultures and the Allure of Race. London: Allen Lane, Penguin Press, 2000

Goldhagen, Daniel (1996). Hitler's Willing Executioners. Ordinary Germans and the Holocaust. London: Little, Brown and Co.

Gundel, Kay (1986). Reborn, Memoirs of a Camp Survivor, (unpublished), copy available in USHMM, 1986.019.2 | RG Number: RG-02.004.0

Haikal, Mustafa (2002). Einige Bemerkungen zur Auseinandersetzung mit der Geschichte der Hugo Schneider Aktiengesellschaft (Hasag). In fremd- und Zwangsarbeit in Sachsen 1939-1945. Beiträge eines Kolloquiums in Chemnitz am 16. April 2002. Herausgeber sächsisches Staatsministerium des Inneren. Halle (Saale), Dresden: Mitteldeutscher Verlag. S. 81-88

Hansen, Valerie (2016). The Silk Road: A New History with Documents, Oxford: Blackwell

Harari, Yuval (2014). Sapiens, London: Penguin Press

Haus der Geschichte Baden-Würtemberg (Hrsg.) (2008). Mythos Rommel, Ulm: Süddeutsche Verlagsgesellschaft

Herbert, Ulrich (1991). Europa und der Reichseinsatz ausländischer Zivilarbeiter Kriegsgefangene und KZ-Häftlinge und Deutschland 1938-1945, Essen: Klartext Verlag

Hoberman, John (1997). Darwin's Athletes: How Sport Has Damaged Black America and Preserved the Myth of Race. Boston: Houghton Mifflin

Hooks, Bell (1992). Black Looks: Race and Representation. Boston, MA: South End Press

Jacob, Sybille-Christin & Drewes, Detlef (2001). Aus der Waldorfschule geplaudert: warum die Steiner-Pädagogik keine Alternative ist. Aschaffenburg: Alibi Verlag

Karay, Felicja (2004). Death Comes in Yellow: Skarzysko Kamiennna Slave Labour Camp, Abingdon, Oxfordshire: Routledge

Klein, Tobias (2009). Fremd- und Zwangsarbeit im Raum Leipzig 1939-1945, zum Forum Geschichtswerkstatt Europa 1938-1949 – Dekade der Gewalt, Nordted: Grin Verlag

Knigge, Volkhard (2020). Buchenwald. Ausgrenzung und Gewalt 1937 bis 1945. Göttingen: Druckhaus Gera

Knobloch, Charlotte (2012). In Deutschland angekommen – Erinnerungen München: Deutsche Verlags-Anstalt

Krystal, Henry (1968). Massive Psychic Trauma. New York: International University Press

Krzyzanowski, Lukas (2020). Ghost Citizens. Jewish Return to a Postwar City, Cambridge MA: Harvard University Press

Lee, Thomas H. C. (1991). China and Europe. Images and Influences in Sixteenth to Eighteenth Centuries. Hongkong. The Chinese University Press

Levy, Primo (1988). Drowned and Saved. New York: Summit Books

Linebaugh, Peter (1991). The London Hanged. London: Verso

Maier, Lily (Hg.) (2018). Die Möhlstraße – ein jüdisches Kapitel der Münchner Nachkriegsgeschichte. Münchner Beiträge zur jüdischen Geschichte und Kultur, Jg. 12 Heft 1, München

Marcus, Paul & Rosenberg, Alan (1989). Healing their wounds. Psychotherapy with Holocaust survivors and their families., New York: Praeger Publishers

Martin, Ben L. (1991). From Negro to Black to African American: The Power of Names and Naming. In Political Science Quarterly Vol. 106, No. 1 (Spring, 1991), S.. 83-107, The Academy of Political Science

Maurer Zenck, Claudia, Petersen, Peter & Fetthauer, Sophie (Hg.) (2017). Lexikon verfolgter Musiker und Musikerinnen der NS-Zeit, Hamburg: Universität Hamburg

Morgan, David (1991). The Mongols. Hobroken: Wiley-Blackwell

Niederland, William G. (1961). The Problem of the Survivor, *Journal of the Hillside Hospital*, 10, 233-247

Niederland, William G. (1981). The Survivor Syndrome: Further Observations and Dimensions., *Journal of the American Psychoanalytic Association* 29.2 413-325

Nordau, Max (1909). Zionistische Schriften. Köln und Leipzig: Jüdischer Verlag

Neuman-Nowicki (1998). Struggle for Life During the Nazi Occupation of Poland. Lewiston NY: Edwin Mellen press

Owusu, Kwesi (red.) (2000). Black British Culture and Society, Routledge, London, 2000.

Paterson, Tony (2011). Was the Desert Fox an honest soldier or just another Nazi?, The Independent, 04.12.2011

Rao, Zhen, Fink, Elian & Gibson, Jenny (2020). Dyadic association between aggressive pretend play and children's anger expression, in British Journal of Developmental Psychology, 5.10.2020

Richardi, Hans-Günther (1986). Schule der Gewalt. Das Konzentrationslager Dachau 1933-1934, München: C. H. Beck

Reuth, Ralf Georg (2005). Rommel, the end of a legend. London: Haus Publishing

Rose, Susan and Garske, John (1987). Family Environment, Adjustment and Coping among Children of Holocaust Survivors. A Comparative Investigation, *American Journal of Orthopsychiatry* 57, 3, 322-344

Rost, Christian (2010). Ausverkauf beim König der Pelze, Aufstieg und Fall eines Münchner Unternehmens: Die Geschichte der Firma Rieger, die ihr Geschäft jetzt schließen muss, Süddeutsche Zeitung, 23. März 2010, *https://www.sueddeutsche.de/muenchen/insolvenz-der-firma-rieger-ausverkauf-beim-koenig-der-pelze-1.13367* (accessed on 06.07.2020)

Schiller, Kay & Young Christopher (2012). München 1972. Olympische Spiele im Zeichen des modernen Deutschland, Göttingen: Wallstein Verlag

Schriftreihe des Museums der Stadt Borna,(2007). Band 2, das Jahr 1945 in Borna, Borna: Druckhaus Borna

Schreiber, Gerhard (1996). Deutsche Kriegsverbrechen in Italien: Täter, Opfer, Strafverfolgung, München: C. H. Beck

Singer, Peter (1975). Animal Liberation, New York: Harper Collins

Sofsky, Wolfgang (1997). Der Orden des Terrors: Das Konzentrationslager. (Übersetzt von William Templer) Princeton University press

Steiner, Rudolf (1966). Die Welträtsel und die Anthroposophie, GA 54. Dornach: Rudolf Steiner Verlag

Strigler, Mordechai (1949). in di Fabrikn Fun toyt, Buenos Aires: Union Central Israelit Polaca en la Argentina

Strigler, Mordechai (2017). In den Fabriken des Todes (deutsche Ausgabe), Springe: zu Klampen Verlag

Strigler, Mordechai (2019). Werk-C, ein Zeitzeugenbericht aus den Fabriken des Todes, Springe: zu Klampen Verlag

Sussman, Robert (2014). The Myth of Race: Cambridge (MA). Harvard University Press

Szwajcer, Isroel (Ben-Awrom) (2010). Pinkes Szczekocin Księga Pamięci Szczekocin, Tel Aviv, [5720 – 1959]: polnische Ausgabe, Marek Tuszewicki, Szczekociny

Terezinska Pametni Kniha, Terezinska Iniciativa, vol. I-II Melantrich, Praha 1995, vol. III Academia Verlag, Prag 2000

Tyson, B. Timothy (2000). Radio Free Dixie, Robert F. Williams and the Roots of Black Power, Chapel Hill, N. C.; London: University of North Carolina Press

Verein Gedenkstätte KZ-Außenlager Schlieben-Berga. Ev (2001). Schlieben Force Labour Camp. Memorial Association Schlieben. Schlieben

Westphal, Uwe (1992). Berliner Konfektion und Mode: die Zerstörung einer Tradition, 1836-1939, Berlin: Edition Henrich

Williams, Robert F. (1962). Negroes with Guns, NY: , Marzani & Munsell, Inc.

Wardi, Dina (1992). Memorial Candles, Children of the Holocaust, London: Routledge

Watt, W Montgonery (1994). Influence of Islam on Medieval Europe, Edinburgh University Press

Williams, Eric (1944) Capitalism and Slavery: Chapel Hill, University of North Carolina Press. worldcat.org

Yehuda, Rachel, Lehrner, Amy & Rosenbaum, Tali (2015). PTSD and Sexual Dysfunction in Men and Women, Journal of sexual Medicine, Sex Med 2015;12: S. 1107–1119

Zelman, Leon (1995). Ein Leben, nach dem Überleben, Wien: Verlag Kremayr &Scheriau

Zylbersztajn, Daniel (1997). Hey Jude… ,in *Jewish Socialist* 39, Winter 1998, S. 14-15

Abbreviations

DZL – Daniel Zylbersztajn-Lewandowski

DP – Displaced Person / Displaced Persons

Soas – School of Oriental and African Studies

SPD – Sozialdemokratische Partei Deutschlands

UCL – University College of London

Z"L – hebräische Abkürzung für Zikarohn le Bracha. Trad Namen einer of a passed waay person,"May is memory be a blessing"

ZLB – Zentral- und Landesbibliothek Berlin

Geographical Map.

Descendants

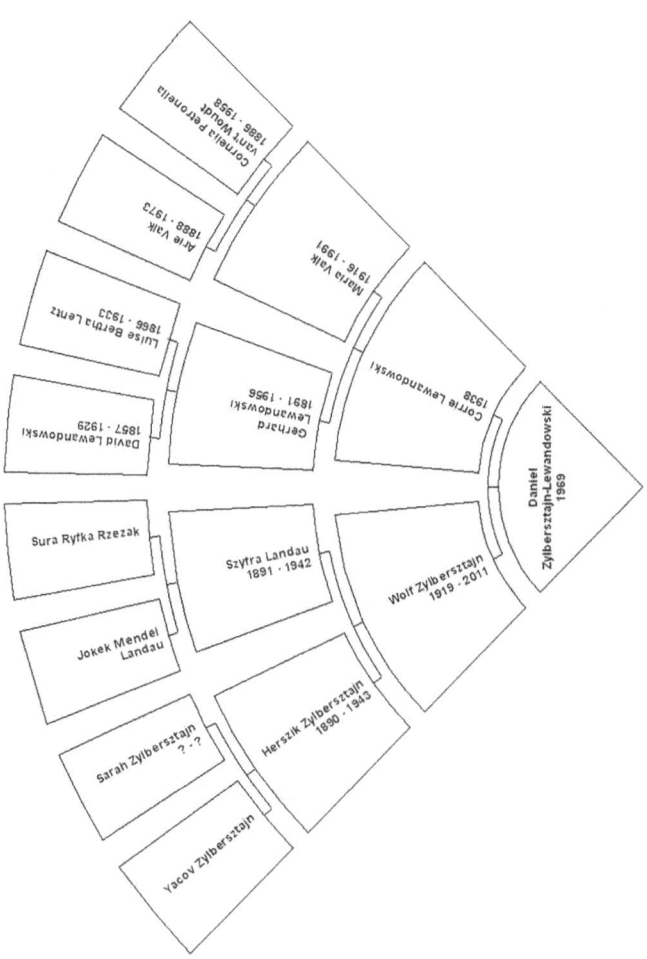

Daniel Zylbersztajn-Lewandowski: Ancestors of the last three generations.

Grafik: MyHeritage

Zol Zayn Shulem I: Zores

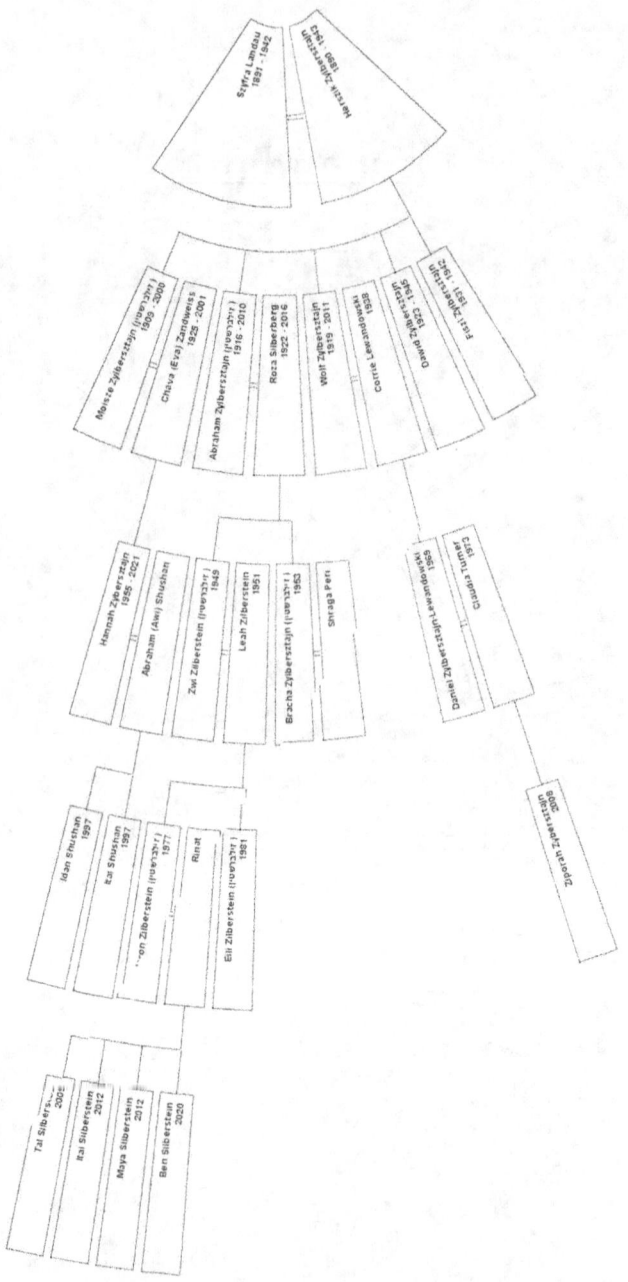

Descendents of Szyfra and Herszik Zylbersztajn.

Graphic: MyHeritage

Descendants

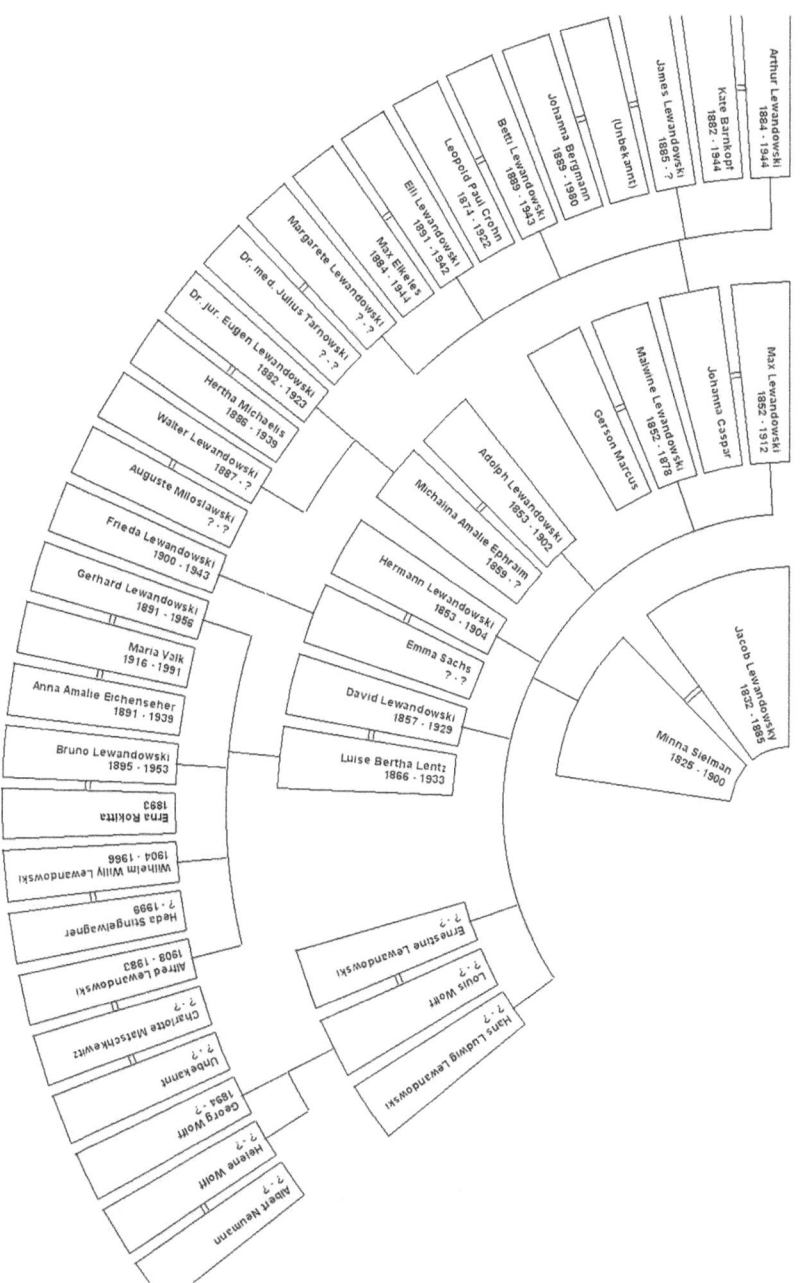

Minna and Jacob Lewandowski: Three Generations of descendants.

Graphic: MyHeritage

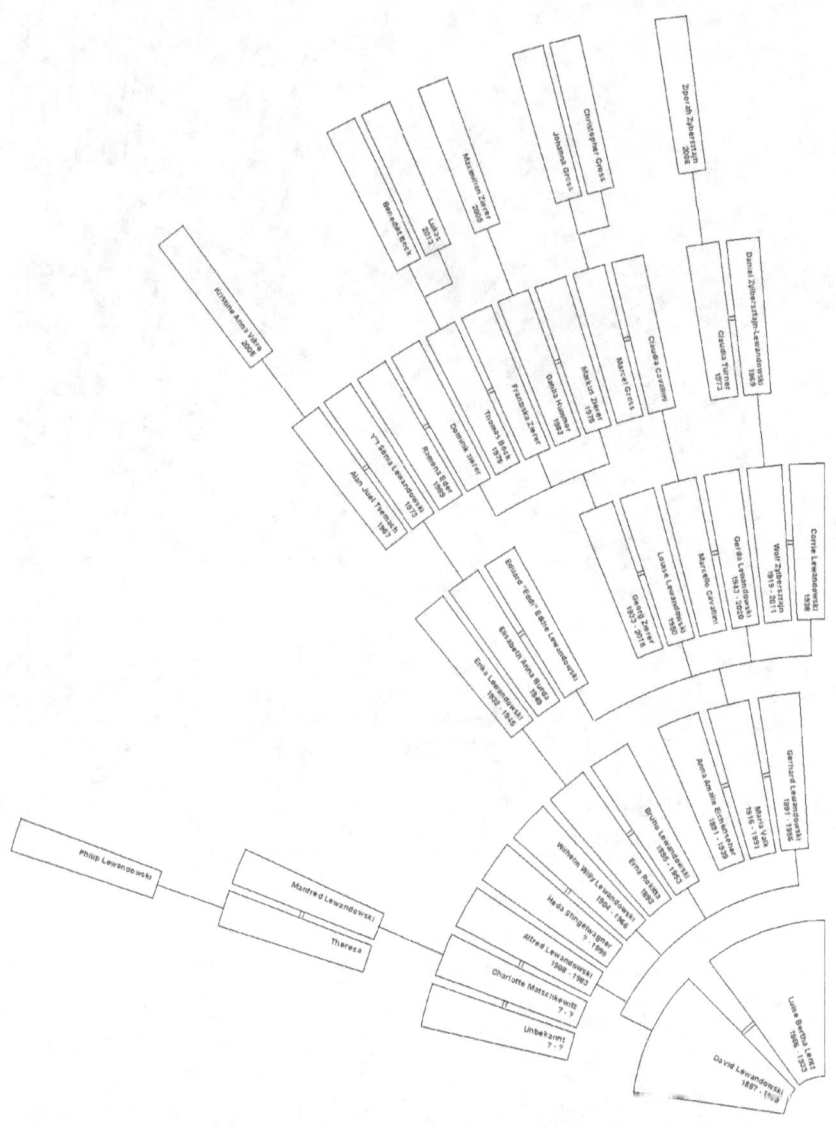

Luise and David Lewandowskis descendants.

Graphic: MyHeritage

Descendants

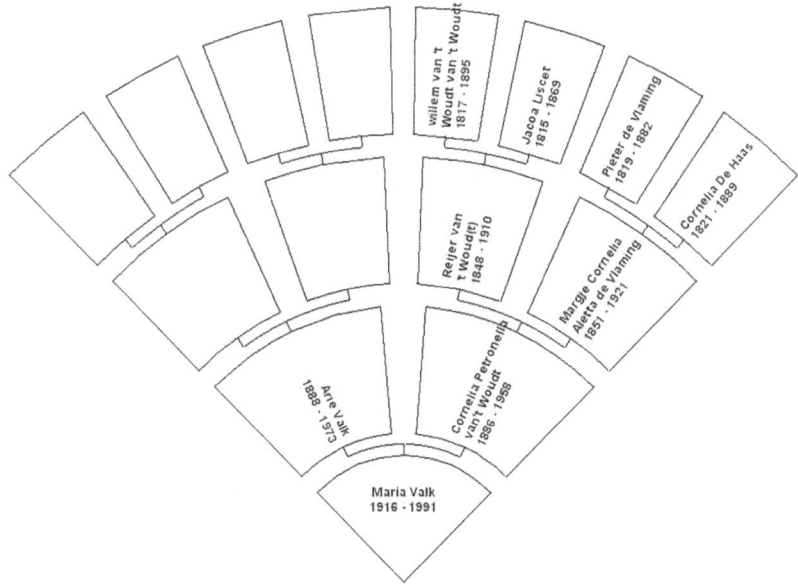

Dutch ancestors of Maria Lewandowski (three generations).

Graphic: MyHeritage

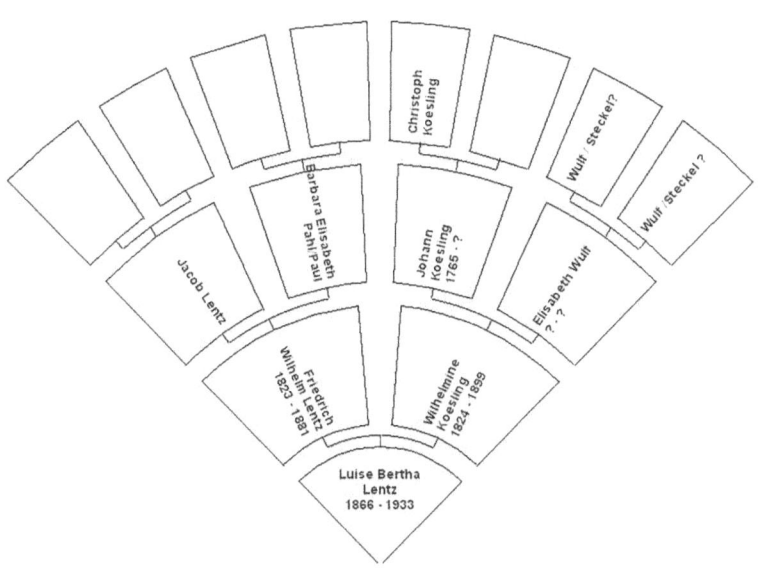

Ancestors of Luise Lewandowski

Graphic: MyHeritage

Zol Zayn Shulem I: Zores

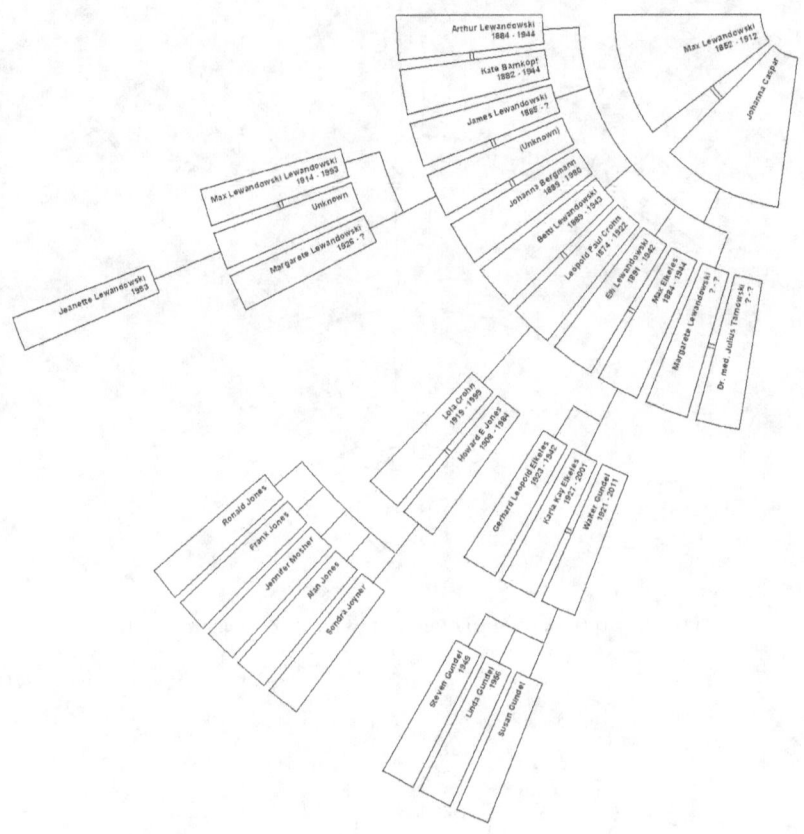

Johanna a Max Lewandowskis descendants

Graphic: MyHeritage

Index

7. Oktober 2023 288
Afrika Korps 58, 96
Agudat Israel 158
Aktion Erntefest 119
Aleppo 9
Altenburg 229
Alsace 51f
American Joint Distribution Committee 313
Amsterdam xiv, 38, 57, 77-79, 81, 84-87, 91-94, 96, 291-297, 301, 325
Haarlemer Straat 85f, 92, 291
Anschluss 86
Antisemitism 6, 28f, 54, 272, 287, 295, 297
April Boycott 61
Auschwitz / Auschwitz-Birkenau xi, 33, 105-109, 111-113, 242, 255, 256, 258, 282, 314
B-94, The Spirit of a Survivor 23
Babylon 9, 12
Bankhaus Aufhäuser 79
Bantenberg 44
Bar Meisel, Rabbi Dov 13
Bayer. Vereinsbank 76, 296
Ben Szlomo, Mordche 8, 17
Beekbergen 92f
Berga 235, 237

Berlin xiv, 32, 34, 35, 37f, 40, 45-50, 54, 57, 76, 96, 98, 103-105, 108-112, 115-118, 206, 209f, 254, 307-309, 323
Schöneberg 104, 110.
Blumenstraße 35, 37
Köpenickerstraße 35
Leipziger Straße 46
Rosenthalerstraße 35
Bernhard, Georg 69
Biderman, Rabbi Dovid 12
Bismarck 32
Bližejov 257, 259-261, 264
Bornstein, Izyk Mendel xii, 21, 23
Braml 60, 70, 71, 74, 294
Braun, Erich 66
Brenner, Michael 54
Breslau 271
Brit Milah 7
Budin, Paul 166, 168-170, 229, 281
Byzantine Empire 10
Carlov 266f
Casey, Steven 286
Casimir IV 9
Challah / Challot 20
Cheder 6, 17
Chelm 291
Cherut (Herut) 17
Červenka, Jiř. 264

Chruzik 128
Ciechanowski, Julian 24f, 148
Cohen, A.B 40
Cohn, Lotte 40
Colditz 229
Compensation 292, 294, 303-307, 318
Corset 31, 34-38, 45-47, 55-57, 76, 86, 92
    98, 168, 302, 306f
Crohn
    Betti 108-114
    Leopold 109, 111
    Lola 109-114
Cukernik, Berisz 128, 130
Cukerman, Isroel Ber 160
Cukerman, Jehudi „Jadzia" 126
Częstochowa 139, 167, 215, 267
Dalski 169
DDR (GDR) 283
Depression 56f. 168, 307
Deutsch Sozialer Verein 39
Displaced Person 314
Dollinger, Hans 287
Domažlice xiv, 256f., 260, 265.
DP-Camp 274, 360
Dresden 31
Dresdner Bank 168
Drezner, Herszl 138f
Drukier, Manny 248, 252-254, 259. 266
Eibl, Ludwig 295
Eicke, Theodor 66, 69
Eisner, Kurt 53-55
El Alamein 98
Elkeles 103, 108, 117, 242
    Elli 103, 108, 117
    Gerd 103, 105
    Karla 103-109, 242
    Max 103

Emancipation 31, 32, 34, 40, 52
Engel, David 272
Enslaved workers 172, 197, 225, 229, 235,
    247, 281
Eulalia of Spain 38, 48
Euthanasia 145
Fajgenblat, Bejlusz 279
Fajwisz, Mojsze Jankew 129, 142
FC Bayern x, 324
Feuchtmann, Pamela Castillo xiv, 186,
    220. 234, 249
Fischer, Samuel 40
Flößberg 229, 231, 246-252, 255-257, 281
Föhrenwald 274
Frank, Anne 86
Freetown xii, 326
Fromer, Awrum 206
Fromer Isroel 140
Garmisch-Partenkirchen 52
Gas-Chamber 113
Gestapo 59, 61, 64, 71,75, 105,111, 141f,
    152, 296
Gibaszewski, Krzysztof xiii, 175, 178, 183,
    192.
Goldberg, Rabbi Lejbl 140
Goldfarb, Abraham 156
Goldszmit, Mojsze Wolf 138f
Goleniowy 141
Gordinia 16
grenade 131-133, 195, 197, 201, 229, 234
Grajpner, Mordchei ben-Szlomo 8
Graipner, Zwi 122, 136, 176
Graipnet Zwi Jeszajahu 136
Gundel Kay 104, 108, 117, 118
    Steven, Susan und Linda 108
Gurtman, Isroel 17, 24
Guterman, Chaim 128

Index

Ha-Noar ha-Zioni 16, 148
Haifa 100
Hammer-Heizung 237-239, 250, 252
Hanukkah 23, 118
Harari, Yuval 12
Hasag xiii, 163, 165-179, 183, 186, 190, 192, 200-202, 204-206, 214-217, 228f, 231, 235, 237f, 247,249, 252 275, 278, 281-79
Haskalah 42
Hebrew Immigrant Aid Society 314
Heidrich, Wolfgang xiii, 247-251, 256
Henech Iczele 132
Henoch Trajan 147
Hep-Hep-Riots 31
Herold, Karl 275
Himmler, Heinrich 61, 118, 145, 226, 311
Hitler, Adolf 54f, 57, 65, 69, 77, 95, 98, 99f. 123, 219, 276, 279, 288, 294
Hitlerjugend 248, 259
Hnatova, Hana 256, 259
Hoffmann, Anton 66
Hollender, Menasze 231
Holýšova 255
Honik, Jankew Szlojme, 133
Horni Břiza 256
Initiative Flößberg gedenkt 247, 248f, 285
Israel 6, 8, 121, 126, 273-276, 276, 279, 288, 311, 317, 320, 323, 325f
Jedrzjow 151
Jerusalem 9
Jewish Agency 313
Jones, Alan 110
  Beckett 110
  Elisabeth 112
  Frank xiv, 110, 112f
  Howard E. 110, 113

Jennifer 110
Lola 109-114
Ronald 110
Joselewicz, Berek 13
Judenrat 137-148, 179, 283-285
Kaddish xiii, 211, 269-271
Kapos 67, 224, 231
Karay, Felecja, 157, 163, 171-174, 178, 180-182, 185-188, 190,194, 197, 202-205, 214-217, 223
Kaulbach, Friedrich 295
Kempe, Hans 228
Kindertransport 109
Kladau 31, 33, 308
Kol Nidre 147
Kolmar 52
Koplowicz, Rab Kopl 279
Kornfeld, Ferenc 286
Kotkowsky, Charles 249
Kościuszko, Tadeusz 13
KPD 66, 236
Krakow 7, 10, 214
Kryman, Efroim 130, 133
Krzeszower, Lejzer 141
Krzyzanowski, Lukasz 272
Kunsthaus Bernheimer 79
Kupferberg (Sparkling Wine) 46
Kupperberg, Yakub 267
KL (KZ) Dachau xiv,59, 61, 64-79, 93, 98, 282, 294f, 298
KZ Venusberg 254
KZ-Bergen Belsen xi, 156
KZ-Buchenwald xi, xiv, 15, 189. 215, 218-229, 231, 244, 249, 251f, 256, 258, 282f,, 285
Champs-.Elysees 224
Koch, Karl Otto 225

361

Kleine Lager 219f
SS-Trophies 226
zoo 225
KZ-Flößberg, see Flößberg
KZ-Majdanek 185, 205, 216
KZ-Mauthausen xiv, 253, 256, 267. 285, 286
KZ-Sachenhausen 117f.
KZ-Schlieben xiii, 215, 221, 227-238, 241, 249-251, 257, 267, 281f, 285
Landau 10
   Josef Mendel 25
   Szyfrah Rayzla 5, 13
   Sura Ryfka 25
Landauer, Gutav 55
Lamkewitz 282
Latkes 23
Lecho dodi 21
Leipzig 166, 229, 237, 275, 278, 281
Lelow xiv, 12, 15, 130, 140f
Lermann, Paul 71f, 75, 79, 297, 298, 303-305
Leopoldstraße 60, 319
Letzte Neijes 320
Leather Worker 5f, 13, 273
Lewandowski
   Brothers 35, 45-47, 54, 57f,76, 308
   David 33, 35, 38-44, 46, 48f, 52f, 56f, 62, 103, 108, 118, 308, 356
   Adolph 33, 40, 47, 115
   Alfred 31, 44, 51, 54, 56-58, 96-98, 100. 102, 197, 302, 308, 309
   Arthur 33
   Auguste 116f
   Blume 31
   Bruno 36, 44, 50, 51, 53f, 56-58, 79, 97, 100-102, 302, 308

Corrie (Zylbersztajn) x-xii, 60 84, 86, 91, 93-96, 290-293, 301, 306, 320-322
Eduard 201, 307
Ernestine (Wolff) 33, 35, 118, 206
Eugen 33, 47, 48, 55, 115f
Gerda xi, xii, 56, 60, 76, 94f, 101, 290f, 293, 301, 306-308
Gerhard xi, 25, 43-45, 49-57, 60.62, 68, 70-73, 76, 84f, 91, 96, 100, 102f, 111, 296, 302-307, 309, 315, 321
Hans-Ludwig 33, 40
Herrmann 33, 238
Jacob 30-32, 40, 108, 118, 308, 355
James 111, 117f
Jeanette 118
Johanna Chaja 103, 109, 110, 117, 118, 358
Käte 108f, 242
Louise 291
Luise 35, 42-44, 91, 103, 356
Malwine 33
Maria 35, 86, 90f, 94, 290, 293, 357
Marcus 33, 109-111
Markus 31
Max (I) 33, 35, 109, 117, 358
Max (II) 118
Minna 31-36, 39f, 42, 108, 355
Phillpp xiv, 56, 309
Walter 33
Willi 44, 54, 58, 302
Liberal Judaism 269
Liebermann, Max 40, 295
Lippert, Michael 69
London 85, 86, 156, 200, 209, 268, 325
Lublin 119, 271

Index

Lütscher, Heinrich 282
Madalinsk, Reb Shmai 158
Maggi 46
Majer, Dowid Manela 128
Majer, Josl 133
Majer, Icze 158
Mangl, Kalmen 142
Mann, Thomas 41
Manzoor, Imran xiii, 199f, 269
Maria Theresa 38
Markowiczowa, Fela 179, 285
Masorti Judaism 269
Mayer Szulmann, Josek 5
Mayer-Zernosovsky 257
Merzdorf 266
Meyer, Otto 57, 61f, 71, 295f
Messiah x, 21
Meuselwitz 226
Miodowa, Jankew 142
Mizrahi 9f
Muselman 193, 207
Müller, Karl Richard 228, 282
München (Munich) x, xii, xiv, 12, 38-80, 90-93, 96, 100-103, 118, 169, 210, 274f, 292, 294-321, 324
    Augustinerstraße 302
    Beichstraße 60, 71, 294, 296
    Caf. Grünwald 70
    Eduard-Schmidt-Str. 316, 320
    Grillparzerstr. 301, 320
    Haus der Kunst 324
    Königsplatz 324
    Landshuter Allee 302
    Marienplatz 38, 302
    Mjelowa 310, 317
    Möhlstr. 310-320
    Neuhauserstr. 38, 56, 302
    Nordbad 324
    Odeonsplatz 324
    Rosenstr. 38, 70
    Schwabing 294
    Hauptsynagoge 52
    Synagogue Reichenbachstraße 289
    Sinai-School 317
    Theatinerstr. 38, 43, 46, 302
Napoleon 12, 31
Nationalism xii
Neuland, Siegfried 297
Neumann, Helene 33, 119
New York 110-113
North Africa 10, 97f, 100, 309
NSDAP 54, 60, 71f, 77, 276
Nurnberg Race Law 74
Oasis of Peace UK xiii
Oppenheimer, Rudi 86
Ottoman Empire 9f
Palestine 54, 77, 86, 99, 273, 288, 313
Panzerfaust 229
Peru 118
Pinchas, Ben 20
Pinkes Szczekocin xiii, 3, 12, 17, 26, 123, 131, 158, 279
Pinschewer, Julius 45
Piskiewicz, Aga (Bornstein) xii, 5
Płatkewicz, Dowid 129f
Pluta, Johann 134, 136-139, 161
Pohl, Oswald 170
Poniatowsk, Jozef 127
ponshkes 23
Pöcking 308
Prikiner 177f
Proste 6
PX-Shops 312
Racism 39, 297, 326

Radom 152, 174, 205, 272, 285
Räterepublik 53f
Rathenau, Emil 40, 43, 55
Reconquista 9
Rauff, Walter 99
Refugee 108, 113
Reichman, Yechiel 153
Reihmann 148f, 157
Rieger, Hertz 315
Rommel, Erwin 96-100
Rosh Hashanah 124, 138
Rost, Arthur 280f
Roßhaupter, Albert 53
Rycht, Jechiel Reb 129, 248
Rusin, Szmuel 129, 137, 141
Russian 10, 12, 19, 52, 108, 173, 234, 241, 249, 254, 256, 264, 272, 286
Rzeszow 271
Santiago de Chile 118
shabbat 8, 16, 19-21, 29, 53, 104, 123f, 313
shamash 19
Schlieben see KZ Schlieben
Schneideman, Philipp 69
Schnellenberg, Martin 168
Schöneck 31f
Schröpfer, Libor xiv, 255-257, 264f
Second Generation 277, 325f
Sedziszow 124f, 152, 158 160
Sefad (Zefad) 10
Seidel, Willi 178f, 281
sexual crime 171, 174, 178, 216, 224
shadchen 24
Shanghai 86, 116
Shoah Foundation xiii, 136, 209-213
Sielmann, Minna 32
silk road 10
Sinti and Roma 100

Skarżysko-Kamienna 142, 164-224, 278-285
  Werk A 176f, 189, 192, 197, 203, 225
  Werk B 176, 178, 185f, 204
  Werk C xiii, 162, 166, 176-179, 183, 192, 196, 215-217, 231
Siodmak, Awrum 141
Sosnowiec xiii, 243, 269-272, 310
Stadelheim 69
Star of David 140, 155
Stark, N. 41
Steinbrenner, Hans 66
Streland, Marie 89-91
Striesa 235
Strigler, Mordechai 166, 178, 185, 192-196, 205
strip search 182
Stückel 136
Stümmler 135f
stybl 16
survivor's guilt 150
Süddeutsche Zeitung 320
Swindon 199f
Swimming Prohibition 62
Szczekociny xii, 2, 4-28, 122-152, 161f, 179, 206, 240, 268, 274, 279, 283-285
  Borech Papiernik 18f
  Melamed Dardacha 17
  Rynek 13, 18
  Sztybelman, Szlojme 129, 135
Szwarcbojm (Schwarzbojm) Awrum 27, 125f, 129f, 141
  Chaim Josef 140
  Orla 15, 125
Tarnow 271
Taucha 364
Tel Aviv 100, 108, 320

Index

Terezin (Theresienstadt) xi, xiv, 105f, 108f, 117, 240-245
Tetryl and Picric Acid 177, 184, 231
Tęgoborz 132, 141
Thälmann, Ernst 226
Torah 6, 17, 26, 135, 148, 161
Tietge, Marianne 280f
Trajan, Rabbi Pinchas 146
Trauma ix, 213, 325
Trawniki 118f, 206
Treblinka 151-163, 171
Typhus x, 204-208, 210, 222, 244
Uhlfelder (Max) 41, 61
Ukranian Helpers 152f, 162, 174, 216
Ukrainian refugees 219, 264
Umschlagplatz 159
Upper Silesia 6, 10
United Nations Relief and Rehabilitation Administration 313
US-Court of Restitution Appeals 297
US-Military Court 282
Uzbekistan 126
Valk Family 87
  Arie (I) 89-91
  Arie (II) 87, 88, 90-92
  Cor 87, 88, 90-92
  Margje 87f, 94
  Maria (see Maria Lewandowski)
  Reyer 87f, 94
Vlaardingen 87f
Volksdeutsch 136, 138, 197, 216, 284
von Kahr, Gustav 54f, 317
von Lanke, Baron 318
von Lenbach, Franz 295
von Maisen-Ponikau, Freiherr 65
Wagner, Alfred 197, 281
Wahat al Salam-Neve Shalom 200

Walburga, Anna Amalie 56
Wasserman, Jacob 49
Wehrmacht 58, 96-99, 136, 168
Weimar 218, 225
Weiss, Helga 255
Weissenbruch, Jan 295
Werkschutz 136, 161-163, 173f, 182, 184, 191, 197, 216, 220, 257
Wiedergutmachung (see also comepnsation) 304, 307
Wiesel, Eli 228
Winsel, Tobias 317
Wisznicki, Mordche 158
Wlodowa 52
Włoszczowa 140
Wodzislaw 152
Wolbrom 140
Wolf, Jürgen xiii 233-235, 241
Wolff Ernestine (see Ernestine Lewandowski)
Wolff Georg 33, 206
Yalana L. 255
Yangiyul 126, 271
Yiddish 6, 24, 193, 210, 231. 316, 319f
Yugoslavia 287, 289
Yom Kippur 53, 138, 146-148, 158, 289
Zahn, Hans 247
Zelman, Leon 6f, 13f, 16-20, 23, 29, 127f, 131
Zionism 16f, 20, 27, 131, 274, 310
Zorneding 307
Zubřina 3
Zylbersztajn
  Abraham xi, 15, 123, 125-134, 137-139, 143, 161f, 179, 187f, 191, 202f, 206, 217, 219-224, 234f, 240-244, 268, 271, 285

Zol Zayn Shulem I: Zores

    Chavtje xii, 273
    Dawid xi, 14f, 125, 160, 162, 177,
        188, 221f, 234, 240, 243f, 245,
        247, 267, 269f, 270, 284f
    Fiszl xi, 15, 146, 149, 152, 157, 159,
        212, 245
    Hannah (Hanni) xii, 275
    Herszik ix, x, 5, 13-15, 17, 27, 137,
        148, 162, 201, 208, 245 354.
    Moisze xi, xii, 14f, 17, 125, 265, 271
        273
    Ruszke (Roza) xi, xv, 271, 289
    Sarah 15
    Szyfra ix, xi, 4, 13, 15, 24, 131, 146,
        152f, 159, 354
    Yaakov 14
    Zwika 271
Żarnowiec 140

www.ingramcontent.com/pod-product-compliance
Lightning Source LLC
Chambersburg PA
CBHW050329230426
43663CB00010B/1798